Twenty-five
Nature Spectacles
in New Jersey

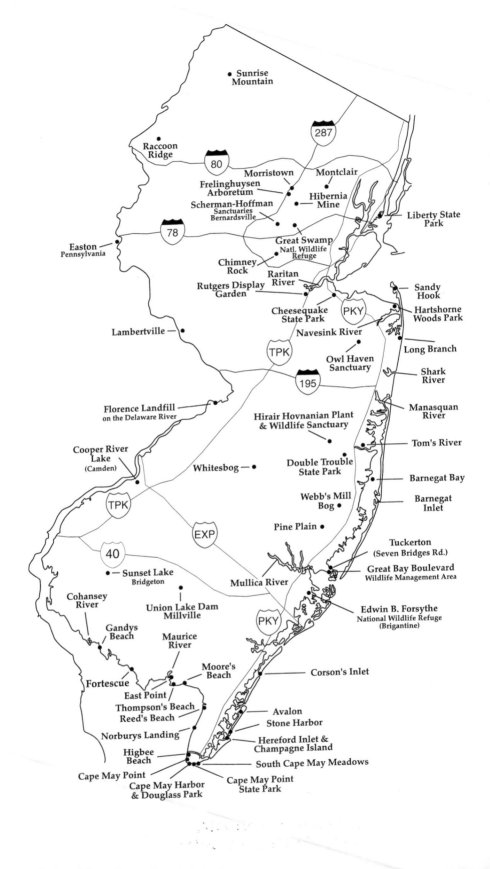

Twenty-five  Nature Spectacles in New Jersey

JOANNA BURGER
AND MICHAEL GOCHFELD

Rutgers University Press
NEW BRUNSWICK, NEW JERSEY

Library of Congress Cataloging-in-Publication Data
Burger, Joanna.
    25 nature spectacles in New Jersey / Joanna Burger and Michael Gochfeld.
    p.   cm.
    Includes bibliographical references (p.   )
    ISBN 0-8135-2791-0 (cloth : alk. paper).—ISBN 0-8135-2766-X (pbk. :
alk. paper)
    1. Natural history—New Jersey.   2. Seasons—New Jersey.   I. Gochfeld,
Michael.   II. Title.   III. Title: Twenty-five nature spectacles in New Jersey.
QH105.N5B863   2000
508.749—dc21   99-43253
                                                                        CIP

British Cataloging-in-Publication data for this book is available from the
British Library

Manufactured in the United States of America

Frontispiece: Map of New Jersey showing locations mentioned in the text.

To our children, Debbie and David, who have provided us with endless delight, and shown us how to see nature with fresh and wondrous eyes, and now ask questions that force us to think about nature in new ways

Contents

Winter

Illustrations

1. Crows form staging groups in trees (*top*) before leaving (*bottom*) to enter their roosts for the night. (Photos by J. Burger)

Preface

Ever since we were small children we loved to wander the woods searching for nesting Great Horned Owls in the late winter, flocks of migrant birds in the spring and fall, and wildflowers and butterflies in the heat of summer. We waded in ponds to catch salamanders and polliwogs, walked along riverbanks looking for Night Herons, and meandered along slow-moving streams peering with wonderment at small minnows. We sauntered slowly through fields flush with flowers, identifying butterflies and searching for dragonflies and "bugs." Exploring the fields, streams, and woodlots provided endless hours of enjoyment, excitement, and discovery. We learned to appreciate all of nature's spectacles, whether it was a tiny Ladybug, a dragonfly nymph underneath a stone in a pond, or hordes of Red-winged Blackbirds and Grackles moving through an autumn cornfield.

Although our parents ignited our interest, showed us the nests of birds and bees, and bought us books to help us identify the wondrous things we discovered, our childhood journeys were largely solitary. They were journeys spent discovering the world around us, the vast diversity that exists in every woodlot, every abandoned field, every flowing stream. Our first love was birds, but even as children we learned that we must understand the plants and animals that make up each bird's world. A Hummingbird on our back porch was inseparable from the Honeysuckle that lured it there. This led us to observe everything around us, whether wildflower, worm, or warbler.

When our paths crossed, they were inextricably intertwined, and we have journeyed far and wide over the world in appreciation and study of biodiversity. We have loved observing and learning about a variety of animals in far-flung parts of the world, and we still feel the thrill of being surrounded by King Penguins on Macquarie Island or nesting sea turtles on the Great Barrier Reef islands, of being chased by a Rhinoceros in South Africa, or of being terrorized one memorable night by a pride of eleven Lions at our campsite in Tanzania. In such exotic places we experienced only a fraction of the natural world, skimming its cream, so to speak.

It is equally exciting to know in more depth the natural history of our own region; to see the changing seasons, to understand from many years of experience how the animals and plants interact with one another, and to cherish the unique natural history of local ecosystems.

Our appreciation for the natural history of New Jersey has increased over the years we have lived here. Most of the country envisions New Jersey as a dense mass of cities and suburbs, polluted as well; but New Jerseyans know better. Ours is a rich and varied state, small and densely populated, but with many well-preserved natural habitats. As our interests have widened from coastal birds to Pine Barrens reptiles, to shorebirds feeding on Horseshoe Crab eggs, to salt marsh fish, to butterflies, we have learned that New Jersey has its own nature spectacles. We have only to look carefully to appreciate the great diversity of natural landscapes in our state. We have spent the last twenty-five years wandering the estuaries and bays, fields and forests, and marshlands of New Jersey, observing, studying, and enjoying our natural habitats.

Our interest in writing this book largely grew out of a desire to share with others the wondrous natural events that happen in New Jersey every year. Often people have commented on our adventures in other exotic parts of the world, without appreciating that spectacles in New Jersey are just as enjoyable. Massive numbers of American Shad migrate into our rivers and streams each spring. Delaware Bay is the center of Horseshoe Crab breeding for the entire Western Hemisphere. The largest concentration of spring migrant shorebirds in the United States occurs along the Delaware Bayshore. Cape May is one of the world's best-known migration points, and hawks migrate in great numbers along the mountain ridges of northern New Jersey. New Jersey has proportionately more salt marshes than any other state, and our coast hosts some of the most diverse breeding colonies of gulls and terns found anywhere. Hundreds of frogs gather at breeding ponds to chorus each spring; thousands of Fiddler Crabs scuttle across the mudflats at low tides, and millions of tiny Glass Eels come into our freshwater streams, having swum thousands of miles from the Sargasso Sea southeast of Florida.

There are other spectacular sights—huge roosts of crows, for example, and immense flocks of grazing geese gracing the nouveau lawns of their reluctant corporate hosts, but they are so widespread we have not included them. We hope we can transmit our excitement about these New Jersey spectacles and events, and that you will visit these sites. The eye of the beholder is very important, and readers are likely to encounter other spectacles that we have not thought of.

Acknowledgments

Many friends and colleagues have helped us see and understand the great diversity of plants and animals, and to appreciate the nature spectacles in New Jersey, from the tiniest Glass Eels making their way upstream, to the hordes of migrating shorebirds on Delaware Bay. We thank Jim Applegate, Ken Able, Kathy Clark, Mandy Dey, Dave Jenkins, Michelle LeMarchant, Fred Lesser, Charlie and Mary Leck, Bob Loveland, Bert and Patti Murray, Larry Niles, Tom O'Connell, Ted Stiles, Guy Tudor, Chris and Paula Williams, and Bob Zappalorti for imparting a wealth of knowledge over the years.

Some of our graduate students have provided knowledge of the organisms they have studied, and we have learned from each of them: Brook Lauro, Kathy Parsons, Greg Transue, Carl Safina, Bill Boarman, John Brzorad, Kevin Staine, Steve Garber, Tom Fikslin, Jorge Saliva, Dave Shealer, Larry Niles, Susan Elbin, Laura Wagner, Nellie Tsipoura, Malcolm Martin, Brian Palestis, Chris Lord, Shane Boring, Michelle Kuklinsky, Mandy Dey, Eric Stiles, and Sherry Meyer. We also thank our technicians and assistants who helped with many of our projects and aided in the preparation of the manuscript: Tara Shukla, Bob Ramos, Mike McMahon, Carline Dixon, Justin Leonard, and Sheila Shukla, as well as Mike Valent and Annette Scherer for allowing us to accompany them on the census of the bats at the Hibernia Mine, and James Faczak for showing us Glass Eels at Cheesequake. Russell Burman of the Pennsylvania Fish and Boat Commission provided additional information on Shad and the fish ladder at Easton, and J. Shissias and Marcia Walton of PSE&G provided information and firsthand experience with river herring at their fish ladders. Fred Lewis, Steve Lewis, and their families provided a demonstration on Shad seining, and the Cadwalders of Waldac Farms allowed access to Lotuses. We thank David Adams for information on rabies, and Alice Boggs for information on Mannington Meadows. We thank JoAnn Humphrey for preparation of the maps.

Several people read earlier drafts of individual chapters, and provided helpful comments on style, natural history, additional interactions, and interesting aspects, and we are grateful to them all: Ken Able, Russellyn Carruth, Kathy Clark, Mandy Dey, Joan Ehrenfeld, David Fairbrothers, Tom Fote, Bernie Goldstein, Stacey Hagan, Dave Jenkins, Charlie and Mary Leck, Robert Loveland, Peter Morin, Patti and Bert Murray, Larry Niles, Benjie Swan, Mark Robson, Robert Soldwedel, Nellie Tsipoura, Mike Valent, and Chris and Paula

2. Tiko, our parrot, resorting to eating a bouquet of Peonies while we work on the book.

Williams. We thank Dave Guston, Charlie and Mary Leck, Bob Loveland, Sherry Meyer, Patti Murray, Mark Robson, and Chris and Paula Williams for contributing photographs, and David Gochfield for printing the bat photographs.

Tiko, our forty-five-year-old parrot, stood faithfully behind us as we wrote, demanding attention when we lingered too long over difficult passages, or disagreed over directions to some of the spectacles. Periodically, he walked across our computer keyboards, reminding us that he, at least, was hungry (fig. 2).

Our interest in nature was stimulated at a very early age by our parents: JB's mother showed her where rare flowers grew in the woods behind her house, cautioning her not to pick them or they would become even rarer; her father stood in the woods with her on cold winter nights, listening for the calls of courting Great Horned Owls, and later showed her the nests of Killdeer and Spotted Sandpiper that were nestled beneath squash plants. MG's mother showed him Hummingbirds coming to Honeysuckle at the back porch when he was three, and his father showed him a Robin nesting in a spruce tree when he was four. These are some of our fondest memories—and they surely affected us profoundly.

Our children, Debbie and David, helped us see the natural world through fresh eyes, and always forced us to address the most simple, yet profound questions of how and why. We have enjoyed their company on many of our field trips throughout New Jersey. Our brothers and sisters shared our love of nature over the years, or at least tolerated it. Our nieces and nephews, who range in age from seven to over thirty, have provided an endless opportunity to see nature through wondering eyes as they went on field trips with us.

Our academic homes at Rutgers University and UMDNJ–Robert Wood Johnson Medical School have provided both intellectual and monetary support through the Biodiversity Center, Bureau of Biological Research, Environmental and Occupational Health Sciences Institute, and Institute for Marine and Coastal Sciences. Our research over the years has been funded by the National Science Foundation, National Institute of Mental Health, National Institute of Environmental Health Sciences (ESO 5022, 5059), Environmental Protection Agency, Department of Energy (Consortium for Risk Evaluation with Stakeholder Participation, AI #DE-FC01-95EW55084), Penn Foundation, Dodge Foundation, and the Endangered and NonGame Program of the New Jersey Department of Environmental Protection.

We share our world with wild things, and must be careful not to disturb them. Field research for studying animals requires permits from various governmental agencies, and we thank the following for permits to work with birds, reptiles, amphibians, fish, and Horseshoe Crabs: U.S. Bird Banding Laboratory, U.S. Fish and Wildlife Service, New Jersey Department of Environmental Protection, and New York Department of Environmental Conservation.

We also thank Marlie Wasserman and Joseph Seneca for encouraging us, albeit with a heavy hand, to write this book, as well as our editor Helen Hsu, copyeditor Alice Calaprice, production editor Marilyn Campbell, and the entire staff at Rutgers University Press for improving the manuscript and making the process enjoyable.

Twenty-five
Nature Spectacles
in New Jersey

3. Mating Horseshoe Crabs stranded on the beach, all that remains of the spawning ritual from the last high tide. (Photo by J. Burger)

Introduction

A ribbon of dark brown shapes tumbles and rolls in the churning surf, stretching far along the shore, beyond the next sandy spit. In some places, the Horseshoe Crabs dissolve into small groups with one female crab surrounded by a dozen smaller males, all agitating, all plowing determinedly toward the female in the center. She is gravid, and the first male to cling to her carapace will win the right to fertilize her eggs, and to carry on the ancient spawning ritual that goes back to a time before the dinosaurs walked the earth. The ritual has remained largely unchanged. Thousands upon thousands of Horseshoe Crabs come to Delaware Bay each year to spawn, more than to any other place in the Western Hemisphere. As the tides recede and the crabs make their way back to the safety of the bay, the ribbon will again pulsate with the movement of thousands upon thousands of shorebirds that converge on the shoreline to feast on the tiny Horseshoe Crab eggs awash in the surf. These eggs are excess, for they will never hatch, but will wash out to sea. Only the eggs buried deep beneath the sand will hatch into miniature Horseshoe Crabs that enter the safety of the sea and grow for nine or ten years before they mature enough to return to spawn.

It is spring on Delaware Bay, but spring arrived earlier at the freshwater streams that empty into the Atlantic Ocean. There, millions upon millions of tiny, threadlike Glass Eels made their way through the estuarine waters, swimming upstream to lakes where their ancestors grew. They hatched in the Sargasso Sea southeast of Florida, and for many months they swam the treacherous, predator-laden waters from the tip of Florida to the New Jersey shore. These clear, fragile threads of life, a little over two inches long, are piled so thick when they pass through the tiny culverts and streams that they look like a pot of simmering angel hair pasta, but they are much more delicate, much smaller, and much more vulnerable. Their transparent bodies are hard for predators to see in the eddying currents of the estuaries, as they catch the light of the sun and glitter slightly, creating the illusion of tiny waves. Once they reach the lakes, the Glass Eels take on the dark brown color of the bottom mud, again to avoid predators.

While spring brings Horseshoe Crabs to their spawning beaches and Glass Eels to their lakes, it comes to the forests of Cape May and northern New Jersey in the form of wave upon wave of neotropical migrant birds. Warblers drop from the sky to decorate the trees just coming into leaf. They alternate their quest for food with chirps and buzzes, each voice characteristic of one of the thirty species of warblers that pass through New Jersey en route from tropical winter quarters to northern breeding grounds. Orioles and tanagers, in their brilliant breeding plumage, stay here to nest. In the summer the forests become quiet, for the migrants have moved on to their breeding grounds while resident birds remain to greet each morning with their endearing contribution to the dawn chorus, then silently pursue their parental roles, thrusting grasshoppers and caterpillars into the open beaks of their voracious babies.

While the large flocks of songbirds are moving through our forests to disperse to their northern nesting grounds, hundreds upon hundreds of terns and gulls have come to the Jersey shore to breed. These birds course over salt marsh islands and sandy beaches, searching for colony sites that will be free from predators and safe from human disturbance. In the early dawn, hundreds of Common Terns leave their nighttime roost on sandy beaches and salt marsh islands to spread out over the coastal bays and ocean, searching for fish. Their white-and-gray bodies glisten in the sun, and they watch one another from afar. When one or two dive directly into the sea and come up with a fish, others are attracted, and soon the sky is filled with circling, screeching, and diving terns. Below them tiny fish, such as Silversides and Anchovies, driven to the surface by unseen predators, careen in panic, assaulted from above as well as below. Some fish even jump out of the water, to be quickly grabbed by the diving terns. There are so many small fish just below the surface that the water splashes and churns, and tiny droplets fly into the air, like glittering sparks in the early morning sun (fig. 4).

Finally, a large, silvery Bluefish leaps from the water, and then another appears. They are in hot pursuit of the small fish they have forced to the surface. These fish are trying to escape the Bluefish and are driven into the waiting beaks of the Common Terns. Terns continue to join the feeding frenzy, from as far away as a tern can see, which is much farther than we can see. Soon a thousand terns hover, circle, and dive above the school of Anchovies. Just as suddenly it ends, the Bluefish dive deep, the tiny fish swim deeper also, out of the reach of the Common Terns, and the terns once again spread out over the ocean.

Within only a few weeks the Common Terns will begin breeding on salt marsh islands, in spectacular groups of up to a thousand pairs. Each will nest less than a yard from its neighbor, and within days they will all lay eggs. So begins the summer breeding season for colonial birds along the New Jersey shore. But the Common Terns are not alone; Black Skimmers nest with them, and Laughing Gulls as well. On other islands there will be large colonies of Herring Gulls, equally noisy but each demanding a lot more space, a larger territory to raise their young. The larger Great Black-backed Gulls that nest among them, however, control the largest territories, and the best ones. They

4. A flock of Common Terns foraging on small fish driven to the surface by predatory Bluefish. (Photo by J. Burger)

are not only larger, but nest earlier than the Herring Gulls. They can command the highest ground, most secure from flooding, with the best vantage point to detect approaching predators, not that there are many creatures big enough to threaten a Black-back.

On nearby salt marsh creek edges, hundreds of Fiddler Crabs go about their business at low tide, all looking like miniature tractors moving across the mud, frantically stuffing algae into their mouths. They have to eat quickly while the tide is low, for when rising tides approach their burrows they must retreat inside and fill the hole with a mud plug, so they can wait out the high tide. They live on the mud banks between the high and the low tideline, where the nourishing waters can bring them new food with each tidal cycle, and where a thin layer of algae covers the mud. Tides are not their only enemy, for Clapper Rails search for them during the day and Black-crowned Night Herons stalk them at dusk and dawn. They must keep a wary eye out for any movement that might spell danger, and dash quickly to the nearest burrow.

Danger for all of these animals can come in the form of severe weather and the predators with whom they have evolved, or it can come in the form of human effects, particularly habitat loss. We have severely altered our environment. We build houses, marinas, and businesses, we bulkhead rivers and the coastline, we dam and change the course of rivers and streams, and we pollute the earth with toxic chemicals of one kind or another. Not only must the plants and animals of New Jersey cope with pollution from our own factories, but there is atmospheric deposition of a number of contaminants, borne by the wind and air currents from volcanic activity around the Earth, and industrial processes and power plants hundreds of miles to the west. The threat of pollution is more severe for animals that are higher on the food chain, for with every step, contaminants accumulate in tissues, and each succeeding step eats food with greater amounts of contaminants. Top-level predators, like hawks, owls, Coyotes, and Bluefish, are the most vulnerable, and in turn have the highest levels in their tissues.

We have altered New Jersey so much that many of us have forgotten that there are still many, many natural and undisturbed habitats here. We live in such crowded places that we have forgotten that many parts of New Jersey are so deserted and empty that people can get lost, even in the summer. When we check the salt marsh islands for nesting terns, skimmers, and gulls, we can see the shimmering silhouettes of distant fishermen on the bay, and the houses on the far-off barrier islands, but no one ever sets foot on the mosquito-infested islands, and we feel alone. When we walk through the forest in northwestern New Jersey we seldom see anyone. And when we wander through the Pine Barrens in the early summer searching for nesting Pine Snakes, we never see another soul (fig. 5). We can find a New Jersey that is not crowded with people and is not a thoroughfare between metropolises.

Nestled uncomfortably between New York and Philadelphia, New Jersey is a state that has often been overlooked. It has been considered a bedroom com-

5. Pine Snake hissing at intruder. (Photo by J. Burger)

munity for other, more bustling and more prosperous neighbors. With a land area of only 7,509 square miles, and a population of nearly 8 million people, the state is clearly crowded—the most densely populated state in our nation. The land area of New Jersey is so small that some ranchers in Wyoming or Texas might consider it only a decent-sized spread, but certainly not a state. Our mountains would make Californians snicker in derision, just as we chuckle at their concept of a river. The image of New Jersey as a giant turnpike, as a necessary link always leading from one place to another, still lingers in our minds. But reality is far better than this image. New Jersey has some of the most diverse habitats in the nation, some of the most intact and unique ecosystems (such as the Pine Barrens), and some of the most spectacular wildlife and plant life of any state in the nation. Nearly 19 percent of New Jersey is wetlands, compared to 5 percent for the nation overall, and some 45 percent of New Jersey is forested, more than was forested a hundred years ago. New Jersey's natural world is a well-kept secret.

About New Jersey

New Jersey has always had trouble establishing its identity. Nestled between New York City and Philadelphia, even in colonial times it was regarded as a pathway. Benjamin Franklin referred to New Jersey as a barrel tapped at both ends. Nonetheless, it had a rich colonial history, as it was one of the original thirteen colonies. It was pivotal during the Revolutionary War, and on two occasions the capital of the nation was here. During the Revolution, both sides marched to and fro, each side threatening or defending New York City and Philadelphia. General Washington and his troops spent more than one-quarter of the war on New Jersey soil, fighting major battles at Monmouth, Princeton, Red Bank, Springfield, and Trenton, to name but a few. South Jersey food and north Jersey iron supplied the armies, which spent three winters in the Jersey hills. Who can forget the image of George Washington standing in a small boat, crossing the Delaware? But who remembers that it was the idiosyncratic winter weather, a bitter freeze followed by a thaw, which Washington understood and the British did not, that allowed Washington to escape with his army from the Christmastime trap at Trenton?

Before the Europeans arrived, the Lenapé Indians roamed the forests, hunting deer and other small game. They burned small patches to provide edge habitats to increase the deer herd and improve their byways. They moved to the shore in the spring to trap fish, dig up clams, and pick up Horseshoe Crabs, returning to the forests when the hordes of mosquitos and biting flies made the shore unbearable.

New Jersey was first settled by Europeans in the 1630s, when the Dutch, Swedes, and Finns arrived, but by 1664 the English had moved in and taken over. Even before the Revolution, the Scots and Germans settled and farmed the fields in north Jersey, set up glassworks in Salem County, and established iron mines in Passaic County. New Jersey was a melting pot, with space and a job for everyone. Part of southern New Jersey, one quarter of the state, is below the Mason-Dixon line, and African slaves labored in the fields and in offices. Masses of Irish immigrants fled the potato famine in the Old Country, to dig the canals and build the railroads in the New World.

Being centrally located, New Jersey was caught in the middle of the slavery debate. Safehouses, strung out from Salem to Hoboken, helped slaves fleeing on the Underground Railroad reach freedom. There were strong New Jersey voices in support of slavery, but the state contributed more volunteers to the Northern army, in proportion to its size, than any other state.

After the Civil War, Italian immigrants arrived, and later the Poles, Swiss, Russians, and French, so that the population swelled, mainly in the northern urban centers. And today they still come, from the West Indies, Latin America, and Asia, each adding to our cultural diversity, a major strength of the state. Because of the great diversity of habitats, many people have found someplace that looked like home. New Jersey was home to some of the world's best-known figures, such as Thomas Edison, Albert Einstein, and the first American yellow fever martyr, Clara Maass.

Much of New Jersey's unsavory reputation derives from the view from the turnpike. The turnpike goes through some of the most highly industrialized portions of the nation, and for many miles the view is of smoke stacks and structures that intertwine and connect like a giant, unending mechanical octopus. Often at night a faint odor engulfs the car speeding past these plants, and flare towers send their flickering flames skyward. However, when the night air is clear, even the chemical plants with their different-sized buildings connected by pipes and walkways, bedecked with myriad patterns of dazzling lights, can be breathtaking. Farther south, the industrial complex turns to houses and apartments, and later to farmlands, forests, and sleepy towns.

New Jersey is a state of contrasts. There are wide, deserted sandy beaches in late October, endless salt marshes brimming with Snow Geese in the winter, peaceful pines intermixed with Scrub Oak in the Pinelands, and deep dark forests in northern Jersey; and there are also factories lining the turnpike, docks and bulkheads lining the waterways, and suburbia sprawling from New York to Camden. This is a densely populated state with many cities that seem to run into one another. But there are also windmills by the Millstone River, lighthouses guarding our barrier beaches, horses in rolling pastures in western New Jersey, and vegetable farms and Cranberry bogs in the south. The diversity is enormous, the possibilities are endless. In the south, the lands are flat and sandy, covered with hardwood forests that host a wide range of migrant birds. In the center is the Pine Barrens, a truly unique ecosystem recognized by its status as the Pinelands National Reserve, protected by the Pinelands Protection Act of 1979. Farther north there are mountains to the east (the Highlands) and to the west (the Kittatinny) that provide even more contrast. On the western edge, the Delaware Water Gap provides lovely views of mountains, and one can enjoy rafting on its waters. On the northeastern edge, the Palisades tower above the Hudson River, providing spectacular views and wonderful hiking trails. Upon this diverse landscape are some enthralling nature spectacles that are wonderful to behold.

Parts of New Jersey have among the highest human population density of any place in the world, yet parts are so deserted no one ever goes there. It remains the most industrialized state in the country, yet almost two-thirds of its land is still in farms and forest. The gross average income per farm is the highest in the nation, and the productive farms visible from any highway in southern New Jersey have given rise to the state's nickname, "the Garden State." It is one of the country's leading producers of blueberries, cranberries, peaches, and nursery plants. But also it is the nation's largest pharmaceutical producer and the second largest chemical producer, behind only Texas. It has the third-highest number of corporate headquarters in the nation, and our megamalls are among the largest in the world. While our industry and farming are world renowned, New Jersey also has the largest wilderness area east of the Mississippi (the Pine Barrens).

Oddly, even though many people think of New Jersey as covered with chemical plants, tourism is the state's second largest industry. Tourism, mostly associated with the Jersey shore, accounts for $11 billion a year in revenues. The shore is a summer place, opening with hordes of tourists on Memorial Day and closing down after Labor Day, with summer cottages boarded up against the cold and wind-swept months ahead. Tourism will continue to increase as ecotourism becomes more popular. New Jersey has some of the most lovely ecotourism spots in the country, and hosts some of the most spectacular natural events, such as the spawning Horseshoe Crabs and migrating shorebirds, unparalleled in the nation. Migrant birds at Cape May have long been a wonder, as thousands upon thousands of ecotourists converge there each spring and fall to watch. For ecotourists, being close to population centers such as New York and Philadelphia is a bonus, for New Jersey is just a short car ride away.

Just What Is a Spectacle?

The word *spectacular* conjures up images of snow-capped mountains, giant canyons, towering waterfalls, and huge herds of animals. It cries for extremes —the largest, smallest, highest, or most expansive. But New Jersey has its own spectacles, along its extensive coastline, its Pine Barrens, and its hilly forests. Our intention in writing this book was to explore and explain some of nature's

6. Great Egret just landing at the edge of a colony in late March. (Photo by
J. Burger)

spectacles that occur on our home territory. In nature, as well as in commerce
and the arts, New Jersey has often suffered an inferiority complex, but it should
not. We have some of the most wonderful assemblages of nesting colonial birds
of any coastal state. We have some of the best places to watch migrating hawks.
We have the Western Hemisphere's center of spawning Horseshoe Crabs and
of migrating spring shorebirds. We have some of the most lovely plants: blaz-
ing pink and white Mountain Laurel, brilliant and showy Yellow Lotus, and
small but spectacular bog plants. We have some of the most diverse scenery,
from expansive beaches, to the Pine Barrens, to hardwood forests, to the Palisades, and to the Delaware Water Gap. New Jersey is a state of great variability,
and it is time to see its beauty, instead of its congestion; to appreciate its great
biodiversity, as well as human diversity. It is time to see its amazing nature
spectacles.

Watching for Spectacles

We have provided you with some spectacles that you can easily find, and that
are relatively reliable in time and space. But there are many other spectacles that
you can discover on your own, when you hike through the mountains, walk
through the woodlands, or comb the beach watching the surf and sea. These
will be the most exciting, because you find them on your own and recognize

their significance. We give you some hints to finding your own natural spectacles, which are helpful for enjoying the ones described in this book as well.

The most important key to finding wonderful wildlife and plants is to look in the right places, at the right times. All animals and plants have preferred habitats, places they normally live. Waterbirds and aquatic plants are found near water, neotropical migrant birds are in forests, and snakes are usually hidden beneath logs and under brush piles. Learn all you can about the habitat of the animals or plants you are searching for. It is equally important to search at the right time of year. Migrant birds, sea turtles, and marine mammals are found in New Jersey only during some parts of the year. Many resident wildlife and plant species occur only in specific habitats, at specific times of the year. Many events occur for a month or less, or occur only at high tide or at low tide. Read carefully the timing of events, and then add your own judgment about the current season. Is it an early or late spring? Did the daffodils flower early, or were they late? Did the migrant birds arrive later than usual? These cues will help you find things in a given year.

It is critical to have the right equipment for observing. Binoculars and telescopes are essential for some activities, while hand lenses may help you see particularly small things. Bring extra film: it is light, inexpensive, and will keep if you do not use it on any given trip. Our car always has a small satchel full of a variety of field guides. The extra weight of a field guide or two is easily repaid when you find an unexpected treasure and are able to identify it. We also find it useful to have a notebook for writing detailed notes, and for making field sketches. Do not worry about the quality of your sketches; they are meant only to remind you about details when you are describing your find to others or are checking against reference books back at home. And of course, bring road maps and the creature comforts, such as insect repellent, sunglasses, sunscreen, water, and plenty of food. Cool, clean, fresh air always makes you hungrier than you think you will be. Watch out for ticks, and in this regard, wearing light-colored clothing makes it easier to spot them. Lyme disease is our most serious plague, although the recently approved vaccine is protecting some of us. In the winter, it is advisable to carry extra boots, warm gloves, extra blankets, and extra food. Though you don't plan to be stranded, it is always wise to be prepared, as the weather can turn bad, or you may have car trouble.

Finding interesting wildlife is often easier than observing it for a long time. Observing it well, from a close distance, requires blending in with your surroundings. Wild animals are sensitive to any disturbances, and this awareness is essential to their avoiding predators. All approaches should be slow, quiet, and as unobtrusive as possible. Wear clothing that blends with the environment, crouch down, and wear a wide-brimmed hat that obscures and shades your eyes. Keep very still, move only when necessary, and then move very slowly, averting your eyes so the animals are not alarmed by direct visual contact. For some animals that are sensitive to vibrations, such as snakes, Fiddler Crabs, and some insects, step very lightly so you create as few vibrations as possible. Watch their behavior, and if they seem edgy, move slowly backward, or stop until they return to their previous activities.

For some wildlife watching, it may be necessary to have a blind, or to use a car, boat, or other object such as a large tree as a blind. Sometimes you can move slowly from tree to tree, edging ever closer to your quarry. If there is nothing you can use as a blind, crouch down, or crawl along the ground slowly. If your body presents a large form on the horizon, animals will bolt. Sometimes carrying a small shrub in front of you, and moving slowly, works. American Indians approached their quarry using trees, shrubs, Buffalo hides, or other objects to hide themselves.

Finally, it is important to respect both the wildlife you are watching, and any other people who are nearby. If your movements and presence seem to disturb the wildlife, move away. This is especially true of animals engaged in sedentary activities, such as foraging in a restricted place, nesting, or bedding down for the night. If you disturb them from the site, you may expose their eggs or young to predators, or make them abandon the only suitable roosting or breeding place available. You should never touch any animal unless you are trained and have appropriate permits, and do not place yourself between a mother and young. Females become very agitated and may attack if you interfere with their babies.

It is equally important to respect the rights of other people, and the habitat. This means making as little noise as possible, and not blocking the view of others. Photographers have a special obligation not to get so close that other people cannot see or that wildlife is disturbed. Stay on the designated trails or walkways, remain on viewing platforms where provided, and try to avoid habitat destruction where there are no designated paths. Avoid trampling or picking vegetation, disturbing animals, disturbing people, or despoiling the habitat. We usually carry a litter bag so that we can leave a place more lovely than when we arrived. If every visitor picked up only one small bit of debris, our view of fields, streams, and woodlands would be improved.

About the Book

It was difficult to select spectacles for this book, not because there are so few, but because we wanted to identify predictable ones so we could describe how and when to find them. Many natural spectacles are difficult to see, and it is nearly impossible to predict exactly when to look for them. Mating Garter Snakes are amazing to watch, as dozens of males gather around a female, writhing and squirming, each attempting to be the one selected for mating. But finding such a mating group is nearly impossible; it just happens. You can pick

7. White-tailed Deer feeding in our backyard in Somerset in the late afternoon. (Photo by J. Burger)

the right time of the year and the appropriate habitat, but actually finding them is another matter. A group of over thirty hibernating snakes is very exciting, but they hibernate under the ground, and it is impossible to see them. Seeing a large "yard" of hundreds of White-tailed Deer gathered amid a pine forest, surrounded by deep snow, is equally exciting. But finding such a yard requires a particularly snowy winter, good deer production, and good luck. More often, we see a lone deer feeding in our yards (fig. 7).

Seeing five hundred Common Terns diving frantically over a school of bait fish driven to the surface by a large school of predatory Bluefish is wonderful. But these are very ephemeral events, and to find one requires spending hours out on the bay or ocean, watching foraging terns at all hours of the day. We have watched all these things serendipitously, and directing you to them is impossible.

Other spectacles are not constant. One of New Jersey's most famous bird spectacles, the egret roost and colony at Stone Harbor, no longer hosts the hordes of egrets and herons who made it their home night after night for decades. The town had set several blocks of woodlands aside for the heronry and built an observation area for tourists, who gazed in awe as flock after flock of these long-necked birds, some dark, some white, pitched out of the sky to settle among the branches, from which their various croaks and grunts bore witness to disputes over optimal perches. But alas, only a few years ago the herons abandoned the roost, and the sky is now silent. Why some birds abandon traditional nesting or roosting sites remains a mystery. It might be due to an increase in predators, to a decrease in habitat quality, or to an increase in disease or insect pests. After so many decades of nest use, the nests may have become hopelessly infested with mites and other noxious creatures, forcing the birds to move elsewhere. The egrets and herons moved to a nearby shore community, and we direct you there as this is one of the spectacles discussed in this book.

We have chosen to describe spectacles that are somewhat predictable, whose occurrence in space and time can be described. We selected spectacles that are so showy (like the Mountain Laurel or the Yellow American Lotus), so numerous (migrant hawks and songbirds), or so dramatic (spawning Horseshoe Crabs, shorebirds feeding on Horseshoe Crab eggs) that we can all enjoy them again and again, year after year. But we have also chosen some that at first might seem less spectacular, because the animals are either so small (Glass Eels) or so common (Fiddler Crabs). These are no less spectacular, however, once you discover the incredible obstacles they have overcome, the distances they have traveled, or the pitfalls they face in their daily lives.

All of the spectacles described in this book have some features in common; all have large numbers of their species gathering together for migrating, feeding, roosting, or reproducing. All of the events depicted play a vital role in the lives, reproduction, and survival of the species. And for many of the spectacles, New Jersey and its habitats are critical for the survival of the species, in some cases globally. For instance, well over 80 percent of the Red Knots in the Western Hemisphere stop in Delaware Bay to eat Horseshoe Crab eggs each spring. New Jersey is the center of the breeding range for Horseshoe Crabs and Laughing Gulls. All of us can appreciate and protect the natural spectacles that occur here in our own backyards, as well as those that are far away.

The book is organized around twenty-five nature spectacles, each having its own chapter, arranged by season. Each chapter begins with a brief description meant to set the mood for observation of the spectacle. This is followed by *key locations, directions,* and the *best time to visit.* The *prime habitat* section provides a brief characterization of the appropriate habitat in which to look for the plant or animal spectacle. The longer description provides the ambiance, natural history, and life history information to help you fully enjoy what you are observing, and to give you an understanding of how the plants or animals spend the rest of their year. A final section gives the name of an agency or organization that can help you get more information about specific timing. While their phone numbers may change with time, these organizations are committed to the natural history and biodiversity of New Jersey and will continue to preserve our heritage. Adventuresome travelers will remember that most of the parks, sanctuaries, and governmental offices have Websites that may have more information on current telephone numbers, visitors' hours, and special facilities or events.

The calendar of events on the next pages provides an overview of the appropriate times to visit and observe New Jersey's natural spectacles. More detailed descriptions can be found in the individual chapters.

Calendar of Events

Spring

Chorusing frogs   Mid-March to early June, the best chorus is in late March to early April when the Spring Peepers are calling.

Shad run on Delaware River   April and May, best the end of April.

Glass Eels at Cheesequake   Mid-March to early June, best last week of March and first two weeks of April, at low tide when they concentrate at creek mouths.

Spawning Horseshoe Crabs at Delaware Bay   Peaks the last two weeks in May, although some spawning from April through June. Peak activity at night on high tide (new and full moon). Peak at Sandy Hook is about two weeks later.

Migrating shorebirds at Delaware Bay   May 15 to June 10, but peaks last ten days in May (best on a falling tide, peaks about two to three hours after high tide).

Mountain Laurel   May 20 until June 20. Usually peaks Memorial Day.

Summer

Nesting Herons at Avalon   Late March to early June, but the peak is in April and May.

Nesting Laughing Gulls at Stone Harbor   Coastal islands, in late May to the end of June, when birds are incubating and feeding young chicks.

Nesting Least Terns and Skimmers   Late May to early July.

Fiddler Crabs at low tide   Late May to late September is best.

Butterflies in gardens   Best in July and August, when the largest numbers fly.

Grass Pink and other orchids at Webb's Mill   For Grass Pink, visit from June to early July. However, the bog is worth a visit at all times.

American Lotus at Mannington Marsh Peaks at the end of July to early September.

Coalescing Terns and Skimmers at Hereford Inlet Late July to early September.

Fall

Migrant Monarchs at Cape May Mid-September to mid-October is best.

Migrant Hawks at inland ridges September and October.

Migrant Hawks at Cape May Last half of September and first half of October for the peak of migration.

Migrant songbirds at Cape May Last half of September and first week of October for the peak of migration.

Bats at Hibernia Mine The large swarming groups can be observed from late August through mid-October.

Winter

Dwarf Pine plains Anytime.

Snow Geese at Brigantine From November until the bays freeze over.

Wintering Gulls in coastal New Jersey September to March, but they concentrate in January and February.

Brant and other waterfowl on the North Shore December to March, especially when they are concentrated by some freezing weather.

Swans at Whites Bog and coastal lakes From late fall until the lakes freeze, usually in late January or February.

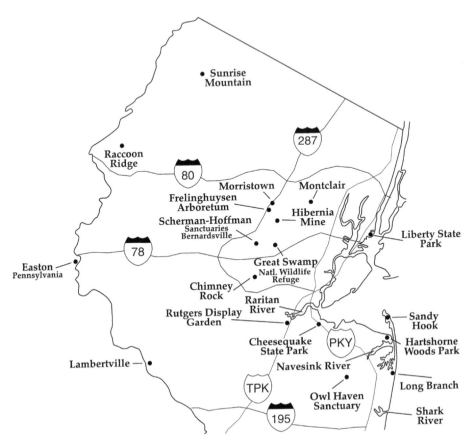

Map of northern New Jersey showing locations mentioned in the text.

Map of southern New Jersey showing locations mentioned in the text.

Spring

8. Two male Green Frogs try to mate inappropriately with a male while another waits nearby. (Photo by J. Burger)

1

Chorusing Frogs
in the Spring

A cool evening breeze rustles through the pines, but it is hardly noticeable above the chorus of Spring Peepers rising from the edges of the pond, each male searching for a mate in an age-old ritual. These tiny, inch-long creatures call from the water's surface or the stems of emerging cattails, expanding their throat pouch to a huge, translucent bubble as they utter their loud musical notes.

KEY LOCATIONS: Almost any woodland pond, even some that are close to suburbia, will have breeding frogs, especially Spring Peepers in early spring and Green Frogs in summer. Key sites to visit include Great Swamp National Wildlife Refuge in Morris County, the Hirair Hovnanian Plant and Wildlife Sanctuary (a N.J. Audubon Sanctuary, Ocean County) and Webb's Mill Bog for Pine Barrens Tree Frog in Ocean County, and the two ponds beside the Bayshore Mall in southern Cape May County. Hearing frogs is easy; seeing them can be very challenging.

DIRECTIONS: For Great Swamp National Wildlife Refuge, take I-287 north to exit 30A (Maple Avenue); take Lord Stirling Road (it becomes White Bridge Road) to Pleasant Plains Road, where you turn left and proceed through the gate to the refuge headquarters.

The Audubon Sanctuary Pond (Hirair Hovnanian Plant and Wildlife Sanctuary) is on Route 530 (Dover Road), 5 miles west of the Garden State Parkway (exit 80).

Webb's Mills Bog is located on the east side of Route 539, about 5 miles south of Route 70, in the Greenwood Wildlife Management Area.

For the Bayshore Mall in South Cape May, take the Ferry Road toward the Cape May–Lewes Ferry, and look for the ponds behind the mall. There are two ponds that were old gravel pits.

BEST TIME TO VISIT: Frogs are chorusing from mid-March (Spring Peepers) to mid-summer, depending on the species, the weather, and the location in the state. In general, the frogs in Cape May are about three weeks ahead of those in the Great Swamp in northern New Jersey. Best time to visit is on a warm rainy night (see table 1).

TABLE 1. Timing of Breeding in Frogs in Three Regions of New Jersey

	Great Swamp	Audubon Pond and Webb's Mill	Cape May
Habitat	Hardwood swamp and forest	Pine Barrens bog	Coastal scrub
Spring Peepers	Late March to mid-April	Mid-March to mid-April	Early March to early April
Wood Frog	Mid-March to April	None	Early to mid-March
Chorus Frog	Late March	Mid-March	Early to mid-March
Gray Treefrog	Early June	Late May to late June	May and early June
Pine Barrens Treefrog	None	May	None
Southern Leopard Frog	None	Mid-April	Early April
Fowler's Toad	None	None	June
Green Frog	Late April to July	Mid-April to June	Mid-April to mid-June
Northern Cricket Frog	June	Late May to June	Late May to late June
Bullfrog	June–July	June–July	June–July

NOTE: Given are the more common frogs found in inland ponds. Trilling Fowler's Toads can be found all along the coasts in late May and June.

PRIME HABITAT: Vernal, or temporary, ponds often have the best choruses because a pond that dries down completely cannot support a population of fish that eat the eggs and tadpoles of frogs. Both Green Frogs and Bullfrogs can be found in permanent ponds, since their tadpoles are large enough and foul-tasting enough for fish to avoid. However, the choruses are not as nice in the spring and they call only sporadically all summer.

On a warm rainy night in late March, when darkness descends on the forest ponds, and clouds hang low in the sky, keeping in the moisture, a lone Spring Peeper calls tentatively, and then all is silent. In the darkness, only a glimmer of moonlight is reflected from the water, and the faint shapes of tangled vegetation are barely visible. Minutes pass, and then the Peeper begins anew, louder and more determined. Another begins peeping, and then a third, and just as suddenly, they pause. Ten minutes pass, and then as if on cue, Spring Peepers begin to call from all around the pond. Patches of ice linger in the shade of low-hanging bushes, but otherwise the water is open, open enough to encourage these first spring frogs to begin anew their ancient breeding ritual.

The chorus of Spring Peepers fills the night with high-pitched, birdlike whistles that can be heard a half mile away. With time, the chorus crescendos even louder, as more and more Peepers join in. It is now difficult to pick out an individual, for when one stops, another takes up the chorus. Though the sound is almost deafening, it is a delightful portent of winter's end.

Occasionally a chorus of quacking breaks the silence, as male Wood Frogs call tentatively. They too begin slowly, until several are alternating their voices. They sound like a distant flock of Mallards, as the loud sounds emanate from their inflated throats. The small, two-inch Wood Frogs are brown with black face masks. Wood Frogs lay their eggs in round gelatinous globules, even while ice persists on parts of the pond.

Spring Peepers are a tiny member of the Hylidae family, commonly called treefrogs. They can climb easily in the tall grasses, shrubs, and trees that line the ponds, using the small disks or suction cups at the end of each toe. They are recognizable by the small dark cross on the back.

Spring choruses serve to attract the females to the ponds, to begin the cycle that will result in egg laying. While the chorus of Wood Frogs lasts only a couple of weeks, Spring Peepers can go on for over a month, as more and more frogs return to the pond from their upland hiding places where they pass the rest of the year hidden in leaf litter. As the last ice melts, Wood Frogs and Spring Peepers are joined by Chorus Frogs, which sound like someone is rubbing a finger over the teeth of a rusty old comb.

Spring Peepers, Wood Frogs, and Chorus Frogs are the vanguard of the many different frogs and toads to come to these ponds. Not all of the fifteen species of frogs and toads native to New Jersey can be found in a single breeding pond, but several may be found together, giving a wide range of trills, whistles, grunts, croaks, and rusty-sounding twangs. In a few weeks, Gray Treefrogs also come down to the ponds, adding their strange, barely melodious trills.

In mid-April, Green Frogs and Bullfrogs begin to call, having awakened from their winter rest in the bottom muds of ponds. The Green Frogs, aptly named because they are green, sound like the plunking of a banjo string, while the Bullfrogs have a deep bass call that sounds like "jug-a-rum." Male Green Frogs have brilliant yellow throats during the breeding season, while the females' throats remain white. They have the distinction of being one of the more diurnal frogs, and it is relatively easy to watch them calling during May and June from their territories scattered around a pond. The males even engage one another in prolonged territorial battles that may last fifteen or twenty minutes. They clasp each other around the middle and jump up and down like boxers. The winner is the one who can force the other frog underwater. Bullfrogs are the largest frog in most of the United States, sometimes reaching a length of eight inches. This is the frog whose legs are served in some southern restaurants.

Finally, Cricket Frogs join the chorus, but they are often overlooked because they sound like an insect or as if someone were banging two pebbles together.

Although they leave the safety of their muddy hibernation places under leaves and other debris at the same time as Spring Peepers, they do not join the chorus until late May or June. They are quite small, never reaching two inches in length.

While most of the frogs discussed above occur in ponds throughout New Jersey, two frogs are limited to Sphagnum bogs and Cedar swamps where the water is more acid: the Pine Barrens Treefrog and the Carpenter Frog. Carpenter Frogs are easy to identify for they sound exactly like a carpenter banging twice on a particularly troublesome nail. As more and more frogs join the chorus, they sound like a convention of carpenters all trying to show how fast they can put on a roof.

The Pine Barrens Treefrog is an endangered species in New Jersey, largely due to the threat of habitat destruction. It is also threatened by off-road vehicles. For some odd reason, when people get behind the wheel of such vehicles, they cannot resist charging through every small puddle and pond they see, splashing Treefrog eggs and tadpoles to the wind. All it takes to protect them is driving around the puddles.

Limited to the Pine Barrens, this little frog is only one and a half inches long, with a bright apple green back and white underparts (fig. 9). Pine Barrens Treefrogs are adorable, with a bright purple pinstripe running from the eye to the groin. They give a low nasal "quonk" sound that is amazingly difficult to locate. Even two people with flashlights triangulating on a calling frog will find it challenging. And as one gets within a few yards, the male stops calling, remaining silent for a quarter hour, severely trying one's patience and resolve.

Though the chorus may contain many different species of frogs, depending on the habitat and latitude, each species has a unique mating call that attracts only females of that species. The males come first to the ponds, and some jostling goes on while they decide who gets what territory, who can perch where. Each male takes up a calling place and begins each night trying to attract as many females as possible. They set about calling, each trying to be louder than the other. Male Spring Peepers can extend their throat into a huge bubble almost as big as their bodies, accounting for the exceptionally loud call emanating from their tiny bodies.

When the chorus reaches a fever pitch, the females are attracted to the pond, and, unmolested by the males, they wander among the chorusers, searching for just the right one. The males usually remain where they are, waiting for the females to approach; but once in a while a male is overly anxious and jumps on the back of a female who has not selected him. She tries to get away, while he tries to cling. Usually, however, the females move from station to station listening to each male in turn.

Sometimes a female is not quite ready to lay her eggs, or the calls are not exactly right, so she hops back into the vegetation at the side of the pond and begins to search for an insect or other food item. The males continue calling, for there are other females hopping among them, and the chorus will go on long into the night.

9. Male Pine Barrens Treefrog sits on a branch it uses as a calling perch. (Photo by J. Burger)

One of the most remarkable things about the spring chorus is that the calls are actually quite difficult for people to locate. Surrounded by calling frogs, one would think it would be easy to walk right up to one. But there are several difficulties. First, the frogs are very sensitive to any noise, movement, or vibration, and they stop calling and remain silent for many minutes. One must tread very, very slowly, and very lightly. Finding frogs, particularly the smaller Spring Peepers or Treefrogs, is a time-consuming process, involving a few steps forward followed by long periods of waiting for the nearest frog to begin calling anew. It usually requires two people to triangulate the sound, standing about fifteen feet apart, because the calling frog is probably farther away than you think. Where the points intersect is a good place to start looking for the calling frog. This can be repeated until the frog is located.

Another difficulty is that the frogs always sound closer than they are. We have spent many a night creeping slowly through the water at the edge of a pond, being sure we were very close to a particularly loud frog, only to turn on our flashlight and discover that no frog was in view. One easy way to find frogs is to sit on a lonely and deserted dirt road close to a breeding pond, on a warm and rainy night. You can often watch them making their way to the pond. On several rainy nights in the Great Swamp in northern New Jersey we have watched dozens of Green Frogs hopping rapidly across the road, each going in seemingly random directions.

Once a male contacts a female, he grabs her around the middle and holds on tightly, and this is called amplexus. He squeezes her steadily to force out the eggs and deposits his sperm as they emerge. While some frogs, such as Spring Peepers and Pine Barrens Treefrogs, lay individual eggs that are attached to vegetation or small twigs, other frogs, such as Green Frogs and Bullfrogs, lay large masses of eggs in the water. The species that lay eggs individually are pursuing a strategy of making it difficult for any predator to find all of the eggs, since they are dispersed around the habitat, and are so small they are cryptic. The species that lay all their eggs in one large mass are counting on rapid hatching with the result that some eggs survive to the tadpole stage. Usually the Green Frogs attach the sticky egg masses to dense vegetation such as Water Lilies or Arrowhead. This partly camouflages the eggs and hides them from terrestrial predators. But the eggs must remain near the surface for the spring sun to accelerate the development of the embryos.

Each tiny black egg is surrounded by a small mass of nearly clear jelly, and the large masses look like strands of beads, all matted together. Depending on the warmth of the sun, it takes only a few days to a week for the eggs to hatch. It is difficult to determine exactly when they hatch, for in the last few hours the round black egg changes to the shape of a small, wriggling rice grain, and then the minute creatures twist and turn, eventually breaking free of the jelly. For a few more hours they remain relatively motionless, close to the jelly and the other hatching tadpoles. Before your eyes the tiny shapes take form, and gradually there is a head with a tail—the tadpoles are hatched. They swim tentatively at first, and then strongly, finding their way to the protection of emergent vegetation.

The tadpoles hide for a few more hours, and then slowly begin to search the sides and bottom of the ponds for algae to eat. They rise to the surface in the heat of the day, often resting at the edge of the pond or emergent vegetation. There they bask, taking in the warm sun, warming their bodies so they can rapidly digest the food they have eaten. Their aim is to grow rapidly, for the larger they are, the fewer predators there are that can eat them.

If their parents have chosen wisely, they are in a pond with no fish predators and few dragonfly predators. This is particularly necessary for the very small frogs, such as Spring Peepers, Gray Treefrogs, and Pine Barrens Treefrogs. They are so small that a wide variety of fish and predacious dragonfly nymphs would eat the eggs, tadpoles, and even the small emerging froglets. Thus these species breed in ephemeral ponds that dry up at least once a year, providing an inhospitable habitat for fish and dragonflies that require water all year around. But they must also have selected ponds that will contain water for at least long enough to hatch, grow as a tadpole, and finally emerge as a terrestrial frog. Occasionally, we have come across hordes of tadpoles, mainly of toads, that were stranded in a drying mud puddle and succumbed before they could metamorphose.

The larger frogs, such as Bullfrogs and Green Frogs, on the other hand, breed in permanent ponds because their tadpoles normally require more than

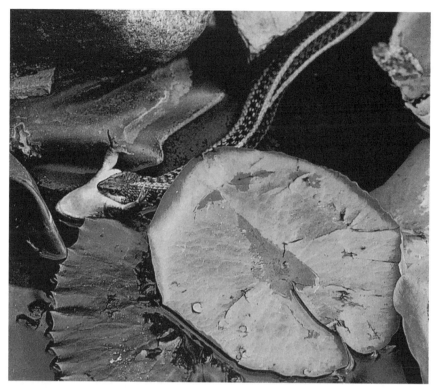

10. Garter Snake capturing a male Green Frog. (Photo by J. Burger)

a year to reach a stage where they metamorphose into adult frogs. In the South these species may emerge in less than a year, but in New Jersey, both species overwinter as large tadpoles in the bottom mud and commence eating again and growing in the early spring. They normally emerge in late spring and early summer, when hundreds of baby Green Frogs can be seen sitting on Water Lilies or other aquatic vegetation, some retaining a tiny remnant of their tail.

Emerging frogs are extremely vulnerable to predators because they have not learned to hide, to watch for predators, to move quickly with any motion, or to forage effectively. Garter Snakes are particularly adept at slithering through the water without making waves, without moving the delicate vegetation on which the recently emerged frogs bask in the sun. They slip up unnoticed and easily capture six or seven young Green Frogs for a nice meal. They can even capture adult Green Frogs (fig. 10). Then they return to the edge of the pond to bask in the sun, allowing the warmth to aid their digestion. After a few days of rest under nearby rocks, they are ready to catch the next wave of emerging Green Frogs.

During metamorphosis, frogs go from eating vegetation, such as algae, to the adult stage of eating insects and other small animals. Their digestive tract shortens, they breathe air, and they become largely terrestrial. They hunt for prey on land, rather than in the water, and spend long hours watching and waiting for an unwary insect to pass close enough for them to whisk out their tongue to capture it.

Recent declines worldwide in several species of amphibians have given rise to great concern. Since the United States was first settled, over half of its original 200 million acres of wetlands have been lost to dredging, channelization, filling, and other operations designed to make them useful for developers. The loss of wetlands continued throughout the twentieth century, slowed somewhat by the Wetlands Protection Act. Moreover, there are very few actual amphibian counts from the early years, so it is difficult to recognize population trends, but wherever people have studied or counted, the trend is downward, alarmingly so for some of the high-mountain amphibians in the West and in the tropics.

Many species of frogs spread out from the ponds into the surrounding fields and woodlands, and if these uplands disappear, so do the frogs. Roads, railroads, and other forms of pavement fragment the habitat, presenting barriers that prevent the frogs from reaching their breeding ponds or kill large numbers as they move to the ponds. Often the wetlands themselves are preserved, but development encroaches on the ponds, leaving scant woodland habitat for the frogs and salamanders to occupy for the rest of the year. Some ponds become surrounded by golf courses, a particularly inhospitable habitat for most forms of wildlife. Most golf courses do not count as open space; they are monocultures of stunted grass from which most animals are excluded, often by the use of toxic pesticides that eventually enter the ponds as well. Yet they offer an untapped potential for wildlife-friendly management.

The causes of the recent worldwide decline in amphibians are not clearly established. Habitat loss and degradation, introduction of exotic species (both competitors and predators), and human disturbance have taken their toll for many years. However, in the early 1990s researchers began to realize that declines were also taking place in relatively pristine and isolated ponds, causing great alarm. A number of frogs in montane tropical rainforests far from industrialization and development all but disappeared, and a few have become extinct. Many frogs vanished from relatively large and protected forests.

Because of their moist, thin, permeable skins, frogs are very vulnerable to pollutants, pathogens, and to changes in ultraviolet radiation. Increased exposure to ultraviolet light has been suggested as one cause of declines. Acid rain has been postulated as another, along with a variety of other pollutants such as PCBs, dioxins, oil, and heavy metals (lead, cadmium, mercury, selenium). Many of the effects are additive; acid rain changes the pH of lakes, which in turn makes it easier for organisms to take up mercury. Thus, levels of mercury that might not have been toxic before acid rain do become toxic or cause sublethal effects.

It is also difficult to determine which stage of the frogs' life is the cause of the decline. It could be the vulnerable egg stage due to low hatching rates. Or it could be the tadpole state; tadpoles store toxic chemicals in their tails during development as a way of ridding their bodies of contaminants. However, during metamorphosis, tadpoles receive a large burst of contaminants as they quickly reabsorb their tails. Or it could be the adult stage, because of the relative permeability of the skin, and the fact that adults spend weeks or months in breeding ponds. Toxic chemicals in the water can quickly permeate their skin, potentially affecting both reproductive rates and survival. Recent studies of several frog species in Central America attribute their demise to a fungus infestation that kills adult frogs; other such infections may soon come to light, perhaps aided by mitigating factors such as changes in ultraviolet radiation or water pH.

At present there is no evidence that any one factor is the cause of the worldwide decline. Instead, the causes vary from one locale to another, with one species or another. What is clear, however, is that most of the immediate factors known to cause declines are a result of human activity, whether it is habitat loss or degradation, pathogens, introduced species, pollution, or increased ultraviolet radiation resulting from ozone depletion. Many of these problems are being addressed both locally and globally, but they are difficult problems requiring cooperation among individuals and nations.

Even more disturbing to ecologists, of course, is the notion that the frogs may simply be an early warning signal of impending danger, much as rapidly declining populations of Pelicans, Eagles, and other fish-eating birds presaged the dire consequences of unrestricted use of DDT and other pesticides. The lack of one key factor in the amphibian decline may indicate a general ecosystem effect, unlike the case of DDT. Amphibian groups that have survived for millions of years have experienced bad times before; assaults by glaciers, drought, and oceanic inundations have all taken their toll. But the human-caused or anthropogenic changes happen so rapidly, in the course of decades rather than centuries or millennia, that populations do not have time to relocate or adapt.

For the moment, most of the frog populations in New Jersey are stable, although the Pine Barrens Treefrog is endangered and Wood Frogs have been declining. We can still go out on a warm spring night and find a thunderous and wonderful chorus of Spring Peepers. When the warm rains start in March and April, the ponds are alive with a changing suite of amphibians that arrive in hordes to call, mate, lay their eggs, and then disappear again into the uplands. Not for another year will they be so audible.

FOR MORE INFORMATION: Contact Great Swamp National Wildlife Refuge (973-425-1222), or New Jersey Audubon (908-204-8998) for information on local breeding ponds. It is best to call your local Audubon chapter for information about your particular area. Also check http://www.njaudubon.org.

11. Shad fishing along the Delaware River by Steve Lewis, his family, and colleagues. Setting the nets (*top*) and hauling them in (*bottom*) at Lambertville in late May. *Facing page:* A catch of mostly Gizzard Shad with a few American Shad (N. Hardpence on the left, T. Kroemmelbein on the right). (Photos by J. Burger)

2

Shad Run on the Delaware River

In mid-April, when the Shadbush trees are covered with white blossoms, punctuating our winter woods with signs of spring, thousands upon thousands of silver-bodied American Shad swim upstream toward ancient spawning grounds, sometimes running so thick they can be scooped out with hand nets.

KEY LOCATIONS: At Lambertville (Hunterdon County). Also, the fish ladder at Easton, Pennsylvania, just across the Delaware River from Phillipsburg, New Jersey, has a viewing platform below water level.

DIRECTIONS: For Lambertville, take Route 202 west to the Delaware River, and Route 29 south to Lambertville. In Lambertville, Route 29 becomes Main Street; take a right onto Cherry Street at the edge of town, and at the end of Cherry Street make a left onto North Union Street. Go south on North Union toward the bridge to New Hope. At the intersection just before the bridge, make a right onto Bridge Street, and just before going across the bridge, turn right on Lambert Lane and park there. Seining for Shad usually occurs at the bridge about five o'clock in the evening during the run.

For Easton Dam, take I-78 west and cross the Delaware River into Pennsylvania. Take exit 22, a quarter of a mile past the toll booth, and follow signs to Route 611. The road winds about 1.2 miles through Easton (Philadelphia Avenue turns into St. Johns Street). After going down a steep hill, the road turns sharply left under the railroad tracks. Immediately after passing under the railroad tracks, take a sharp right onto Route 611 south (ignore the fact that you are actually pointing north). The road curves along the Lehigh River, and after about 0.1 mile (on a curve) there is a parking lot on the left for Hugh Moore Park. The fish ladder or passageway is readily accessible. It lies at the junction of Lehigh River and the Delaware River at the dam. A stairway leads down to a viewing platform, where two large windows allow viewing of the passing fish.

BEST TIME TO VISIT: The Shad "run" is during April and May, but mid to late April is best at Lambertville, and early May is best at Easton because the run is dependent on water temperatures. Some Shad are visible during the day but are most abundant from dusk to midnight. The best time to visit is during the Shad Festival at Lambertville, which is usually the last weekend in April.

PRIME HABITAT: Spawning usually takes place in rivers with gentle slopes and sandy bottoms or very fine gravel. However, the Shad are most easily seen as they move upstream through artificial fish ladders and passageways located next to dams on major rivers or their tributaries, or during the Shad Festival in Lambertville when fishermen catch them in seines.

When the cold winds of March finally give way to the warm sun of April, huge numbers of two-foot-long Shad, our largest member of the herring family, leave the Atlantic Ocean and coastal bays to return to their place of birth. It has been four or five years since the tiny silver fish left their natal streams, traveling downriver to the ocean in large schools. The adults begin to arrive at the very end of March or the first of April, when the water temperature barely exceeds 40 degrees Fahrenheit, and the runs upriver begin in mid-April.

Along the banks of the rivers, the white buds of the Shadbush are opening, and hordes of small Shadflies swarm around our faces, a sign that the Shad are running in the rivers. The delicate white blossoms provide the only woodland color this early in the spring, and they were named after the Shad run. The blossoms are in full bloom in mid-April, just when the Shad run begins in full force. Shadbush is also called Serviceberry and Juneberry, because it produces small red or purplish applelike fruits that people used to eat fresh or make into jelly. Many animals eat these small berries, including Skunks, Raccoons, foxes, squirrels, Black Bears, and many species of birds.

For the next six weeks, large numbers of Shad swim up the rivers to their spawning grounds. Some travel as far as two hundred to three hundred miles upriver, but in many tributaries they are prevented from doing so by dams or other obstructions. In the rush of tumbling water, their silvery sides glisten in the sun; their tops gleam a shiny, bluish green. Males arrive first, the smaller females arrive next, and the very largest egg-laden females arrive last. Females can weigh up to eleven pounds, although most weigh from two to five pounds, and can carry 115,000 to 450,000 eggs each.

Shad are anadromous fish, which means they live in saltwater for most of their lives, but return to spawn in the freshwater streams and rivers of their birth. Other anadromous fish in New Jersey include Atlantic Sturgeon, Shortnosed Sturgeon, Striped Bass, Sea Lamprey, Rainbow Smelt, Blueback Herring, and Alewife. Most swim up the larger rivers, such as the Hudson or the Delaware, for some distance before spawning in the river or its tributaries. Their path is often blocked by dams, but still they come, forcing their way upward. One of the unique features of the Delaware River is that there are no dams on the main river, only on the tributaries, allowing for a run in the main river.

In some places, thoughtful managers have built fish ladders, a staircase of water, for the fish to climb, allowing them to bypass dams. With great thrusts of their powerful muscles, the fish swim up against the turbulent currents, or leap from one step to the next, eventually reaching the top. Other fish passageways are inclined planes, allowing the fish to swim up against the current. Passing these structures, they continue farther and farther upstream until they reach traditional spawning grounds.

In shallow streams the Shad gather by the hundreds, and with vigorous thrashing and splashing near the surface, the females shed their pale amber or pink eggs while the males fertilize them. Since the sperm can live in the water for only a few seconds, the male and female swim alongside each other, allowing the male to fertilize the eggs as they are laid. The swimming motion of the sperm is not activated until they touch water, and then the sperm have only a few precious seconds to find and penetrate an egg. The fertilized eggs sink slowly to the bottom or are caught by currents and carried downstream where they settle in the gravel. The spent adults, now emaciated from their arduous journey, swim slowly downriver. Many die on the way, but some reach the ocean. In Canada, nearly all the Shad are repeat spawners (iteroparous), while farther south than New Jersey, nearly all spawn only once and die (semelparous). Only about 5 percent of the Delaware River Shad live to breed again, although nearly half of those that spawn in the Hudson River return the following year. This ancient spawning ritual is repeated in rivers all along the Atlantic Ocean, from the Gulf of St. Lawrence to Florida.

The Shad eggs are very vulnerable to predators because they are small and are rich in protein, and many of the eggs are eaten by aquatic insect larvae and small fish as they drift passively with the currents. The eggs on the bottom or in the water column hatch in about a week, but it is two or three weeks before the minute larval fish are able to swim. Finally, the tiny survivors swim to nearby freshwater marshes and coves, where they remain hidden from predators in the aquatic grasses near the bottom, and feed on small crustaceans and insects. They grow quickly, and mortality drops dramatically as they become longer and fast enough to avoid predators. Although they spend most of the day ten feet deep or more, at night they rest near the surface.

By September they are fingerlings, three to five inches long. Triggered by decreasing water temperatures, they slowly make their way downstream to the river, and downriver to the Atlantic Ocean, arriving by October or November. The trigger, however, may be their own size as well as water temperature because some young shad in the Hudson River grow extremely fast and make it to the ocean in June and July, while others remain in Delaware Bay even during their first winter.

Once in the ocean, the young mingle and coalesce in schools of thousands of other fingerlings from different rivers, even from as far away as Chesapeake Bay. The center of American Shad distribution is from Connecticut to North Carolina. From colonial times until the early 1990s the most productive fisheries were in Chesapeake Bay and elsewhere along the Atlantic coast. Nowadays, the schools wander along the coast, but the Gulf of Maine is a favorite place for them to forage during the summer and fall, where they have been caught in trawls at 50 fathoms (300 feet), and some individuals have been caught up to 110 miles offshore. Then they move south to overwinter in deeper waters off the Middle Atlantic states and southward. While in these schools they stay near the seafloor, feeding on zooplankton, crustaceans, and occasionally on small fish.

They remain in these schools until they are four or five years old, and then the schools disintegrate into cohorts of adults that were hatched in the same rivers. Like the more famous Salmon of the Pacific Coast, the Shad are guided by chemical odors back to the rivers of their origin, to begin anew the spawning that will produce the next generation.

The migration and spawning of the American Shad is one of the great spectacles in our rivers and streams (fig. 12). Although many outdoor enthusiasts seldom appreciate the event because the fish are hidden beneath the waters, fishermen surely do. The Shad is a herring and is much prized for the table, as are its eggs. Indeed, the species' scientific name, *sapidissima*, means "most delicious." There have been successful fisheries both in the Delaware River and in the Hudson River. The long rows of Shad seines were a characteristic sight in the Hudson River when we grew up. The catch in the Hudson River has varied markedly since colonial times, being over four million pounds in 1909 and 1942, but as low as 40,000 pounds in 1916. The catch in the Delaware

12. The catch of American Shad from one seine haul is still low in the Delaware River, but the shad populations are increasing. (Photo by J. Burger)

River was about 100,000 Shad (about 400,000 pounds) from the 1930s to the 1950s, but it dropped to about 25,000 pounds by the 1970s.

The causes for the declines in the 1950s, 1960s, and 1970s are much debated, but the fishermen attribute the declines to the construction of dams on tributaries that block the migrations, pollution by raw sewage and chemicals, and to lowered dissolved oxygen. Some reluctantly mention overfishing. Habitat loss and habitat degradation have played a part in the declines. There has been widespread destruction of spawning areas for many anadromous species in North America. In the Delaware River, pollution and oxygen depletion near Philadelphia were responsible for the decline of adult Shad swimming upstream, as well as the number of juveniles that could get downstream in late summer and fall.

Serious efforts to clean up the Hudson and Delaware Rivers, along with artificial propagation and restocking, have resulted in increases in the Shad run in the last two decades. The number of Shad counted at Lambertville rose from about 150,000 in the 1970s to 830,000 in 1989, an increase largely attributed to improved sewage-treatment methods that resulted in higher oxygen levels, so necessary for egg development, spawning, and survival of the young. Unfortunately by 1998 this number had dropped to just under 400,000.

Overfishing is one of the major factors in the decline in Shad populations; they are fished both in the ocean prior to spawning and within rivers during the spawning run. Before regulations were passed, commercial fishermen competed for ways to catch more Shad, and some even fished with nets that were a few miles long, catching thousands of Shad at a time. Shad that avoided the massive nets were often caught by recreational fishermen who specialized on the nooks and crannies avoided by the commercial fishermen.

The building of dams also had a severe effect on spawning because the shad are prevented from reaching their spawning grounds. The shad are programmed to return to the place where they hatched, and dams prevent this, leading to heavy mortality. As dam after dam was constructed, Shad and other anadromous species were barred from accessing their traditional streams, and population after population simply died out, affecting the upstream ecosystem in many rivers and tributaries. At some dams, recently constructed fish lifts, fish ladders, and passageways allow the Shad to run in rivers such as the Susquehanna and the Lehigh in Pennsylvania. Fish ladders are water stairways, allowing the fish to continue moving upstream. In other places, lifts or elevators allow fish to swim into a box which is then transported upward, where the fish are released.

The fish ladder south of Easton, adjacent to Hugh Moore Park in Pennsylvania, is an example of successful management (fig. 13). The ladder is a series of compartments, each slightly higher than the next, that raise the fish from the

13. View of the fish ladder at Easton, Pennsylvania. Fish swim toward the fastest-moving water, which takes them upstream. (Photo by J. Burger)

Delaware River to the level of the Lehigh River. A series of baffles maintains the turbulent water that is necessary for the upward movement of Shad and other fish. The current must be swift enough for the fish to detect it as they move up the Delaware. The fish ladder is visible from above as well as from an underground viewing room where you can see the Shad moving upstream through the passageway. Other fish also use the ladder, and it is exciting to see them moving swiftly through the bubbling water. Hugh Moore Park is also worth visiting because it has a museum that is a replica of a lock tender's house containing historical information on the canal era.

Hatching fry in fish hatcheries is another management tool for increasing populations. This method is practiced in Pennsylvania by the Fish and Boat Commission, but not in New Jersey. American Shad adults are caught just before they spawn, their eggs and sperm are artificially squeezed out, and the two are mixed to achieve fertilization. After the eggs hatch, the larval fish are raised in captivity until they are large enough to be past one of their most vulnerable periods. In Pennsylvania, small eighteen- to twenty-day-old fingerling Shad only a few millimeters long are released into the Lehigh River. Here they grow for several months, imprinting on the river's chemical composition, or "smell," before migrating downriver in the fall.

The fish ladder at Easton was constructed by the Delaware River Shad Fisherman's Association and the Pennsylvania Department of Conservation and Natural Resources in 1993. So far, between two thousand and three thousand Shad make the run up this passageway each year, and the numbers are increasing, indicating the success of this management effort. Future management can increase the number of stream tributaries with viable Shad populations.

Some hatcheries mark the fish they release so they can tell whether any survive to spawn, and to identify from which hatchery they came. Being able to identify whether Shad are from a hatchery or whether they are wild is extremely important in their conservation and management. Such discrimination is essential to allow management of weak and declining stocks and to curtail their harvesting. Today, molecular techniques are being used to identify specific fish stocks. Molecular data indicate that although there is genetic variation within the populations, the populations of the Connecticut, Hudson, and Delaware Rivers are homogeneous overall. This suggests that colonization of these rivers must have occurred after the Ice Age, less than 10,000 years ago.

The Bureau of Marine Fisheries of New Jersey's Department of Environmental Protection is participating in a multi-agency American Shad tagging program for the Hudson and Delaware Rivers. So far the tagging program indicates that Delaware Bay is a mixing area for various stocks of American Shad from all along the Atlantic. The Bureau also monitors the commercial landings of Shad, which amounted to 212,552 pounds in 1996; 70 percent were obtained from coastal waters.

Because of its commercial and recreational importance, the American Shad was introduced into the Columbia River in the Pacific Northwest in the late 1980s, and by 1990 the population of shad entering the river was four million. As might be expected, this introduction is still controversial because of potential competition with species native to the Columbia River.

Reports on the status of American Shad populations in New Jersey are mixed. Sophisticated underwater equipment (hydroacoustic) mounted at Lambertville counted approximately 792,000 Shad in the run from April 1 to May 31, 1996, with similar counts in 1997, but counts were down to just under 400,000 in 1998 and to 24,700 in 1999. Current estimates put the adult Shad population in the Delaware River at about 500,000. Using nets, the state also monitors young Shad migrating out from the Delaware. They averaged 456 young Shad per seine haul in 1996, more than double the seventeen-year average of 207, but in 1998 it was down to sixty-two, far below what it should have been from the count of adult spawners. Barring catastrophes, the record production in 1996 and 1997 should result in good runs when these age classes return to the Delaware in 2000 and 2001. However, the low production in 1998 will be reflected in lower adult runs in 2003.

The low 1998 adult Shad count may have been a cyclical aberration, or it could reflect a serious decline due to unrecognized problems. The Atlantic States Marine Fisheries Commission voted for stricter regulations on commercial fishermen, and imposed a ten-fish-or-less recreational limit for all states from Maine to Florida in 1999. Since Pennsylvania already had a six fish per season limit for Shad, New Jersey did likewise. Even before this limit, many fishermen enjoyed the thrill of catching Shad and released them immediately. Even as early as 1995, the Division of Fish, Game and Wildlife estimated that about 90 percent of the Shad were caught and released.

Others enjoy the fishery by attending the Lambertville Shad Festival and watching the fishermen seine at this time. The Leni-Lenapé Indians taught the Europeans to use nets that are set today. Not only is the festival a piece of New Jersey history, but Lambertville is worth seeing, with its Victorian houses, federal row houses, and graceful church spires. Hopefully American Shad will recover with the stricter catch limits and continued management, and we will have increasingly larger runs of these magnificent fish, swimming determinedly upstream to spawn as they always have, in splashing frenzies.

The Shad fishery along the Delaware River can be seen at Lambertville, where Fred and Steve Lewis and their family still set seines around 6 P.M. during the Shad run.

When the seining crew of four first assembles near their dock, they check their huge net, folding it carefully into the boat in piles that will be easy to feed out when the net is set. Steve Lewis rows the boat upstream nearly a quarter of a mile. The other three walk along a well-trodden path to meet the boat. The

14. Steve Lewis and crew setting the net for an evening Shad run. (Photo by
J. Burger)

Shadbush is in bloom, its brilliant white flowers glowing in the pale dusk. Two
men join the paddler, while one man remains on shore to hold the end of the
net line. One person rows the boat out about a hundred yards to the middle of
the Delaware River, while the others slowly feed the piled net overboard. They
stop before the main channel; then they bring the boat slowly around in a wide
arc heading back to shore, slipping the net into the water (fig. 14). The weights
on the bottom drag the net to the bottom, while floats on the top line keep the
upper edge at the surface. The river is shallow and the net creates a mesh wall
sufficient to capture large fish. Once the net is set, forming a large half-moon,
it is dragged slowly toward the dock by the boat. It takes all three men, two
rowing and one using a pole to guide the boat, to haul the net slowly toward
shore near the dock. At the same time, the man on shore moves toward the
same spot, keeping the end of the net close to the bank. It takes four people
standing on the bank to haul the net to shore because of the weight of the net,
fish, and other debris. They lean backward, slowly winding the net into two giant coils, each pull making the trap smaller and smaller. Eventually the net is
nearly on shore, the trap only eight to ten feet long, and the men lift the top,
forcing the jumping, squirming fish on shore.

They catch many different species, including Bullheads, Gizzard Shad, and
American Shad. In a good haul, in a good year, they can get over five hundred
fish. Nowadays, they often get only five or ten at a time, although they sometimes catch forty or more. They return all but the American Shad to the river

and keep only enough of the Shad to fill their orders, phoned in by locals who know when the Shad are running. The six dollars they get for each Shad does not pay for their work, but it is a family tradition, a local happening, and a bit of the past for us all to enjoy. We can attest to the thrill of watching them haul in the nets, to the delicious taste of fresh Shad, and to the fun of the Lambertville Shad Festival.

FOR MORE INFORMATION: Call the N.J. Department of Environmental Protection, Division of Fish, Game and Wildlife (number for information on Shad is 908-236-2118, www.state.nj.us/dep/fgw), or call the Shad Hotline for spawning information (610-954-0577 or 610-954-0578). For the Shad Festival, call Lambertville Chamber of Commerce (609-397-0055) or check www.lambertville.org. For information about Hugh Moore Park in Easton, call 610-250-6700 (open only from May 1 to Labor Day).

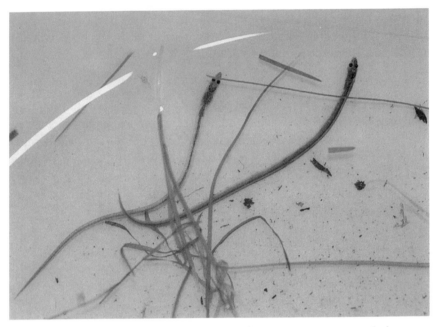

15. Two tiny Glass Eels, the same size as Spartina stems, start to turn darker as they enter the freshwater. (Photo by J. Burger)

3

Glass Eels (American Eels) at Cheesequake

By the light of the moon, a million glassy threads with beady black eyes swim frantically up the narrow stream, against the current, bound for water they have never known.

KEY LOCATIONS: Hooks Creek Lake at Cheesequake State Park in Middlesex County.

DIRECTIONS: Take the Garden State Parkway to exit 120, follow directions to Cheesequake State Park. Once in the park, pass the park guardhouse; make the first angular left down a dirt road, and make a right into the Nature Center. There you can ask directions to the spillway, where the eels can be seen. The spillway is on Hooks Creek Lake, a favorite local fishing spot.

BEST TIME TO VISIT: Glass Eel migration occurs mainly from late February to late April, although the eels can show up in December. The greatest numbers pass through on high tides, but they are easier to see at low tide when they concentrate at creek mouths or pass through the water trickling over the spillway. Glass Eels generally hide in the gravel during the day and mostly move at night under the cover of darkness, but some movement is visible during the day.

PRIME HABITAT: Creeks near estuaries leading from the Atlantic Ocean, where freshwater comes into saltwater. Although they can be found in many coastal streams and tributaries that lead to the Atlantic, the eels are easiest to see when they are forced through a narrow channel or culvert when the water level is low.

Slivers of light dance off the bottom of the creek and seem to disappear in the advancing tide. On a closer look, the slivers seem to wriggle and dissolve into hundreds of small threadlike Glass Eels making their way upstream. They are enacting one of the oldest rhythms of nature, moving upstream to lakes where they will remain for many years, growing slowly to the adult eels we are more familiar with. But for now, they are not much larger than a few inches of thread, caught in the flow of the creeks, swimming upstream with tremendous force.

These tiny threads have made their way thousands of miles from their hatching grounds in the Sargasso Sea, between Bermuda and the Bahama Islands, to streams where their parents bred. Remarkably, the European Eels also swim from the shores of Europe to the Sargasso Sea, where they intermingle with eels from North America. Each baby eel finds its way back to the continent of its mother's origin and then seeks an appropriate stream, though it is not known whether this is partly by chance or if they deliberately return to their mother's stream.

The life cycle of the eel is opposite that of the Shad (previous chapter). They are catadromus, breeding in the ocean and maturing in freshwater. In the fall of the year, the small larvae start their long journey from the Sargasso Sea northward through the ocean, to bays and streams where their mothers spent their youth, streams they have never known. They are then Glass Eels, so named because their bodies are crystal clear, when they reach the coast several months later. By early spring, Glass Eels are spread out all along the Atlantic Coast, waiting in estuaries and bays to make their way into streams. They are less than a year old. The female eels come into freshwater, but the males lag behind in the bays and estuaries. Their clear, glasslike appearance no doubt shields them from predators because they look like light glancing off bits of debris rather than a tasty meal. There is safety in numbers, and by traveling in the hundreds and thousands, many avoid being eaten.

When the females reach freshwater, their bodies change from clear to dark, but here in Cheesequake the water is still a bit salty and the eels are crystal clear. The males remain in the estuarine waters for another year or two. The tiny black female eels (now called elvers) remain in freshwater lakes and grow to twice the width of a garden hose. They can weigh up to eight pounds and grow to five feet long, unless they are caught by a predator or a fisherman. Males, by contrast, are much smaller. Since eels often remain near the bottom, their dark body helps them blend in with the mud, so they escape most predators.

By now it should be clear that American Eels have different names for their different stages of development (see table 2).

American Eels have a very complicated life history, and it takes a long time before they reach sexual maturity and breed, up to nineteen years for females and twelve years for males. Even in the estuaries, some black eels begin to change into silver eels. When the adults enter the sea, they start their spawning migration southward, completing their change into the silver eel stage. Their eyes enlarge, their internal organs atrophy, and their pectoral fins change shape. It may take them two to three months to reach the Sargasso Sea, where spawning takes place in the spring.

Little is known of their spawning behavior, but the small Leptocephalus larvae occur only in the Sargasso Sea. The larvae drift at sea for up to a year, during which time they are carried around by the Gulf Stream. At this stage they have teeth. As they leave the Gulf Stream and approach the North American coast they transform into Glass Eels, losing their teeth and becoming shorter. If they can successfully negotiate the streams and go past dams, some will enter the lakes, where they will spend at least the next five to ten years. Older and larger eels avoid light more than younger eels, meaning that they become noc-

TABLE 2. Stages of American Eels

Silver Eel	This is the oceanic, breeding adult that migrates to a spawning area in the Sargasso Sea.
Leptocephalus	The oceanic larval stage, in the Sargasso Sea.
Glass Eel	The larval stage in transition from oceanic to estuarine, and the stage caught by fishermen for the Asian market.
Elver	The larval stage once its body has darkened.
Whip	A juvenile eel up to two years old, mostly in freshwater lakes, but some remain in estuarine waters.
Yellow Eel	The freshwater stage, which lasts from nine to nineteen years for females, and seven to twelve years for males.
Green Eel	The freshwater stage (summer) just before the eels migrate back to the ocean to breed.
Black Eel	The freshwater stage (fall) that is migrating to the ocean.

turnal, so older individuals are found at deeper depths. They are more abundant in dark habitats, under and around piers and sheltered docks.

For most of their life history, the eels face another problem besides predators. Fishermen pursue them from June through November, when they are swimming about the lakes. During these months the eels feed and travel for twenty-four hours a day, moving so quickly that an "eeler" needs a fast boat, a strong body, and a good memory for the location of the eels' feeding grounds. In the past some eelers kept an eye out for small holes in the bottoms of clear streams and speared the resident eels with a split-oak fork.

Not only are there commercial "eelers," but there is also a lively recreational fishery for American Eels. In the upper Delaware River, for example, American Eel is one of the most popular sport fish because it is tasty, but the taste partially comes from fat, which accumulates contaminants. New Jersey officials have issued a statewide consumption advisory, which also includes all of the Delaware River, because of the contamination of American Eels with PCBs, dioxins, and chlordane. Pennsylvania has also issued an advisory for the Delaware River, which is "Do not eat."

Today, eel pots are set and baited with half of a female Horseshoe Crab, preferably one with eggs, leading to another major conservation issue described in the next chapter. There has been a tremendous increase in the number of eelers and eel pots set in the last decade, leading to an increasing demand for harvesting female Horseshoe Crabs. The Horseshoe Crab bait is changed every day or every other day when the eel pots are checked. While it has been difficult to determine the take of Horseshoe Crabs from direct information on catch, it is possible to estimate take based on the number of eel licensees engaged in full-time eeling. Eelers often use a variety of eel traps, in different sizes and shapes, to attract the eels, which enter tail first. Small eels caught early in the season are salted and sold as bait to crabbers, but large ones are shipped to cities for use in stews or for smoking. Eels are also used by recreational fishermen as bait for Striped Bass, which is increasingly important as bass become more abundant and bass fishing increases. Thus eels are faced not only with a substantial harvest at the Glass Eels stage early in their life history, but also with significant commercial and recreational fishing pressure on the adults.

Many elude fishermen, however, and continue to swim rapidly about their freshwater haunts. When they are five to ten years old, the females leave their freshwater steams and lakes, swim down to the estuaries, and are joined by the males. They swim slowly out to sea and down the Atlantic Coast toward the Sargasso Sea. There the males and females breed, releasing thousands upon thousands of eggs and sperm into the sea, and the cycle begins anew. The eggs hatch and grow slowly, first as larvae and then as tiny, threadlike Glass Eels.

While their small, thin, glasslike bodies have protected them against predators for thousands of years, they now face their most serious threat—humans, for whom they have become a rare delicacy. Having exhausted the Glass Eels in most of Asia, the Japanese are now offering U.S. fishermen over $300 a pound for Glass Eels. Of course, the Glass Eel species in Asia are different from those along the East Coast, but the problems are similar. It takes two thousand Glass Eels to make a pound. Moreover, in Japan growers are paying as much as $2,500 per pound for Glass Eels to restock ponds, so all of the middlemen are obviously making good money. This kind of money is hard to resist for fishermen who may have lost other fishing opportunities, and it is easy to take Glass Eels by the bucketful when the tide is right. Such fishing can occur at high tide in the dead of night, away from the wary eyes of conservationists and law enforcement officers.

The Japanese then transport the Glass Eels back to Asia, where they put them in large fish farms, feeding them for five years until they reach adulthood, when they are used for sushi and other favorite dishes. Adult eels also command high prices and are much in demand. Several Asian countries have so overexploited their Glass Eels of a closely related species that their populations are nearly gone, which accounts for their willingness to pay exorbitant prices for American Glass Eels. This situation illustrates the potential fate of our Glass Eel stock unless we implement and enforce conservation measures.

In 1998 for the first time, New Jersey temporarily closed the legal harvest on Glass Eels, through the hard work of many individuals and many conservation and scientific organizations. Outdoor writers played a key role in bringing the issue to the public, illustrating the importance these writers can play in conservation issues. Some conservationists are proposing a six-inch limit on American Eels, which would effectively protect the Glass Eels, but many want to close the season on young eels completely. Since many states along the East Coast have closed the Glass Eel fishery, it is important to do so also in New Jersey, or all the fishing pressure diverted from elsewhere will come here. This happened in 1997 when poachers caught Glass Eels in Delaware and transported them to Cape May for sale. It is thus critical to have a coastwide plan, so bootleggers cannot transport eels to states where it is still legal to land them.

The Atlantic States Marine Fisheries Commission has set up a Glass Eel Committee to develop a management plan for American Eels all along the Atlantic, but it may take years for the plan to be approved—years during which Glass Eels can continue to be transported to Japan.

The tiny threadlike Glass Eels that swim slowly through the narrow entrance into Hooks Creek Lake are a spectacle not because they are large and showy, but because millions of these fragile creatures make their way into New Jersey creeks and lakes every year, almost unseen by most naturalists. These wriggling threads of light have already swum thousands of miles from the Sargasso Sea to reach their maternal home, which they alone will recognize. Some, however, seem at the mercy of tides and currents and go upstream wherever they reach shore. Although they have many years to grow to adulthood, they will once again make the long journey to the Sargasso Sea to breed, along with millions and millions of other eels.

Only thirty miles from metropolitan New York City, Cheesequake Park is one of the most urban of New Jersey state parks, and it is easily accessible from the Garden State Parkway. The name Cheesequake was taken from the Lenapé Indians who used the area for hunting and fishing for at least five thousand years. Sitting along the quiet, peaceful lake on a cool spring evening in late April or early May, when the park is relatively deserted, it is possible to imagine a Lenapé family camped along the water's edge, trapping fish in the shallow waters of the lake, and creeping slowly through the underbrush in search of deer or small game. It is unlikely that they bothered the Glass Eels, which are so small they would provide little energy.

Cheesequake is at the northern edge of Pine Barrens habitat. For a relatively small park, it has great diversity in habitats, including Pine Barrens, open fields, freshwater and saltwater marshes, and a White Cedar swamp, in addition to more familiar hardwood forests. Three main trails crisscross the park, providing the visitor with an opportunity to see the different habitats. There are also picnic areas and campgrounds, as well as opportunities for fishing, swimming, hiking, jogging, and bicycling. Portions of the park are accessible for people with disabilities.

At dead low tide, one scoop with a dip net at the intake to Hook's Creek Lake in Cheesequake State Park yielded three hundred Glass Eels. We put them in a shallow white pail so we could see in more detail their small wriggling, nearly transparent bodies. Some were up to two and a half inches long, with a small head and dark eyes atop the long, thin, threadlike body. We did not keep them long, returning them after a few minutes to the swift flowing water, where a steady stream of swimming eels made their way into the lake.

FOR MORE INFORMATION: Call Cheesequake State Park (732-566-2161) or the N.J. Department of Environmental Protection, Division of Fish, Game and Wildlife (609-292-9400), www/state.nj.us/dep/fgw.

16. Three groups of mating Horseshoe Crabs at the surf line just after high tide. (Photo by J. Burger)

4

Spawning Horseshoe Crabs on Delaware Bay

A mass of swirling dark brown shapes boils in the shallow surf, stretching far along the beach. Thousands upon thousands of Horseshoe Crabs have come to mate and lay their eggs in the intertidal waters.

KEY LOCATIONS: Several beaches along the lower reaches of Delaware Bay, from about two miles north of the bay entrance to Cohansey Point, mainly along the lower thirty miles of the bay in Cape May and Cumberland Counties. It is especially important to go to beaches where close scrutiny of Horseshoe Crabs will not disturb foraging birds. The best places to watch and study Horseshoe Crabs is East Point Boat Ramp, Cape May Harbor, and Douglass Park. Places where both shorebirds and Horseshoe Crabs can be viewed include Gandy's Beach, Fortescue, Moore's Beach, Reed's Beach, and Norburys Landing.

Horseshoe Crabs can also be seen at Sandy Hook, on the beaches along Raritan Bay in Monmouth County, and on the exposed sandbars and mudflats at Barnegat Inlet.

DIRECTIONS: For places where Horseshoe Crabs can be viewed without disturbing feeding shorebirds, go to East Point Boat Ramp (at the western end of East Point Road), Cape May Harbor (in Cape May; take Pittsburgh Avenue to the Nature Center of Cape May, 1600 Delaware Avenue), and Douglass Park (take Route 9 to Ferry Road in North Cape May, just beyond the Cape May Ferry).

Below are detailed directions for East Point, Fortescue, Moore's Beach, Reed's Beach, and Norburys Landing, which are the best places to view mating Horseshoe Crabs along with shorebirds; but in these sites you must stay at viewing platforms and not go down to the water's edge.

For East Point: from Route 47 about one mile north of Delmont, take Glades Road west to Heislerville, continue to follow signs to East Point Lighthouse (about 6 miles).

For Gandy's Beach and Fortescue, take Route 555 from Millville about 10 miles south to Route 553 and go north to Route 629. Or take Route 553 from Cedarville south for 2 miles to Route 629, turn west, and make the next right onto Baptist Road; after 0.3 mile take the left onto Fortescue Road. In four miles you will reach the town of Fortescue. As you cross the bridge, Fortescue

Road becomes Downe Avenue; at the next T junction, turn left and travel just over a mile to the bulkhead.

To reach Moore's Beach (Heislerville Wildlife Management Area) from the southern end of Route 55 where it joins Route 47, continue south on Route 47 for 8.5 miles to Delmont, turn right onto Moore's Beach Road, and proceed to parking lot (road may be impassable at high tide).

For Reed's Beach, take Route 47 to Reed's Beach Road (about 4 miles north of Norburys Landing Road). Turn left (west) into Reed's Beach, turn right on Beach Avenue in town, and continue to parking lot at end of the road.

To reach Norburys Landing, return to Route 47 and go about 4 miles south or take exit 4 off the Garden State Parkway and follow Route 47 west and north for about 5 miles; turn left on Norburys Landing Road at the sign for Villas, stay right at the yellow light. Continue to end at Norburys Landing (road becomes Bay Shore Road).

BEST TIME TO VISIT: Horseshoe Crab spawning peaks from the last two weeks in May to the first two weeks in June, particularly during the two highest tides of the month. Good viewing is within one hour on either side of high tide.

The peak of Horseshoe Crab spawning at Sandy Hook is two weeks later than the peak on Delaware Bay.

PRIME HABITAT: Shallow sandy beaches on southern half of Delaware Bay, on both New Jersey and Delaware sides. Also mud banks along salt marsh creeks.

In the warm sun of late May, the beaches along Delaware Bay are littered with hundreds of dark brown bodies looking like overturned brown bicycle helmets jammed into the sand, with a sharp spike sticking slightly upward from the shiny shells. Some of the dark brown shapes are quite large, measuring as much as twenty-four inches from the front end to the tip of the spike, but here and there are smaller ones that are a third the size. The Horseshoe Crabs on the beach are half buried into the sand to keep moist, for the receding tide has left them stranded. They must await the next high tide to slip back into the waters of Delaware Bay, otherwise they will dry out and die. The gentle slope of the beach indicates to them where the bay is, and from there they move slowly downward toward the gentle surf of the open bay. On flat beaches the crabs have considerable trouble finding their way back to the bay waters; they need a slope of about 6 degrees to orient correctly. Behind each stranded crab a trail resembling miniature bulldozer tracks leads to the retreating tide.

In the receding surf, a few female Horseshoe Crabs are still laying eggs, but for the most part they have gone back in the water. Those remaining are barely visible, for the large females are surrounded by many of the smaller male crabs, all jumbled together, vying for the chance to fertilize the female's eggs as she deposits them in the wet sand. On the receding tide, the surf is gentle as it

17. Horseshoe Crabs strewn on the beach during low tide. Most stranded crabs go out with the next high tide, but some die on the beach. (Photo by J. Burger)

slowly seeps down the beach. It will be several hours before the tide turns and begins to rise again on the shores of Delaware Bay. The beach is almost deserted, save for the hundreds of motionless Horseshoe Crabs strewn around and the few solitary gulls strolling among them (fig. 17).

The front section of the crab, shaped like a horseshoe, is called the carapace. It contains the digestive, circulatory, and respiratory organs and protects the crab from predators as it walks along the bottom of the bay. The second segment, behind the carapace, is the abdomen, which contains the reproductive organs. Finally there is a long, spikelike tail. Some of the carapaces are smooth and shiny, but others are rough and encrusted with a variety of marine creatures. A wide range of animals hitchhike on the Horseshoe Crab shells, including bacteria and algae, Barnacles, Blue Mussels, Slipper Shells, and sponges. The more creatures attached to a Horseshoe Crab, the older it is likely to be. Most of these are harmless and pose no real threat to the crab.

As the males pursue the females, sometimes they accidentally turn over or are pushed over by more aggressive males, and if the surf recedes quickly, they can be stranded upside down on the drying sand. In an attempt to turn over, they press their tail into the sand, using it as lever to push over, moving in an endless circle (fig. 18). When this fails, they curl their body at the hinge, but it is not enough to keep them moist against the drying sun or to prevent their exposure to predators.

18. Stranded Horseshoe Crabs try to right themselves by pushing the sand with their tails. When they are turned upside down, as in this photo, they are vulnerable to predation by gulls and to drying out. (Photo by J. Burger)

A Great Black-backed Gull pecks at the hard brown shell of a large female Crab but moves on when there is no movement. From the top, the crabs are invulnerable, for no soft parts are uncovered. The gulls search for one that is turned over, exposing a vulnerable body. Finding one, the gull pecks harder and harder until it dislodges bits of flesh from between the joints of the legs. The legs are encased in a horny material, but the gulls can crack it and extract the meat. Ultimately this spells death for the crab.

Overhead the sun is high in the sky, and the warm rays continue to dry the sand, forcing the crabs to bury themselves deeper and deeper, protecting their bodies from the searing rays. Those that remain buried in the sand will survive until the next high tide, but many will perish as predators eat them, or thoughtless people turn them over, leaving them exposed to the drying sun.

It is late May on the Delaware Bay beaches, and the Horseshoe Crabs have returned for one of the oldest mating rituals known. Each new high tide brings with it a wave of crabs, jumbled groups of males crowding each female. Horseshoe Crabs have remained relatively unchanged for over two hundred million years and are known as a "living fossil." They were around before the dinosaurs. Many different species of Horseshoe Crabs once roamed the Earth, but now only four remain: the one we see here, and three that are limited to Asia, from Japan through India.

Along with insects, spiders, scorpions, and crabs, Horseshoe Crabs are arthropods, and their closest relatives are spiders and scorpions. They are not true crabs because they lack two pairs of antennae and a pair of jaws (called mandibles) and have seven pairs of legs, while true crabs have only five.

Waves lap the sands, and just offshore a ribbon of Laughing Gulls feeds on a sandbar barely covered with water. The gulls are noisy, but for the most part they are so engrossed in looking for tiny Horseshoe Crab eggs that they hardly notice our approach. With a stretch of open water separating them from shore, they feel safe enough to continue searching for food without interruption.

Along the edge of the water, a flock of five thousand shorebirds crowds into the narrow band where the receding surf boils with millions upon millions of Horseshoe Crab eggs. Even if these eggs were not eaten by the shorebirds or gulls, they would never hatch, for without the protection of surrounding sand they quickly disintegrate or are washed out to sea. The shorebirds are feeding on excess eggs dug up by hundreds of female Horseshoe Crabs digging their own nests on top of those of earlier-spawning females. The shorebirds stop at Delaware Bay on their northward migration because of this abundance of Horseshoe Crab eggs (see the next chapter).

A wide variety of fish also eat the eggs and young larvae of Horseshoe Crabs, including American Shad, Killifish, Striped Bass, Weakfish, and Winter Flounder. The excess eggs of Horseshoe Crabs thus play an important role in the food web of the estuaries and bay. If the numbers were to decrease, there would be a cascading effect on many other organisms.

As the tide begins to rise, the Horseshoe Crabs that are waiting just offshore begin to swim toward the surf, moving higher and higher with the tide. When the surf is high and boiling, the crabs frantically engage in their mating ritual, oblivious to the surf and predatory gulls waiting nearby. The Horseshoe Crabs no doubt lay their eggs in the sand between low and high tide as an antipredator strategy—there are fewer predators here. The water teems with the bodies of thousands upon thousands of Horseshoe Crabs mating, digging nests, and laying eggs. The shorebirds and gulls walk among the jumbled crabs, pecking at the eggs, but it is difficult to feed in the confusion, so most birds move to other beaches or to salt marshes during the high tide, or they rest along the high-tide line. Some feed on the salt marshes while others simply wait for the tide to recede.

Thousands upon thousands of Horseshoe Crabs breed on Delaware Bay beaches each year, as they do along the Atlantic Coast from southern Maine to the beaches of the Yucatan in Mexico. Delaware Bay, however, is the center of their breeding range, and it is here that the greatest numbers congregate. These large masses of mating crabs are limited to Chesapeake and Delaware Bays, where just the right conditions exist, with wet sand protected from the onslaught of the driving surf. Horseshoe Crabs have declined everywhere else.

The mass of breeding Horseshoe Crabs is one of the most magnificent spectacles of nature in the United States, one not to be missed. Although breeding peaks in the last two weeks of May on the spring tides in Delaware Bay and is highest at full moon, egg-laying can occur from April through September.

During the winter, Horseshoe Crabs live half-buried in the muds and sands beneath the sea on the continental shelf, just off the Atlantic shore. Their metabolism slows down, which allows them to eat very little and move so infrequently that they avoid predators. When the days of spring begin to lengthen, the changing light cycle stimulates the crabs on the sea bottom and awakens them from their winter stupor. Slowly they start to swim toward the beaches. While moving languidly in the water, the crabs are vulnerable to a wide variety of predators. They are the most common prey of Loggerhead Sea Turtles in many bays and estuaries, and smaller ones are taken by fish.

Spawning takes place primarily at night, although hundreds come up on high tide during the day as well. Peak numbers spawn during the full moon, and again at the new moon. They avoid windy weather and linger offshore for several days following the full moon, waiting for a calm night. While they spawn primarily on the beaches of Delaware Bay, lack of habitat and winds can force them up into the creeks, such as Dividing Creek, Kimble's Creek, and Moore's Creek. Most of these crabs make it back to the bay, leaving with the next high tide, but some become stranded.

The smaller males arrive at the beaches a week or two before the females, and they wait quietly just offshore. The arriving females release into the water a pheromone that attracts the males. Sometimes a large female will have up to twenty males trailing after her, and the first to arrive—not necessarily the largest one—is usually the successful mate. Since the largest are not more successful than the others, there is no selection for size in males, and they are usually only a third the size of females. Females can weigh up to six pounds.

Each male patrols the water, searching for a female, and when he finds her, he clasps her abdomen with his first pair of legs, specially adapted for this purpose. She swims toward the beach, dragging the male with her. Once she reaches the beach, she scoops out a shallow nest at the wet tide line and deposits up to twenty thousand pale green pea-sized eggs in the eight-inch hole. She moves very slowly ahead, allowing the male to deposit his sperm over the eggs. She lays the eggs in clutches, which are somewhat glued together by a liquid she extrudes; as she moves forward, she may lay several clutches. The eggs are mixed with sand grains in a mass not much larger than a plum tomato.

The opaque eggs, looking like tiny bits of lime-green tapioca, are quickly covered by the sand boiling in the surf. The female and her entourage quickly move out of the gentle waves, back into the shallow bays. Females time their egg-laying for the new and full moon, when the tides are the highest. Remaining close to the spawning beaches, they may return to the surf during the next day or two, or they may wait until the next new or full moon to lay two or three more clutches before swimming off into the deeper reaches of the bays. Females, which do not start to breed until they are ten years old, can lay up to eighty thousand eggs each spring. Of the thousands of eggs a female lays each year, only one or two may survive to adulthood.

Although the females lay their eggs in nests well below the sand surface, the impressions remain in the sand when the tide falls (fig. 19). The eggs often do not remain there. In succeeding days, other females, frantic to dig nests, dislodge the nests of others, releasing these eggs to the churning surf. The eggs collect in the millions in the simmering surf, forming a foam of tiny green eggs that attract the migrant shorebirds and gulls.

The moisture of the bay and the warmth of the sun incubate the eggs buried eight inches below the sand, and they double in size within a few days. The eggs hatch in about thirty days, during the next new or full moon. The trilobite larvae look like miniature adult crabs, except they are only one-eighth of an inch across. They remain in the sand for another two weeks, and then the young larvae emerge and are carried out with the tide to the bay. While buried in the sand, they live on the yolk remaining from their egg stage; shortly after emerging from the sand, they begin to search for tiny marine worms and clams to eat. They plow slowly along the bottom muds, feeling for tiny prey, using their legs to crush the worms or clams they capture. They will also eat dead fish they find lying on the bottom.

As the tiny crabs grow, they molt periodically, simply splitting the front of the carapace from the bottom of their shell and walking out. The discarded shells usually remain buried in the mud, but sometimes the winds are just right and thousands of these paper-thin Horseshoe Crab shells are left in windrows on the beach. The shells are light brown and translucent, and each is a perfect replica of the crab, with the tiny tail and all the leg coverings intact; the crabs themselves are safe in the bay. After it sheds its shell, the tiny crab pumps water to expand its new soft shell by about 30 percent, so that the shell is big enough to allow growth. The new shell of the small crab slowly hardens over the next twenty-four hours while the crab continues to patrol the bottom muds in search of food.

At first, the crabs molt several times a year, but as they age, they molt only once a year. When the young crabs crawl along the bottom, the carapace faces upward, but they can also swim rather quickly by turning on their back and churning their legs. The larger they grow, the more slowly they can swim, until as adults they mainly shuffle along the bottom, plowing ahead like a bulldozer pushing dirt.

The males do not breed until they are nine years old, but females wait at least until they are ten. Although the full lifespan is unknown, they live for at least thirty years. Unlike most other arthropods, Horseshoe Crabs have a life history strategy that involves delayed maturity and late age of first breeding, and a long lifespan. Most crabs, such as Blue Crabs, have a lifespan of only one

19. After the tide recedes on sandy beaches it is impossible to see where the female Horseshoe Crabs laid their eggs. However, on mudflats the depressions left by the females as they burrowed down are visible (*bottom*). Here there is a large group of nests on a mudflat at Moore's Beach. The darkened depressions are where the female burrowed in to lay her eggs. (Photos by J. Burger)

or two years. The breeding strategy of Horseshoe Crabs places them at risk because they have to survive for at least ten years before they reproduce. Thus any increase in mortality can have dire consequences for Horseshoe Crab populations, and the recovery time for the population is at least ten years.

Young Horseshoe Crabs face a number of enemies, largely because they are small and are quite vulnerable when they are molting. Small Horseshoe Crabs are eaten by a variety of fish and invertebrates, but larger ones are vulnerable only to large fish, sea turtles, and humans. Like all coastal and marine animals, they are threatened by loss of habitat due to development, bulk-heading, beach erosion, and global warming. Global warming is particularly problematic, as it is associated with sea level rise. As the seas rise, tidal waters move higher into marshes and uplands, and even today some Horseshoe Crabs are already being stranded in forested areas. Horseshoe Crabs need sand for egg deposition, and they avoid beaches with extensive peat formation. The last two decades have seen a net loss of sand from Delaware Bay beaches, forcing some crabs back into the salt marsh creeks.

Horseshoe Crabs have been exploited by people for as long as they have lived along the coasts. American Indians ate them, fashioned the tails into fishing spears, and used them as fertilizer for crops. When the European settlers arrived, they quickly adopted the habit of using Horseshoe Crabs as a source of nitrogen and as a feed for hogs and chickens. Between the 1800s and the 1930s, nearly two million crabs a year were harvested in New Jersey. In 1871 alone, some four million crabs were gathered for fertilizer. This harvest was not sustainable, and by the 1880s it had dropped to two million a year; by the 1930s it was down to one million. The crabs were gathered on boats and stacked along the shore to dry in the sun. Some old-timers report that the crabs were stacked waist high, as far as the eye could see. In the fall they were taken to the factories to be pulverized and put into sacks.

There was a thriving fertilizer business in Cape May into the 1950s, when the hapless crabs were ground up by the thousands, and some farmers today still plow dead Horseshoe Crabs into their fields as fertilizer. The industry ended because other sources of fertilizer became available, there were fewer crabs to exploit, and residents complained bitterly about the stench of the crabs drying for months in the hot summer sun. The last plant, located in Millville, closed in the 1960s. This longtime exploitation had devastating results, and by the 1930s the entire Horseshoe Crab population of Delaware Bay was estimated at less than 50,000.

Horseshoe Crabs are very important to medicine because they are a model animal for the study of eyes, and they are easy to work with in the laboratory. They have large compound eyes with an accessible optic nerve. The chitin in the shell of the crabs is used to make filaments for suturing wounds; chitin-covered sutures heal 35 to 50 percent faster than other sutures. By far the most important medicinal use, however, is to detect endotoxins in pharmaceuticals. The copper-based blood of Horseshoe Crabs contains a clotting agent that attaches to bacterial toxins, the poison produced by infectious bacteria. Limulus Amoebocyte Lysate (LAL), the clotting agent, is produced by several companies in New Jersey and elsewhere. To collect the blood, the companies capture female Horseshoe Crabs, bleed them in the laboratory, hold them overnight, and release them back to their native bay. Estimates are that less than 10 percent of the females die in this process, a relatively small take given the huge medical benefits. The worldwide market for LAL is estimated to be $50 million a year, based on bleeding 280,000 crabs each year. The companies pay up to $3.00 per crab.

For many years, fishermen in South Jersey have used crabs as effective bait for catching eels and Conch. The fishermen picked them up off the beaches for their own use, and the few they took did not create a problem for the crab populations. However, in the late 1980s and early 1990s, the shortage of Horseshoe Crabs along Atlantic beaches outside of New Jersey made them very valuable, and people would come to Delaware Bay in small trucks to pick up the helpless and unprotected crabs in larger numbers. They preferred the females because they produce the pheromone that acts as an attractant for eels. Within a year, commercial crabbers arrived in larger trucks and picked up all the crabs on beach after beach. Their activities disturbed the migrant shorebirds, who were forced to leave the beaches to forage where food was less abundant. The increase in crab harvest in the mid-1990s was not only due to overexploitation but to an increase in the demand for Conch bait in the U.S. and Asian markets.

Finally, New Jersey set regulations to decrease the harvest and stop disturbance to the shorebirds. It became illegal to pick up crabs during the day when the shorebirds were foraging and to pick them up on consecutive nights. This stopped the interstate trucks because it was impossible to fill up a large truck in only one night, and the crabs rotted too quickly to stop over for several nights. The traditional fishermen of Cape May were not hurt by these regulations because they could pick up enough crabs on one or two nights a week to keep their eel pots working.

The fishermen were more clever than the regulators, however, and they soon devised methods to trawl for crabs just off the spawning beaches. They could then "take" Horseshoe Crabs every day without removing them directly from the beaches, thus increasing the harvest in succeeding years. Counts of spawning Horseshoe Crabs and counts of the number of eggs in the sand showed alarming declines, although these numbers are often disputed by the crabbers. Soon the number of migrant shorebirds feeding along Delaware Bay also decreased, alarming conservationists worldwide.

The alarm spread to Delaware and Maryland, states with high Horseshoe Crab harvests, and the governors of these states ultimately placed moratoriums on further takes. This action upset the fishermen who sell Horseshoe Crabs for

Conch and eel bait. Thus the Atlantic States Marine Fisheries Commission set up a committee to evaluate the health of the Horseshoe Crab "stock," the term used for any resource that is fished commercially. In the meantime, New Jersey and several other states put more severe regulations into effect that would ensure a lower harvest. The commission has established a modest plan for Horseshoe Crabs, although many feel that the regulations are not stringent enough to protect either the Horseshoe Crabs or migrant shorebirds. One important provision of the plan is that all states must monitor the take of Horseshoe Crabs, and that standardized methods of assessing populations must be developed.

The states have maintained these regulations, protecting the crabs on their major spawning grounds in Delaware and Chesapeake Bays. The ecosystems where the crabs spawn are vulnerable also to oil spills and other catastrophic chemical spills that could hurt the spawning populations. For now, however, the mass movement of Horseshoe Crabs to Delaware Bay goes on as it has since the Paleozoic, with over a million arriving each May to lay their lime-green eggs beneath the wet tidal sands. If numbers recover, it will be possible to see as many as 200,000 per mile of prime beach—truly spectacular. As the spawning mass of dark-brown domes sway in the boiling surf, we are reminded that some parts of our distant past are still with us—and that we hold the key to their continued survival.

FOR MORE INFORMATION: Call the Endangered and Nongame Species Program of the New Jersey Department of Environmental Protection (609-292-9400) for information on Horseshoe Crabs on Delaware Bay; www.state.nj.us/dep/fgw. For information on crabs at Sandy Hook, call the Littoral Society (732-291-0055 in North Jersey; 609-294-3111 in South Jersey); www.alsnyc.org.

20. A group of Red Knots and Turnstones in late May along the Delaware Bay-shore, part of a flock that exceeded ten thousand. (Photo by J. Burger)

5

Migrant Shorebirds
at Delaware Bay

Five thousand small bodies dart in a frantic dance along the tide line, follow-ing the waters as they recede, each shorebird pecking furiously at the tiny lime-green Horseshoe Crab eggs rolling in the surf. The scene is primeval.

KEY LOCATIONS: Gandy's Beach, Fortescue, Thompson's Beach, and Moore's Beach in Cumberland County, and Reed's Beach and Norburys Landing in Cape May County, all on Delaware Bay. Directions to the best viewing loca-tions are given below.

DIRECTIONS: For Gandy's Beach and Fortescue, take Route 553 from Cedar-ville south for 2 miles to Route 629, turn right, and make the next right onto Baptist Road; go 0.3 mile to a Y junction. For Gandy's Beach, go right on Route 643, which soon bends west; bear left to Gandy's Beach and follow Cove Road to the beach. For Fortescue, take the left at the Y junction, onto Fortes-cue Road; in 4 miles you will reach the town of Fortescue; as you cross the bridge, Fortescue Road becomes Downe Avenue; at the next T junction, turn left and travel just over a mile to the bulkhead.

For Thompson's Beach, take Route 47 to the turnoff for East Point and fol-low the signs for East Point. The road goes through a marsh area, and then through a small group of houses. In town, make a left on Thompson's Beach Road; follow to the parking lot and viewing platform.

For Moore's Beach from the southern end of Route 55, take Route 47 south to Delmont (8.5 miles), turn right (south) onto Moore's Beach Road, and fol-low to the end.

For Reed's Beach, take Route 47 to Reed's Beach Road (about 4 miles north of Norburys Landing Road). Turn left (west) into Reed's Beach; turn right on Beach Avenue in town, and continue to parking lot at the end of the road.

For Norburys Landing, take exit 4 off Garden State Parkway; take Route 47 west and north for 3.2 miles, turn left on Norburys Landing Road at the sign for Villas, and continue to Norburys Landing (road becomes Bay Shore Road).

BEST TIME TO VISIT: May 15 to June 10, but shorebird numbers peak in the last ten days of May. The best viewing is on a falling tide; numbers peak about two to three hours after high tide. This usually corresponds to the peak laying period of the Horseshoe Crabs.

PRIME HABITAT: Sandy beaches of Delaware Bay, primarily on the lower thirty miles of the bay. The birds gather where the Horseshoe Crabs are concentrating to lay eggs.

Pressing against one another, each pecking rapidly at the swirling Horseshoe Crab eggs, the mass of shorebirds ebbs slowly with the receding tide, separating awkwardly around the few plodding Horseshoe Crabs still spawning in the sand. Grays, blacks, russets, and browns intermingle. The shorebirds are strewn into a thin mottled ribbon along the surf, as far as the beach goes, vying for space amid the windrows of eggs washing at the wave's edge. They are so dense that the much larger Laughing and Herring Gulls are unable to penetrate the mob. Instead, they remain on the edge, running wildly about, searching for a tiny spot where they have access to the simmering surf. Some have given up, and a dense flock of Laughing Gulls works the edge of the sandbar just off the beach where other Horseshoe Crabs deposited their eggs. Here the Laughing Gulls are dense and frantic, forcing the larger Herring Gulls to the edge once again. For the most part, only the gulls on the edge peer about, looking for predators; the rest feed hurriedly without glancing up.

The shorebirds are noisy, and occasional fights break out. But time is too precious to waste on aggression, and they soon return to feeding as rapidly as possible. Some whirl in tight circles like a wind-up toy; others peck resolutely, moving in a straight line. With a closer look, it seems that the undulating nature of the paisley pattern is caused by differences in sizes, colors, and textures of the birds, for they are not all the same species. Larger and redder birds are Red Knots; those mottled with reds, browns, blacks, and whites are Ruddy Turnstones; while the smaller brown ones are Semipalmated Sandpipers. Although each usually remains with its own kind, in many places they are intermixed, as if the time required to find your own species was too high a price to pay for missing feeding time.

They jostle each other for the best place. They are not competing for the eggs, for there are millions rolling in the surf, but for a place to stand where they can feed uninterruptedly (fig. 21). While the eggs may not be limited, time is, for the eggs will wash out with the next tide, and the shorebirds have only about two weeks to double their weight before their long northward migration. Many of these birds have flown nonstop from South America, from places like Surinam, Peru, the palm swamps of Paraguay, the pampas of Argentina, and the desert coasts of Chile. Their voyage may have taken several days, with a long nonstop flight, and their fuel resources are now totally de-

21. A flock of shorebirds and gulls on Reed's Beach in late May. The shorebirds are so dense that the gulls cannot penetrate. (Photo by J. Burger)

pleted. When they leave Delaware Bay, they will fly nonstop for another two thousand miles to their Arctic breeding grounds, often flying at altitudes of 12,000 to 18,000 feet. They must eat enough to have the energy to fly that long distance, with sufficient reserves left over to defend their Arctic breeding territories or to lay eggs. When they arrive in the Arctic, cold winds will whip across the tundra, and snow still lies in low places. Insects are scarce. Females that still have enough fat reserves to lay eggs quickly will be the ones more likely to raise young during the short Arctic summer. Those that cannot accumulate enough fat during their stay on Delaware Bay will arrive depleted, if they arrive at all, and will probably not breed successfully.

The intense competition among the feeding shorebirds is borne of the need to eat the most food possible in the least amount of time, and to store enough fat to breed successfully in the short Arctic summer. For example, many shorebird females lay four eggs within days of returning to the tundra, and the eggs represent 60 percent of the female's fat-free body weight. Imagine giving birth to a sixty-pound baby after completing a sixty-mile hike!

Shorebirds, an ancient and diverse group of birds, occur worldwide, as breeders and as migrants. Although they are cosmopolitan in distribution, their migratory paths are often restricted to a narrow band along the coasts, where there are major concentrations in only a few places, called "stopover sites."

A stopover place is one where birds pause during their long migration to rest and refuel for the remainder of their journey. They need to make use of seasonally abundant food resources to build up their fat reserves for the next long-distance flight. Delaware Bay provides superabundant resources in the form of Horseshoe Crab eggs, which are available by the millions from early May until mid-June, and the shorebird migration is timed precisely. The shorebirds moving through in late May consume up to one hundred tons of Horseshoe Crab eggs before they fly north to the high Arctic. A hundred tons of crab eggs, if converted into adult Horseshoe Crabs, would cover most of New Jersey. The importance of Delaware Bay to shorebirds was recognized by the governors of Delaware and New Jersey in 1986 when they nominated it for a charter site in the Western Hemisphere Shorebird Reserve Network—a designation that carries international significance.

The pattern is the same every year. A few shorebirds begin to arrive in mid-May, the numbers crescendo to a peak the last week in May, and by the second week in June the shores are almost devoid of shorebirds. The Laughing Gulls remain, for many breed on the salt marshes at Stone Harbor, but even most of the Herring Gulls have moved on to their breeding grounds.

The Horseshoe Crabs deposit their eggs in the sand of the bay's beaches (see previous chapter), providing a massive food resource for the migrating shorebirds. Delaware Bay hosts the largest concentration of spawning Horseshoe Crabs in North America, and consequently it also hosts the largest concentration of spring migrant shorebirds. This is possible in part only at Delaware Bay because elsewhere, such as in Chesapeake Bay, the bulk of Horseshoe Crab egg-laying occurs a month later, too late for the shorebirds, which are already on their Arctic breeding grounds. While records of the massive concentrations of spawning Horseshoe Crabs go back for several centuries, information on the shorebirds is nearly lacking, largely because the farmers interested in the crabs as a source of fertilizer did not comment on the birds.

In the early 1980s the first aerial surveys of Raritan and Delaware Bays found over 350,000 shorebirds on one day in late May on Delaware Bay, with individual species counts of up to 130,000. Subsequently, the New Jersey State Endangered and Nongame Species Program has been conducting aerial surveys annually. The sparrow-sized Semipalmated Sandpipers are the most abundant migrant on Delaware Bay, followed by Ruddy Turnstone, Red Knot, and Sanderling. These four species alone account for over 95 percent of the shorebirds counted. Other species present in smaller numbers are Short-billed Dowitchers, Dunlin, Semipalmated Plovers, and Black-bellied Plovers. High counts for Semipalmated Sandpipers can reach nearly 270,000, with peak counts of Turnstones and Knots of about 100,000. In total, counting the many additional birds that use the marshes, a million to a million and a half shorebirds move through Delaware Bay in just two weeks.

It is not unusual to have counts of 5,000 to 10,000 shorebirds feeding along Reed's Beach or Thompson's Beach during the last two weeks of May. The shorebirds generally form a dense foraging flock along the falling tide, or rest in a tight mass on the high sandy beach, waiting for the tide and the spawning crabs to return. While they are here they concentrate on the beaches whenever Horseshoe Crab eggs are available, but when the tide is high, the shorebirds move up onto the salt marshes, where they can continue to feed.

On the beaches and marshes they pick up invertebrates and sand that aids in the breakdown and digestion of the Horseshoe Crab eggs. Analysis of stomach contents reveals that all shorebirds examined have the chitinous remains of Horseshoe Crab eggs in their stomachs, along with sand. They feed day and night, taking only short breaks to sleep briefly, before continuing to feed. The fact that they feed most of the day, whether on the beaches or in the backbays and salt marshes, indicates the intense pressure they are under. Anything that disturbs them while they are foraging may have dire consequences; they may not obtain enough food to migrate to the Arctic or to breed once they get there.

Disturbances to shorebirds can be caused by people who move too quickly or approach too closely, forcing them to fly briefly or to abandon that beach. In a year-long study of shorebirds on Delaware Bay, an average of 30 to 70 percent of the shorebirds flew when approached on the beach. Remarkably, during spring migration, when thousands of shorebirds were always present, over 50 percent flew when disturbed. While one or two disturbances are not disastrous, several in succession can severely restrict foraging time and may force the birds into suboptimal habitat.

While the high counts of shorebirds are interesting, more important is the relative role that Delaware Bay plays in the migration of some of the species. The peak counts of Red Knots, a bird the size of a Robin, suggest that a relatively high proportion of the North American population of this species migrates through Delaware Bay. For example, the one-day count of Red Knots represents over 50 percent of the North American population, and given that not all Red Knots using Delaware Bay were there on that day, the bay is even more significant to that species. Some people estimate that on a peak day, 80 percent of the New World population of Red Knots, and half of the New World's population of Sanderlings and Ruddy Turnstones, are in Delaware Bay. Having such high concentrations of shorebirds in one place is a problem because it means that a high proportion of each species' total population is vulnerable to any catastrophic event, such as an oil spill or an avian cholera outbreak, that could devastate them.

To decrease the disturbance on beaches caused unwittingly by joggers, walkers, bird-watchers, and photographers, the New Jersey Endangered and Nongame Species Program constructed viewing platforms and signs at some of the

22. Viewing platform at Reed's Beach. (Photo by J. Burger)

prime shorebird beaches (fig. 22). This serves to keep people in one place and allows the birds to learn that people stay on the platforms; thus, they habituate to the presence of people. It is therefore very important for visitors to remain on the platforms. On beaches without platforms, visitors should stay well up on the dunes away from the birds. It is completely wrong to approach close enough to encourage them to fly, either to identify a strange plumaged bird or to get good photographs. Five thousand, or more, shorebirds feeding in one long ribbon along the shore should be a spectacular enough sight.

While the record high populations indicate that Delaware Bay is extremely important as a spring stopover area, they also show that any threat to the food resources on Delaware Bay may severely endanger the North American populations of Red Knots and Sanderlings. The relative importance of Delaware Bay to the migratory ecology of these two species is cause for alarm given their dependence on Horseshoe Crab eggs and the apparent decline in spawning Horseshoe Crabs over the last ten years. While there is some controversy over the spawning Horseshoe Crabs' decline, several lines of evidence suggest that the numbers have indeed declined, some think precipitously, and prudent management dictates that measures be employed to restore these populations.

There are two issues with Horseshoe Crab spawning that bear consideration: (1) the populations and spawning rate of Horseshoe Crabs necessary to maintain stable populations; and (2) the spawning population of Horseshoe Crabs necessary to fulfill their role in the ecology of these estuarine habitats. Horseshoe Crabs fill a niche that includes the overproduction of eggs to provide a superabundant food source for the migrating shorebirds and enough food for finfish and sea turtles that depend on the crabs. Several different species of fish feed on the eggs and larvae, including American Eel, Striped Bass, Summer Flounder, and Weakfish, and Loggerhead Sea Turtles feed on adult Horseshoe Crabs as well.

There have been disturbing trends in populations of some of the shorebirds on Delaware Bay over the last ten years that suggest that both Red Knots and Sanderlings are decreasing in number. The decreases could be due to the decline of suitable habitat on Delaware Bay, such as loss of beaches, loss of feeding sites on salt marshes and mudflats, and local pollution. Our studies examining levels of toxic metals in the tissues of shorebirds, and in the eggs of Horseshoe Crabs, suggest that pollutants are not the problem. Most of the land lost to development in the last twenty-five years on Cape May peninsula consists of uplands rather than salt marshes and sandy beaches, although there is some loss of beaches due to water level rises. This is most evident from the deserted beach houses standing out in the water at Thompson's Beach; some are already long gone, having fallen into the bay.

The most serious and catastrophic threat for the shorebirds feeding along Delaware Bay may well be the possibility of an oil spill during the peak of migration and spawning of the Horseshoe Crabs. The number of tankers and the amount of oil that pass by the spawning beach each year is phenomenal. More tons of petroleum enter the port of Philadelphia each year than any other port in the United States except for New York and Valdez (Alaska); Philadelphia has the fifth-highest number of tanker calls (a single visit) in the United States. There is a lot of traffic, and with so much traffic, accidents can happen. Bad weather and fog can cause collisions, particularly given the many miles it takes for a huge tanker to stop or change direction. While some of this can be avoided by having local captains who are familiar with the other tanker traffic, the bay, and local weather as they pilot the tankers through Delaware Bay, other accidents still can happen. Tankers can spring a leak, run aground, or dump bilge water tainted with oil into the bay or just offshore.

Having a response plan in place is essential to dealing with an oil spill, as it is with any disaster. Such a plan has been developed by New Jersey and Delaware, and a workshop on oil spill response was convened to examine existing procedures. The final conclusion was that there really is *no* way to protect the Horseshoe Crabs and shorebirds once a spill occurs. For small oil spills, "booms" (long rolls of absorbent material) can be placed around sensitive areas to prevent oil from entering creeks or other spawning beaches. However, the bay is so large that it would be nearly impossible to place booms quickly enough to prevent oil from getting to the beaches. The sheer number of beaches to be protected is very large, and the foul weather that would likely accompany an oil spill would make placing and maintaining booms difficult. The only effective measure is prevention.

The unthinkable happened on May 9, 1996. The *Anitra*, a French-owned tanker, spilled Nigerian light crude oil into the mouth of Delaware Bay. The spill occurred when the tanker was transferring some oil to another ship to lighten its load before entering the bay. High seas broke the boom, and about 40,000 gallons drifted free. This is a small spill by oil spill standards. The oil spill in 1990 in the Arthur Kill was 567,000 gallons, the *Exxon Valdez* spilled 10.8 million gallons, and the terminals and tankers during the Gulf War released 240 million gallons. However, the Horseshoe Crabs were just beginning to spawn and the shorebirds were just arriving. It took several days for the oil to start washing ashore, and then it continued to do so into June. Fortunately, the spill was small, and it occurred offshore, giving the oil some time to weather and some space to disperse. Still, oil droplets littered the beaches, and oil response teams worked well into June. Most of the oil washed ashore along the Atlantic coast, where there were fewer shorebirds. By the last week in May, nearly 90 percent of the Sanderlings and other shorebirds feeding along the Atlantic beaches had some oil on their plumage, oil that they ingested when they preened. Since the oil continued to wash ashore, the birds were exposed day after day. Our research in the laboratory indicated that even the slight oiling experienced by the Sanderlings along the shore was enough to cause weight loss at a time when the birds were under severe pressures to gain weight.

Several Piping Plovers, a federally endangered species, were oiled and had to be removed to rehabilitation centers where they were cleaned. They lost their clutches, mostly because the eggs were so oiled they did not hatch. Compared to the number of birds in Delaware Bay, the damage was slight, but only because we were lucky. The oil spill was small and occurred where the oil did not flow directly into Delaware Bay where it could foul the beaches. The *Anitra* brought home the lesson, however: *prevention* is the only viable option.

While decreases in the populations of Red Knots, Sanderlings, and other species could be due to many factors, such as predation, pollution, weather stresses on the breeding or overwintering grounds, or global warming, they could also be due to stresses caused by the declining availability of Horseshoe Crab eggs during the critical stopover on Delaware Bay. The last ten years have seen a sharp decline in the number of Horseshoe Crab eggs, both below the sand and at the sand's surface, where shorebirds and gulls feed. Some counts of spawning crabs have also shown declines, although it is difficult to obtain accurate counts because the spawning crabs peak on the full and new moons, when it may not always be possible to census.

The overwhelming concern for the shorebirds led to the development of a Comprehensive Management Plan for Shorebirds on Delaware Bay, prepared by a coalition of scientists, conservationists, and naturalists in conjunction with personnel from the Endangered and Nongame Species Program. Designed to protect and enhance the shorebird migration, the coalition meets each year to discuss progress, new problems, and new initiatives. The group determines management needs for the next year, as well as organizing a public outreach program. Anyone is welcome to the workshop held each year in Cape May in early May.

While there is a groundswell of concern for the well-being of the shorebirds, it is not only a conservation issue. Economics is involved as well. The spectacle of thousands upon thousands of shorebirds feeding on Horseshoe Crab eggs, along with the massive spawning of the crabs themselves, draws a large number of ecotourists. Although many are making day trips, the vast majority come for the weekend or longer, staying in hotels, eating in restaurants, and shopping in the little boutiques just behind the Victorian gingerbread houses that line the ocean in Cape May. In 1988, for example, over 90,000 birders spent $5.5 million in Cape May to watch the interaction between the Horseshoe Crabs and shorebirds. Now, ecotourism is over a $30 million business each year in Cape May. In 1996, the Fish and Wildlife Service estimated that over 400,000 people living in New Jersey watched shorebirds. The economic benefit for southern New Jersey is substantial and is clearly worth more than the revenue from the sale of Horseshoe Crabs within the state. Loss of the Horseshoe Crab food base for the shorebirds would jeopardize some of this ecotourist influx.

Concern for the Horseshoe Crabs and shorebirds on Delaware Bay has prompted the Atlantic States Marine Fisheries Commission to set up a committee to write a management plan for Horseshoe Crabs that takes into account the role of excess crab eggs to migrating shorebirds, as well as other ecosystem effects. This was a landmark decision by the Commission because it recognized that fisheries plans should include multispecies considerations. While they failed to set take limits, they did recognize the importance of collecting hard data on the harvest of the crabs, which will provide reliable information to evaluate population trends and to reevaluate the need for regulating the harvest in the future. The plight of the shorebirds on Delaware Bay is one of the most important ecological issues in coastal New Jersey. The Horseshoe Crab–shorebird interaction is not only a matter of a small local resource dispute, but of a shorebird population recognized as internationally important, one that is being watched around the world.

23. Semipalmated Sandpipers feeding on Horseshoe Crab eggs in the shallow sand. (Photo by J. Burger)

The spectacle of the swirling shorebirds during their stopover on Delaware Bay in late May is unparalleled anywhere in the world, except perhaps in the Copper River Delta in Alaska and Texel Island in the Netherlands. Both of the latter sites serve as funnels for much of the Arctic, just as Delaware Bay does for the Canadian Arctic. The difference is that the Copper River Delta and Texel Island are primarily funnel points for the southward migration, while Delaware Bay is the stopover point for their northward migration, when they are pressured to reach the Arctic on time, in good condition, or they will be unable to breed. During their southward journey, time is less of a problem. Shorebirds can take more time to migrate south, can stop at more places, and will eventually arrive where more food is available. The shorebirds moving through Delaware Bay have a scant two weeks to obtain enough food reserves to take them another two thousand miles and into the breeding season. Delaware Bay may be the most vulnerable link in the entire life cycle of the shorebirds. The cost of not having enough food is starvation on the way to the Arctic, and being unable to breed successfully once there (fig. 23).

These issues are weighty, but for the moment, the shorebirds seem to be holding their own, particularly if we reduce the harvest on Horseshoe Crabs, as New Jersey regulations currently require. The swirling mass of shorebirds gathered in a dense ribbon along the surf is one of the most amazing concentrations of migrants in the world—right in our own backyard.

FOR MORE INFORMATION: Call the Endangered and Nongame Species Program of the New Jersey Department of Environmental Protection (609-292-9400) or Cape May Bird Observatory (609-861-0700); www.nj.com/audubon/.

24. Mountain Laurel growing along the side of the Garden State Parkway.
(Photo by J. Burger)

6

Mountain Laurel

In the spring of the year, the understory is ablaze with a wash of vibrant white and pink flowers that stretches for miles. A delicate sweet smell caresses the air, and the lower branches sweep to the ground, forming a wall of pink and white.

KEY LOCATIONS: The Pine Barrens and Hartshorne Woods Park (Monmouth County).

DIRECTIONS: One of the easiest places to see Mountain Laurel is along the Garden State Parkway, from mile 70 to 94. There are particularly good patches from milepost 70 to 75, and from milepost 93 to 96, where the blooms are visible on both sides of the road and the bright white and pink cascades contrast sharply with the deep green of the pines and of the Laurel leaves.

Hartshorne Woods Park overlooks the Navesink and Shrewsbury Rivers and Sandy Hook. From Route 36 in Highlands, turn right on Navesink Avenue and drive a half mile to the park entrance.

BEST TIME TO VISIT: May 20 to first week in June. The color usually peaks around Memorial Day.

PRIME HABITAT: Interestingly, Mountain Laurel grows in three very different types of habitats in New Jersey, in the flat Pine Barrens of central New Jersey, on Oak, Sycamore, and Tulip Poplar woods in the Highlands overlooking Sandy Hook, and in the hills of northwestern New Jersey, where the snow lingers and the blossoms are delayed until early June.

A blaze of rose, pink, and white flowers forms a mass of color against the deep green needles of the Pitch Pines. The color undulates, forming large mounds of color that sweep from the forest floor and heap twenty feet up into the air. Growing toward the sunlight, the Mountain Laurel trunks twist sideways until they look like they will fall over, forming a spectacular wall of color. Nearly all of the blooms face the sun, particularly at the edges of narrow sand roads, rocky outcroppings, or the Garden State Parkway.

The unopened buds look like dollops of frosting with tiny ridges leading to a point. Even before the flowers open, some buds are a brilliant rose that turns to a delicate pink as the five petals open to form a delicate cup, with as many as thirty flowers on a single stem. In the more shaded places, the flowers are always white; it takes the brilliant sun to produce the brilliant rose. With the warm rays of springtime, the pink fades to a radiant white. The overall effect is of giant scoops of strawberry and vanilla ice cream plopped down amid the forest. Some have melted more than others, dissolving into the understory, while others are still tall and erect. Mostly, the dazzling flowers form a colorful ruff on the tips of the branches (fig. 25).

25. Each Mountain Laurel flowerhead contains many delicate flowers. (Photo by J. Burger)

The flowers are highly specialized for being pollinated by bees and other insects. The insides of each flower are like tiny parasols, and near the outside of each rib a tiny pit has a straplike stamen, one of the male flower parts. The stamens arise from the center of the flower but bend delicately to be inserted in their own pit. When a bee touches the edge of the pit, the stamen springs from the pit to slap pollen all over the bee's head and back. Sprinkled with pollen, the bee leaves to visit another Mountain Laurel, thus cross-pollinating the species, a perfect case of coevolution between a plant and an insect.

The evergreen leaves of the Laurels are hidden just below the blooms, clinging to strong but gnarled, wooden trunks that can be two inches in diameter. Evergreen leaves remain on the tree for several years, saving the tree energy, as it does not have to produce new leaves each year. The older leaves are a deep forest green, thick, leathery, and tough enough to last for many years. The newer leaves are smaller, more delicate, and are a light lime-sherbet green. With time they will thicken, darken, and curl to preserve moisture during droughts.

Farther in the woods, where the sun penetrates only in shafts that illuminate the dust and fall on the brilliant blooms, the Mountain Laurel grows taller and straighter as it reaches up for the light. Some of the branches are twisted where they have tried unsuccessfully to reach the sun. It must be harder for new Laurels to grow here, for there are fewer here than along the road, and they are more scattered.

In the Pine Barrens and along the Garden State Parkway, a wall of Pitch Pines rises above the Mountain Laurel. In the Atlantic Highlands, the Laurel is framed by stately Sycamores and Oaks, while in northwestern New Jersey near the Delaware Water Gap, dark green Hemlocks, Beeches, and Maples shade the flowers. While the canopy varies, the understory is similar. Beneath the decaying leaves, the soil is usually well drained and quite acid, and the lowest understory consists of the closely related, thigh-high Sheep Laurel, less showy and less spectacular but no less beautiful. It blooms at the same time as the Mountain Laurel but has smaller and deeper pink flowers, the color of raspberry sherbet. Unlike the Mountain Laurel with its large, showy blooms at the ends of the branches, the blooms of Sheep Laurel are two to three inches from the top of woody stems that are thinner than a pencil. Each deep pink blossom has a reddish dot on the inside of the cup. It does not bend to face the sun, but grows straight, and no branches sweep the forest floor.

Scattered among the Sheep Laurel are Bracken Ferns, forming a feathery vision of lacy leaflets, each plant having three stout and flattened fronds. In some places the Bracken forms dense stands, while in others only a few are found. Some of its delicate fiddleheads have not yet opened. Although the fiddleheads can be eaten, the mature fronds are slightly toxic to people and livestock. Here and there, the Bracken crowds out the Sheep Laurel, but both are dwarfed by the sheer size and majesty of the Mountain Laurel that sweeps from the forest floor, mature trees reaching twenty feet high in a display of delicate flowers that face the sun. Each bush is more lovely than the last, each one more pink, or more white, or more covered with flowers.

Mountain Laurel grows from New England west to Indiana and south to northern Florida. It was familiar to the early settlers, and was one of the plants that was sent to Carolus Linnaeus in Sweden in the 1700s; it was named personally by him. In the South, where Mountain Laurel grows taller, the colonists were able to use its branches for small tools, bucket handles, and even for pipes. It is the state flower of Pennsylvania.

The bush grows in both oak and pine forests. Sometimes it is mistaken for Rhododendrons, which are members of the same Heath family, the Ericaceae. But Rhododendrons have larger leaves, grow even taller, flower about a month later, and usually grow only in hardwood forests. Rhododendrons thrive best in wet places, in ravines, and along streams. They occur in the hills of northwestern New Jersey, but not in the Pine Barrens.

As beautiful as the Mountain Laurel is, its leaves contain a substance that is poisonous if eaten, leading to symptoms including salivation, nausea, vomiting, diarrhea, pain and cramping of the intestines, and dizziness. Besides humans, goats and other domestic animals can also be poisoned by eating the leaves. Mountain Laurel is well known to herbalists, and American Indians used the leaves in small quantities both as a sedative and as an astringent. Mixed with lard, it was used as an ointment for skin irritations. Some people get an itching or burning of the skin when exposed to it; the symptoms usually pass, and there is no known cure. One herbalist's volume reports that the American Indians used it to commit suicide.

Although Mountain Laurel has the reputation of being poisonous to livestock and people, wildlife seem to be immune. In some places, Ruffed Grouse and White-tailed Deer feed extensively on the leaves, buds, and twigs. During harsh winters, Mountain Laurel provides cover for deer and other wildlife, and was the background for a famous painting by John James Audubon. America's most famous bird artist of the nineteenth century, Audubon painted several birds that have never been seen since. Some say he painted from memory and simply made mistakes. Others say he painted birds that were rare hybrids, and some suspect that he encountered and painted birds which soon became extinct. One of these mystery birds, or *aves ignotae,* was a tiny kinglet which Audubon called Cuvier's Regulus; he chose to portray it on a Mountain Laurel.

Mountain Laurel are so beautiful that they are often used as ornamental plantings, particularly in large gardens. They require well-drained, acid soil and are therefore not well suited for most suburban lawns, which are regularly limed to promote grass growth. Nonetheless, wherever they grow, they are a stunning addition to the understory. To see the related Rhododendrons and Azaleas in bloom, visit the Rutgers Display Garden in late April (see chapter 11 for directions).

FOR MORE INFORMATION: Call the Hartshorne Woods Park to obtain detailed information on peak color in any given year (732-872-0336).

Summer

26. Adult Common Egret flying (*top*), and Common Egrets arriving at a colony on a salt marsh island in Barnegat Bay (*bottom*). (Photos by J. Burger)

7

Nesting Herons at Avalon

Bushes of Cherry and Poison Ivy sway in the harsh winds of late March. Winter has barely departed, but the trees are laden with tall stately white Great Egrets, smaller Snowy Egrets, and an occasional Black-crowned Night Heron, facing stoically into the wind. They crane their necks, peering through the branches for a closer view. Satisfied that danger is past, they hunker down, or drop to lower branches, and some disappear. A lone Great Egret glides in to land on an exposed perch, symbolizing the massive heronry forming among the branches.

KEY LOCATIONS: Avalon (Cape May County), Third Avenue at 70th Street.

DIRECTIONS: Take the Garden State Parkway to exit 10, and go east on Stone Harbor Boulevard; take a left (north) on 3rd Avenue, to 70th Street. Herons nest and roost in the trees beyond the playground.

BEST TIME TO VISIT: Herons and egrets breed from late March to early June, but the peak is from late April to late May. Birds are active all day, but the early morning egress of feeding birds and the return to the colony at dusk are most spectacular.

PRIME HABITAT: Herons and egrets require vegetation for nesting, such as the chest-high Marsh Elder on salt marsh islands, Poison Ivy thickets, and small Cherries on bay islands, or tall and stately Birches, Oaks, and Maples of mainland heronries. They usually prefer clumps of bushes or woods that are isolated from people and other disturbances.

When the snow melts from the salt marshes, the barrier islands, and the dredge-spoil islands in Barnegat Bay, when the noisy Herring Gulls take up territories amid the grasses and low shrubs, egrets and herons begin staking out their territories. The tentative long call of the gulls, indicating that courtship is not far behind, mingles with the harsh croaks of herons. For the most part, the herons stand motionless, huddled down against the wind. The vegetation is still brown from its winter rest, and the white-and-gray Herring Gulls are visible from afar. They seem to be the only life on the islands, but they are not.

Black-crowned Night Herons have settled on their heronries. They arrived in early March, when snow still lingered under the bushes and in shaded crannies. They return to the same nest site they used last year, hoping to find the nest still intact. With any luck, they only need to repair the nest by adding a few twigs and tucking in the loose pieces. The old platform serves as a place to rest during the day and to sleep in the late hours of the night, after an early night of searching for prey along the shore. They well earn their name, for they are mainly nocturnal.

By early April, other species begin to arrive. Great Egrets and Snowy Egrets are conspicuous, not only because they are white, but because they like to sit on the tops of the bushes where they can watch for approaching danger. Nine species of herons, egrets, and ibises nest regularly in coastal New Jersey, with Snowy Egret and Glossy Ibis accounting for more than 70 percent of the individuals. Other species that breed in New Jersey heronries include the Black-crowned Night Heron, Great Blue Heron, Great Egret, Little Blue Heron, Tri-colored Heron, Cattle Egret, and Yellow-crowned Heron. Great Blue Herons usually nest in inland colonies by themselves, preferring groves of tall trees. Other species, such as bitterns and the diminutive Green Heron, nest solitarily.

Herons, egrets, and ibises are some of the most dependable of all nesting birds. Some heronries have been used for years, decades, and, in some cases, even centuries. Some of the writings in Europe from the 1700s and 1800s describe heronries that are still there today. If this passage were written five years ago, we could have reported that Witmer Stone wrote of the Stone Harbor heronry in the early part of the 1900s, and that it was still there. But after decades of using the same heronry in the very center of Stone Harbor, the birds picked up and moved to the middle of a nearby town, Avalon. Someday they may return to their traditional Stone Harbor colony, or move elsewhere.

The reason for their desertion has generated much discussion but few concrete ideas. It cannot be space, because they moved to a block that is not as large as the one they occupied at Stone Harbor. It could be an increase in Fish Crows and Great Horned Owls, which prey on their eggs and chicks, but the increase in these avian predators was not large and they are surely able to find the new colony only a few miles away. Herons, after all, are conspicuous birds. It could be that Red Foxes were wandering beneath their nest trees, or that Raccoons have taken over the large trees for their own winter dens; the foxes do not climb, but the Raccoons certainly do. It could also be that the habitat just degenerated over the years due to the deposition of guano, which kills vegetation, or the breaking of branches and twigs for nest material. It could be the steady increase in human disturbance, though fences prevented intrusion at Stone Harbor. Or it could be the slow buildup of nest parasites, such as ticks, mites, and biting flies, an explanation we favor. There is precedent for colonial birds abandoning colony sites when there is a large infestation of nest parasites such as mites. They become so annoying that the birds simply cannot stand it, much as we avoid Snake Bight Trail in the Everglades because of the millions of mosquitoes all biting at once. Similarly, the American Indians, and later the early settlers, avoided the Jersey shore because of the hordes of mosquitos and green-headed flies in July—so why not the birds?

Usually, however, the herons stay where they are because they selected wisely in the first place. The birds usually return to last year's colony site, inspect it, and settle down. They selected sites that were far removed from people and predators. Since they usually nest in trees, they can avoid most ground predators, and their high elevation removes them from the reach of flood tides. Heronries we have studied in Barnegat Bay have remained on the same salt marsh islands for many years, and those that shifted did so only after a Red Fox got on the island. The Marsh Elder and Poison Ivy bushes on salt marshes are only waist to shoulder high, and any self-respecting fox can easily catch chicks or even unwary adult birds at that height.

Settling on the heronry, however, is no trivial matter, for the birds must choose their nest site judiciously. There are major battles over old nests from last year, as well as new nest sites, as each individual tries to get the best spot. If there are few trees or low shrubs, as often happens with the colonies on salt marsh islands, then there is intense competition for them, and the Glossy Ibis, which loses out to the more aggressive species, is often forced to nest on the ground in the dense Phragmites, the tall Common Reed that invades our wetlands. Our studies with heronries indicated that the preferred places are high in the bushes or trees, for the highest places offer the best view of approaching predators and are the farthest from ground predators and high storm tides. Competition for high sites is intense, and birds may lose their site to others if they cannot adequately defend it. In birds, the biggest individual usually wins. This results in a stratification in the heronry that is based on size among our native species: Great Egrets nest the highest, followed by Little Blue Herons, Tri-colored Herons, Yellow-crowned Night Herons, Snowy Egrets, and finally Black-crowned Night Herons and Glossy Ibises, which are often forced to nest on the ground. Black-crowned Night Herons sometimes succeed in nesting higher because they eat the eggs and chicks of nearby species, thus providing abandoned nests for them to take over.

The exception to this nice neat pattern is the Cattle Egret, a non-native species from central Africa that first bred in Florida in the early 1950s and nested in New Jersey shortly thereafter. Since Cattle Egrets arrive at heronries much later than our native species, and are smaller, scientists and conservationists were not worried about competition. However, the Cattle Egrets did not listen to the scientists and outcompeted the larger species for nest sites by harassing them, stealing twigs from their nests while they incubated, and directly attacking them. They are relentless, slowly causing other species to abandon their nests, and then taking them over. Thus, Cattle Egrets nest higher in the bushes and trees than their size would predict. But otherwise, the size-related nesting pattern is intact.

As the weather slowly warms, the herons and egrets begin to repair their nests in earnest, adding twigs they have stolen from neighbors or picked up from the ground. Any nest that has not been claimed is quickly dismantled as the birds discover that it is easier to steal a few nice twigs from nearby than to fly a long distance and hunt for ones that may be too large or too heavy to carry back.

In early May the first pale blue egg, about the size of a chicken's egg, appears in a nest on the ground. Within a few days there are four, and a Black-crowned Night Heron is incubating quietly, barely visible above the bulky nest. All over the colony, egg-laying begins in earnest, with nearly all of the species initiating egg-laying at once, soon after the Night Herons, including the late arriving Cattle Egrets. The herons, egrets, and ibises all lay eggs that vary from the pale blue of Night Herons to the sky blue of egrets and the deeper greenish blue of the Ibises. The eggs of Great and Snowy Egrets are a clear, Robin-egg blue, and the former are distinguishable because of their large size. Those of the Glossy Ibis are nearly green and smaller than those of the Night Herons. The Little Blue and Tri-colored Herons are bluish green, but since their nests are smaller and higher than those of Night Herons, they too can be identified. The differences are subtle, but with time and practice, they are distinguishable. For the whole colony, egg laying is highly synchronous, meaning that all the pairs start at about the same time, and finish at the same time.

When the peak of egg laying passes, the colony becomes nearly silent, as the birds incubate quietly. It is still a bit chilly on mid-May mornings, and the herons and egrets sit low in the nest, deriving a little protection from the cold winds that sometimes sweep across the water. A mate may linger nearby, preening or sleeping, but usually only one member of each pair attends the nest. The nests are well below the tops of the bushes, otherwise the branches could not hold the weight of the nest and adults. Thus there is barely a sign of the heronry from the outside. The larger the colony, of course, the more sign of activity, as mates fly back to take their turn at incubation or climb to the top of the trees to look for predators or any other disturbance. Any slight disruption, and more birds fly up to the higher perches until the colony is dotted with the varied colors and shapes of the herons and egrets.

The nasal call of a Fish Crow causes a disturbance, and several nesting egrets stand up, climb to a nearby branch, and peer around. It is a safer strategy to remain on the nest, however, for Fish Crows quickly swoop in to take eggs from unguarded nests. In inland colonies, the larger Common Crows can be even more of a nuisance as they are less easily intimidated by the egrets. The crows hide quietly in nearby bushes or in a dense Red Cedar, waiting for a nest exchange, when the arriving mate will be unaware of its presence. Then, when the new-arrival mate flies up and circles around to defecate far from the nest, a

27. Snowy Egret foraging in the shallow water. (Photo by J. Burger)

crow seizes the opportunity to steal an egg, taking it to the edge of the colony where it can break it open and eat in peace.

The colony is mostly quiet during the day, except for occasional harsh notes indicating an altercation. Parents that are not guarding young are out on the creeks or salt marshes, searching for fish or other foods for their chicks (fig. 27). At dusk, however, when many birds arrive to roost for the night, there is constant noisy activity until each has found its perch. This continues for many minutes, and even when it is too dark to see, there is bickering when the Night Herons leave, uttering loud "quonks" as they fly to distant feeding grounds. At last, the day arrives when very faint calls can be heard from incubating birds. They become restless and spend more time standing up, peering at their eggs, and then returning to incubate, as if their quiet has been interrupted. Within a day or two, the cause of their anxiety is clear. The first tiny chicks have hatched—chicks only a parent could love, for when they first hatch their down is sparse and very wet, and they look like little fat balls with sickly green-and-gray translucent skin (fig. 28). Their closed eyes are large, their heads are small, and their necks are too weak to support the weight. Yet within a day or two they can raise their heads and even thrust their bills upward to seize food or strike at an intruder. The chicks of each species are identifiable, based on body color, down color, and size.

Since the herons began their incubation as soon as their second egg was laid, the first two chicks hatch a day or two before the next sibling, and by the end of the week, there are four chicks that differ strikingly in size and strength. As

28. Young Black-crowned Night Herons only a few days old. (Photo by
J. Burger)

with the Black Skimmers discussed in chapter 9, asynchrony is an adaptation
to variations in food supply. Depending on the clutch size, which in herons
and egrets can vary from two to six depending on the food available during egg
laying, there can be quite a difference in the size of chicks in the same nest. Five
or six days can elapse between the hatching of the first chick in a nest and the
last days, when the oldest chick has been well fed and has grown rapidly. The
last chick to hatch is at a serious disadvantage; not only is it smaller and less
able to compete for food, but it is competing with four or five older chicks that
show it little mercy. The first chick to hatch did not even have to compete for
food; everything its parents brought back, it ate.

While many heronries in New Jersey are hard to visit because they are on
dredge spoil islands in the Kill van Kull or on salt marsh islands along the
shore, some are located on the mainland, such as the one at Avalon. Visiting
the heronry at Avalon can be exciting at any time during the nesting season, for
different things are visible. Early in May, many of the herons and egrets are sitting on the tops of the trees and bushes, their white almost brilliant against the
drab green trees. With time, the birds settle in to incubate, and then fewer birds
sit on top of the vegetation, although a few stand guard duty, and there are
always returning parents, waiting to take over incubation duties from their
mates. Still later, as the chicks age, they begin to get impatient for their parents'
return, for they are always hungry. More and more climb to the tops of the
branches, peering around, searching for parents. They flap their wings and

jump up and down, exercising their wing muscles; they begin to make short flights, landing awkwardly, flopping down into the branches. Finally, the day arrives when the first chicks fly from the heronry to the nearby water, often landing clumsily or even tumbling down head first.

By mid-July, many heronries are empty—the herons have all departed. There is nothing to suggest that a noisy heronry was active except for the stick nests hidden in the branches, and perhaps the bodies of hapless chicks that failed to make it. Family groups feed in the marshes, searching for fish in the shallow pools and creeks. For a few days, the herons and egrets concentrate in the marshes around the heronry, for the young are learning to fish; but within a week they begin to fan out along the coast, searching for new places to forage where the competition is less. Many actually move northward, exploring habitats where few herons breed.

FOR FURTHER INFORMATION: Contact the colonial waterbird coordinator for the Endangered and Nongame Species Program, either at the Trenton office (609-292-9400) or at the Tuckahoe Wildlife Management Area (609-628-2436). For specific information on the Avalon heronry, call the Wetlands Institute, which keeps track of this heronry (609-368-1236); http://www.wetlandsinstitute.org/.

29. A flock of Laughing Gulls flying over a breeding colony, early in the nesting season when all have black heads. (Photo by J. Burger)

8

Laughing Gulls at Stone Harbor

Stiff green Cord Grass borders the muddy banks of tidal creeks, and in between, a wide expanse of pale green Salt Hay lies in swaths across the marsh, forming a soft blanket festooned with hundreds of Laughing Gulls incubating their eggs in the warm sun. Overhead a hundred more Laughing Gulls swirl, calling loudly, and dive down to chastise a Fish Crow that has intruded into their midst. The crow departs, trailed by a retinue of gulls that escort the marauder away from the colony.

KEY LOCATIONS: Marshes near the Wetlands Institute in Stone Harbor (Cape May County), and along Stone Harbor Boulevard.

DIRECTIONS: Take the Garden State Parkway to exit 10, and take Stone Harbor Boulevard east toward the coast. The Wetlands Institute is on the right before you cross the bridge over the Intracoastal Waterway.

BEST TIME TO VISIT: Late May is best because the gulls are incubating, but early June is also interesting because they are feeding their young chicks. However, they are more vulnerable to disturbance when they have chicks, and the colony should not be approached closely at this time.

PRIME HABITAT: They nest on the highest spots in salt marshes, preferring to nest on wracks of Cord Grass or Eelgrass strewn there by the highest winter tides.

A cold April wind blows across the brown salt marshes of south Jersey, and only a hint of the green tips of new growth indicates that soon the marsh will be lush and the grass tall along the creeks. Long wracks of dead and brown Cord Grass stems lie strewn on the high parts of the marsh, deposited there by high tides during the winter and early spring. The marsh is dotted with hundreds of Laughing Gulls, each facing into the chilly wind, waiting for the calm to resume their courtship activities. When the wind dies down in the late afternoon, the birds begin their elaborate and vocal courtship displays and start to defend territories.

Laughing Gulls are familiar to anyone who visits the Jersey shore. They are dark gray above and immaculate white below, with a black head and a dull red bill. Their "kek-kek-kek" calls are omnipresent sounds throughout the summer. But Laughing Gulls do not spend the entire year in New Jersey; they migrate in October and return at the end of March.

A male begins to give plaintive "long calls," bending his head down until it nearly touches the wrack between his feet. Then, raising his head slowly upwards and over his back, he utters a series of soft "kah" calls. Turning his head, he looks upward from side to side, watching for any unattached females that might be flying overhead. On and on he goes, giving long call after long call. Finally, a female lands ten feet away from him, and begins to peck at the wrack, tossing aside a few straws, as if unaware of the nearby male. He watches for a moment, and then gives another long call, taking a few tentative steps, edging ever closer to the female. With each long call he moves nearer, until he is about three feet away; but he misjudged her interest, and she leaps into the air and flies way across the marsh.

Undaunted, he returns to his original spot and continues calling, searching the sky. Hundreds of gulls course over the marsh, some searching for old mates, some for new mates, and some for available territories. Laughing Gulls usually stay with the same mates from year to year. But there are some divorces, and of course, some fatalities. Those that must find new mates spend nearly all the time calling, courting, and careening over the marsh in their quest. It may take a week or two to find a new mate, but in the meantime, the male is defending his territory and assessing the highest point suitable for a nest.

Most of the Laughing Gulls bred last year, so now they need only find their mate, who likewise has returned to where they nested last year. Once both are on their familiar territory, they engage in pair-bond maintenance by displaying and calling to each other. Courtship activity is highest in the colony in the early morning and late afternoon, when prolonged bouts can go on for several minutes. The reunited pairs engage in courtship by long-calling to one another and giving head tosses (fig. 30). The male brings back fish, crabs, and other food to the female who waits in the territory. This courtship feeding accomplishes three things: it allows the female to defend the territory, it is an integral part of courtship and pair-bond maintenance, and it provides the female with additional food stores that she uses to produce her eggs. Thus the male can affect the quality of his mate's eggs. Courtship feeding is often followed by copulation.

Territorial Laughing Gulls also walk about the territory to assess its suitability. But the winter months have taken their toll on the habitat, and some of last year's sites are no longer usable, for stiff winds and high tides blew or washed away some of the banks, eroded the marsh itself, and shifted the wrack, removing the old and depositing the new, but not necessarily in the same places.

30. Pair of courting Laughing Gulls. The male on the left is giving a head toss to his mate. (Photo by J. Burger)

Although the gulls have come to select a territory in the Stone Harbor gullery, they need not worry about the colony site because this site is generally safe from predators. The Stone Harbor marshes are extensive, with many smaller islands surrounded by creeks and channels of various sizes, enough to discourage any but the most persistent predator. Islands are ideal for colonies of nesting birds because they are surrounded by water, providing protection from mammals that would have to swim long distances to reach them. One of the advantages of using the same colony site from year to year is the knowledge that it is generally free from mammalian predators, and that some places are above the high tides.

Each gull selects a territory, hoping to acquire one that is large enough to support successful breeding. Choosing a territory is a tricky business for a gull, because it must select a site that is high enough to avoid high tides, yet low enough to have no mammalian predators. To accomplish this, the gulls spend a month on their territory before they begin to build a nest. During this time they assess where the highest place is by moving every time their feet get wet during high tide. Waiting a month ensures that they have been there during the highest tides of the new and full moon. In some seasons, however, there are unforeseen floods, with prolonged winds and rains or even early hurricanes.

Only when they have found a good site will they begin to construct their nest, interlacing together bits of old Cord Grass and Eelgrass that have washed

31. Laughing Gull with nest material in its bill. (Photo by J. Burger)

up on the marsh. Building a substantial nest is very important, because it is a hedge against some high tides. Not only does the additional height help, but when the marsh is covered with water, the nests float up, keeping the eggs above water. Since the nest is attached to the upright stems of marsh grasses, it does not drift away unless there are gale winds.

Both males and females bring back material for the nest (fig. 31). Nest building is accompanied by more courtship, including courtship feeding. While the male is away, he must find enough food for himself as well as some large pieces to bring back for his mate. If food is scarce in the salt marsh creeks, it is only a short flight, eighteen miles as the gull flies, from the Stone Harbor gullery to the Delaware Bayshore, where food is often abundant.

In mid-May on the Delaware Bayshore, thousands of Laughing Gulls form dense flocks on sandbars not far from shore, pecking furiously at the mud, looking much more like sandpipers than gulls. These dense flocks are feeding on Horseshoe Crab eggs washed up by the gentle surf after hundreds of female crabs have dug up the nests of others who nested before them. The abundant supply of eggs is only possible because there are so many Horseshoe Crabs that each succeeding wave of arrivals digs up the nests of others. If the density of crabs decreases, then fewer excess eggs will be available for the gulls and shorebirds. When Horseshoe Crab eggs are available in abundance (see chapter 4), the gulls and shorebirds have a field day, gorging themselves on the surplus eggs. For the shorebirds, food abundance is a crucial resource that allows them to continue migrating, but for the gulls it is mainly a bonus.

The thousands of shorebirds have formed their own tight flock at the high-tide line, so thick that the larger gulls cannot intrude, so the gulls are forced to the nearby sandbar. The dense flock of gulls is fairly quiet as the birds busily search for the pale green eggs, and there is little jostling, except at the edges. For the most part they feed without interruption, although occasionally an edge gull looks around, making sure no predators are nearby.

Although in the feeding frenzy the gulls are at a disadvantage and are forced to the edges of the shorebird flocks or out on the sandbar, they have one major advantage: they do not have to travel thousands of miles to breeding grounds in the high Arctic. They are near their breeding sites, for most breed in the salt marshes of New Jersey, although a few may travel north to breed at Jamaica Bay Wildlife Refuge at the end of the runways of J. F. Kennedy Airport, much to the consternation of airport officials.

Many of the gulls picking up eggs so frenetically nest at the large colony at Stone Harbor. They have only a few hours to feed, and then they must return to the colony to their waiting mates who are guarding their territory or are incubating. Egg laying in Laughing Gulls usually begins in early to mid-May, and each female lays three dark brown eggs splotched with black. These eggs are cryptic, blend with the Cord Grass nests, and are difficult to see when the nests are placed on Cord Grass wracks strewn about the marsh.

By mid-May, many of the pairs at Stone Harbor have settled into a calm rhythm of incubation. Each member of a pair incubates for three to four hours, and then is relieved by its mate. The incoming parent gives a long call on approach, warning its mate that it will land. After a short exchange of long calls and head tosses, the relieved bird flies off to forage, perhaps making the flight to Delaware Bay, or searching in the nearby salt marsh creeks for clams, crabs, or other delicacies.

When storm tides build up slowly over a few hours, the gulls feverishly add material to their nests, raising their eggs higher, hoping to keep ahead of the tide. Our research has shown that this behavior is also triggered by wet nests. We put little plastic cups, like those used under houseplants, just below the top layer of grass, and filled them with water. When the parents came back to incubate, their feet were wet, and they quickly set about finding nest material and slowly raised the height of the nest until the eggs were well above the water. Gulls given plastic cups without water did not add any new material.

Most of May passes in quiet incubation, interrupted only by an occasional Fish Crow that flies low over the marshes, searching for an unguarded nest. Then the gulls fly up in dense, noisy flocks (see fig. 29). Leaving a nest unguarded is a dangerous business because the eggs are not only vulnerable to predators, but the nest itself can be torn apart by neighboring gulls in only a few hours. It takes a lot of work to keep up a nest, and gulls flying over the colony find it easier to steal a few pieces from an unguarded nest than to find their own. Besides, the pieces in a nest are already the right size, and it is easy to pick up several pieces at once.

In late May, incubating birds become nervous, standing up now and then to peer at their eggs. They give more and more soft mewing calls and then return to incubation. They are more reluctant to give up their nests to their mates, and linger longingly, peering at their eggs. Within a day or two the reason for their concern is clear, as the first tiny chicks hatch.

The hatching process itself takes more than a day. First a series of cracks called a star appears, where the chick has begun to work the eggtooth on top of its beak against the unyielding shell. With increasing vigor the chick expands the star into a small hole. At this pipping stage the chick's pink bill and white egg tooth are visible, and its soft peeping notes can be heard. The parents take great interest at this time. Soon the chick, working from inside, breaks off the top of the egg and wriggles free. At this point it is wet, bedraggled, and appears naked, but this is an illusion because it has a lot of down. It takes the newly hatched chick more than an hour to dry off, but then it is covered with fluffy brown down, splotched with black and darker brown spots, another antipredator adaptation because the young also blend with the marsh vegetation.

The anxious parents fly up from the nest carrying the eggshell in their bill and drop it far from their nest. This too is an antipredator behavior, for the white inner surface of the eggshell is very visible from the air and might attract a passing crow or Herring Gull. Incubation continues as the parents have two more eggs to hatch. Since they started incubating with the first or second egg, the third chick always hatches a day or two later. This asynchronous hatching, which occurs in herons and egrets as well, is an adaptation to limited food supplies. If food supplies are low, only the first and second chick survive, but if food is abundant, then parents raise all three chicks.

Almost immediately the parents begin to bring back food to feed the tiny chick. The Laughing Gulls at Stone Harbor feed their chick mainly Horseshoe Crab eggs, supplemented with clams, crabs, fish, worms, and insects (fig. 32). Insects and worms are gathered from inland wet meadows and farm fields, particularly following rains, when they are abundant. Although the Horseshoe Crab eggs are still plentiful on the Delaware Bayshore in late May and early June, they cannot feed their young entirely on the eggs because they are insufficient for growth. In fact, we have shown in laboratory experiments that Laughing Gull young lose weight and might eventually die if fed only Horseshoe Crab eggs.

Initially the parents brood the young chicks to keep them warm, for the chick's thermoregulatory abilities are not fully developed. However, within a week the chicks no longer require brooding, and the parents merely stand nearby, guarding them from predators or shielding them from the hot sun. When the winds begin to blow and rain pelts the marsh in sheets, however, the

32. Laughing Gulls feeding on Horseshoe Crab eggs on Delaware Bay. (Photo by J. Burger)

chicks quickly crawl under their parents for protection. Although their down can withstand mild rains, a driving rain can quickly penetrate to their skin, chilling them, and within a few hours they die from exposure. Disturbance during these periods, either by predators or thoughtless people, keeps the adults away from their nests and can cause widespread chick mortality. If the rains continue for several days, the result is often a high mortality, because eventually the parents must leave to forage, both for themselves and to bring back food for their chicks. Parents are faced with hard choices; do they remain and brood the chicks or go out to forage? Usually one parent can remain and the other can go forage, but if the weather has been especially severe, it may be difficult to find food and both parents may leave.

Within a week the chicks learn to recognize the calls of their parents, an adaptation to being able to find their own nests amid a colony of hundreds. This individual recognition occurs at the time the chicks first begin to move about their territory and ensures that they do not wander into a neighboring territory, where they might be viciously chastised or even killed.

The chicks grow quickly, and within three weeks the down begins to give way to feathers. The cute, cuddly, down-covered chicks now look gangly, awkward, and prickly. With each succeeding day they require more and more food, and their parents must spend many hours each day foraging. Soon the chicks are completely covered with feathers and are nearly as big as their parents. They are now able to defend themselves and their territories against neighbors.

Both parents spend more time away from the colony, gathering food. They return to the colony for brief periods to feed their chicks, preen for a while, and then leave once again.

When it is warm and sunny, the chicks stand on their nests, picking up stray pieces of vegetation, working at the nest, and guarding their territory against neighbors. They rest, and during the middle of the day, they hide in the vegetation to avoid the searing heat of the sun. When any gull gives a warning call, all the chicks dive for cover, and they can easily hide in the Cord Grass that is now knee-high.

When they are about four weeks old, they begin to strengthen their wings by jumping up and down and flapping vigorously. They are nearly fully feathered, and are quite handsome, though they are mainly brown rather than gray and white. They wander about their territory, but they still return to the nest to be fed. By five to six weeks of age they can make short flights, although they often crash-land in a neighbor's territory and have to run quickly back to their own, amid the attacks of neighboring chicks and adults.

With time, their flights become longer and stronger, as well as more directed; they can now land where they choose. They fly to nearby muddy creeks, sit in the sun, and return to their territory only when they hear the familiar long call of their parents announcing feeding time. By mid-July, most of the chicks are flying, and only a few small ones remain on their nests, waiting for parents to return with food. Their chances of survival are not high, for soon their parents might abandon them; even if they fledge, they may be so underweight that they will not survive for long.

Most chicks, however, are strong and able to fly to the nearby creeks or beaches. Gradually, the colony becomes quieter and quieter, as more and more gull families leave the colony. Chicks remain with their parents for several weeks while they learn to forage on their own. It is difficult to learn foraging techniques, appropriate foods, and suitable foraging sites. They tag along with their parents, begging for food, and watching and learning. They pick up many inedible items at first, but gradually they improve their skills.

By mid-July, many gull families leave the Stone Harbor marshes and spread out along the Jersey shore. Some fly as far north as Jamaica Bay Refuge in search of food. With so many birds concentrated around Stone Harbor for the breeding season, it is advantageous to disperse as soon as it is possible. This means there is less competition for food in any one place. For several years the gulls that flew to Jamaica Bay faced the threat of death. Many thousands of Laughing Gulls banded in New Jersey were killed at J. F. Kennedy Airport in New York as part of its gull control program to prevent collisions with planes.

The young gulls forage for several months, learning new foraging skills and laying down fat for their southward migration. By early September, some Laughing Gulls begin to migrate south, and by early October most are en route to the wintering grounds. Only very few remain in New Jersey. The rest spend the winter in Florida, the West Indies, or in South America.

New Jersey is the center of breeding for Laughing Gulls, and more breed here than in any other state. For the present, they are doing well, although they face competition with Herring Gulls for the highest nest sites in marshes. Laughing Gulls have been displaced from many of their traditional sites, forcing them into lower areas of the marshes where they are vulnerable to flood tides. Not only do the Herring Gulls arrive earlier by several months, but they are three times larger, putting the Laughing Gulls at a severe disadvantage in direct encounters.

Still, large and vigorous Laughing Gull colonies exist on many of the Jersey salt marshes. Their long calls echo across the marsh, and they swoop and soar over the marshes and beaches along our shores. The laughing long call of these gulls is the signature sound of our coasts, and their colonies are well worth visiting, particularly the one at Stone Harbor.

The Wetlands Institute is always interesting; it not only gives you a nice view of the marshes and Laughing Gull colony, but there is a children's discovery room, exhibits, and telescopes. There is also a self-guided tour of the marsh, with a boardwalk across part of it.

FOR MORE INFORMATION: Call the Wetlands Institute (609-368-1236) for information on the nesting cycle in any given year; http://www.wetlands institute.org/.

33. Black Skimmers nesting on Tow Island in Barnegat Bay. (Photo by J. Burger)

9

Nesting Least Terns and Black Skimmers

The pale sandy beach is alive with white waifs that tilt and dart overhead, uttering shrill, piercing shrieks as they dive toward us to discourage our approach. Least Terns are aggressive and protective of their young. Abruptly, a whirl of sleek black bodies with long tilting wings lifts from the barren sand, wheeling low over the beach, and out over the water, only to circle and return, uttering loud barking calls. The flock of Black Skimmers parts, passing on both sides, coming so close there is a faint woosh of their wings. Some skimmers drop to the ground in front of us, falling flat on their breasts and flailing helplessly with their wings, seemingly unable to rise, while the terns dive-bomb us even though we are well away from the colony site. It is time to retreat.

KEY LOCATIONS: Sandy Hook (Gateway National Recreation Area, Monmouth County), Barnegat Inlet (Barnegat Lighthouse State Park, Ocean County), Corson's Inlet, and Hereford Inlet or nearby (Cape May County). However, winter storms change the face of the sandy beaches and spits, making it necessary to check for colony locations each year. Nesting areas are "off limits," but the birds can be observed from a distance of one hundred yards.

DIRECTIONS: For Sandy Hook, take exit 117 (southbound), or exit 105 (northbound) off the Garden State Parkway, follow Route 36 to Highland Beach; there is a well-marked entrance to the recreational area. Ask at the Visitor Center where the Least Terns can be observed nesting.

For Barnegat Inlet, take the Garden State Parkway to the Manahawkin Bridge exit, take Route 72 east to Long Beach Island, and just over the bridge take Main Street north about 5 miles to the end, where you will see the lighthouse at Barnegat Lighthouse State Park (birds usually nest out on the sandy spit).

For Corson's Inlet, take the Garden State Parkway to exit 25. Drive east on Roosevelt Boulevard (Route 623) to the end and turn south on Central Avenue (Route 619), which becomes Ocean Drive. Follow this to Corson's Inlet State Park. Park and walk out toward the ocean. When the terns and skimmers nest there, they are usually on the north side of the inlet.

For Hereford Inlet, take the Garden State Parkway to exit 6 and drive east on Route 147. Just before entering North Wildwood, Ocean Drive (Route 619) goes left (north) across Nummy Island toward Stone Harbor. The location of the skimmer colony changes from year to year. Look for them on exposed sandbars, which may be quite a distance from the road. Both species are endangered in New Jersey.

BEST TIME TO VISIT: Least Terns and Black Skimmers are incubating eggs and raising chicks from the end of May to early July.

PRIME HABITAT: Both species nest together on open and sparsely vegetated sandy beaches, above the high tide. They prefer wide beaches with an open view of predators. Least Terns also nest on wide patches of dredge spoil on islands or abandoned gravel pits. Black Skimmers also nest with Common Terns on wracks of dead and dried Eelgrass and Cord Grass on salt marshes, particularly in Barnegat Bay.

Sun glares off the smooth sand, bordered by a swaying sea of pale green Beach Grass, undulating sensually in the light onshore breeze. In the distance we see a tiny black dot, almost as a mirage, and then another, and another, until, as we approach, the sand is strewn with a hundred pairs of Black Skimmers, each facing the same direction, into the wind. They are crouched down, motionless, their brilliant blood-red bills laying on the sand, their eyes closed. The sun is hot, and the skimmers raise their back feathers slightly to release excess heat. Most of the incubating skimmers have their mate standing next to them. The mates sleep with their heads turned over one shoulder, their bills tucked neatly into the back feathers. They seems to sleep most of the day, for skimmers are mainly nocturnal, and as the sun goes down they wake up, stretch their wings, and begin to preen. Soon the nonincubating mates will leave the beach to skim the nearby creeks for food. But for now, most are asleep, barely moving; only one or two peer around, watching for predators.

One pair standing at the edge of the colony is engaged in courtship. The male, much larger than the female, presents her with a fish. She takes it and immediately turns away from him. He mounts her, while she adjusts the fish in her beak and then swallows it. He raises his wings to help maintain balance and tilts his tail to the side to make sexual contact. The mating ritual is brief, and the female steps out from under the male. Both shake and adjust their plumage, preening quietly for a few moments.

Behind the skimmers is a small colony of Least Terns, the smallest tern in New Jersey. Their nests are also mere depressions in the sand. Their activity betrays their location, for they are very diurnal and very noisy, and are busily establishing territories, defending them with displays and shrill calls, and courting. Most are merely reestablishing their pair bonds from last year, for

34. Least Tern shading eggs in a nest next to a clamshell on Brigantine Beach. (Photo by J. Burger)

like most seabirds, they are monogamous, maintaining the same mate from year to year unless one dies or they have a run of low reproductive success. Only then will they divorce and search for a new mate.

The Least Terns choose nest sites that are a bit higher than the surrounding sand, and are often closer to the Beach Grass or to weathered driftwood or large clamshells, which will provide shade for the chicks in the heat of the day (fig. 34). Although skimmer chicks can seek vegetation cover from the hot sun, they usually bury down until they reach cool sand, and then go to sleep. Choosing a nest site is a trade-off for both the terns and the skimmers. They select nest sites that are high enough to avoid high tides, but are away from dense vegetation that could conceal predators such as domestic cats, Raccoons, and foxes. Abandoned cats that have become feral are a particular threat to nesting birds along the shore. They take a heavy toll of chicks throughout the nesting season. Cats are equally lethal in our backyards, for during the day they wait at feeders to pounce on birds, and by night they stalk sleeping birds in low shrubs or ground nests.

Skimmers and Least Terns prefer the open sand on barrier beaches for nesting because it gives them a long view. They can always see a predator approaching a long distance away, and fly off, to return when danger has passed. These habitats with expanses of unoccupied beaches are decreasing because they are exactly the habitats that people prefer for bathing beaches, homes, marinas, resorts, and restaurants. Following the stock market crash of 1929, the federal government developed several public works programs to employ people and help end the depression. One of the key public works programs was to drain the salt marshes along the Atlantic Coast as a means of reducing the hordes of mosquitos that plagued visitors to the shore. Lines of men with shovels dug trenches that crisscrossed the marshes, draining the water off the marsh, into the ditches, and out to the bay. Mile upon mile of East Coast salt marshes from Maine to Florida were drained, mosquito populations did indeed diminish, and the adjacent barrier beaches became more inviting.

Development along the shore was slow until after World War II, largely because money was scarce, and many mosquitos remained. People joked that the mosquito was New Jersey's state bird. But in the postwar period, chemical insecticides, initially developed as warfare agents, became readily available. Pesticide use was adopted with incredible enthusiasm, and large areas of salt marshes were sprayed to cut down the populations of mosquitoes and Greenhead Flies even further. Mosquito populations declined, beach life was enjoyable, and beach communities thrived. Before that time, people had to escape to the mainland in June when the Salt Marsh Mosquitoes emerged or in July when the hordes of vicious-biting Green-heads made life unbearable, just as their Indian predecessors had done centuries earlier.

With these insect pests under control, massive development began on the Jersey shore, and it continues today, virtually unabated despite legislative attempts to stem the "progress." The small, shacklike summer cottages that dotted the shore at the beginning of the twentieth century were replaced by permanent homes, and more recently by massive, elegant beach houses, many sitting on stilts to obtain a better view of the tempestuous raging ocean or to avoid flooding that comes with the occasional hurricane that batters the Jersey shore. The birds nesting on the barrier islands came in direct conflict with development, and for many decades the birds lost out. Few mourned the passing of colonies of nesting terns and skimmers. A few people shook their heads in alarm, but most merely thought the birds would go elsewhere to other beaches. Pretty soon the supply of unused beaches dwindled; people were everywhere. Common Terns and skimmers did indeed go elsewhere, moving onto salt marshes to nest. But the new habitats were often less suitable than the old, and finally the day came when there was nowhere else to go. Least Terns never did adapt to salt marshes. Only vigorous management and protection of the few colonies that remain allows these striking birds to persist on our shores. But it was not always this difficult for the species that nested along the coasts.

Long before the Indians first visited these shores to trap fish in the springtime, to search for Ribbed Mussels along the salt marsh creeks, or to dig Soft-shelled Clams in the exposed mudflats, terns and skimmers were nesting on the barrier islands along the Jersey shore. Then there were fewer predators. There were no bridges to allow Raccoons to cross from the mainland to the islands and beaches. The Red Fox, a scourge of seabirds in Europe, had not yet been transported to North America. And there were no abandoned cats or dogs, left to search for food on their own. There were some native predators to cope with, but their numbers were low.

Now there are Raccoons and Red Foxes, as well as feral cats and dogs, roaming the dunes of barrier islands, maintained by a constant supply of food from abandoned garbage and feasting on nesting birds when they are available. Common Crows that never flew out to barrier islands now make feeding trips to the shore, feasting on human refuse and bird eggs. Feral cats skulk about at night, abandoned by well-meaning people who cannot stand to kill anything; their only option for survival is to kill our wildlife, including species that are endangered or threatened. Both Black Skimmers and Least Terns are endangered in New Jersey, largely because of habitat loss and because they nest in so few colonies. The Piping Plover, a small shorebird that nests solitarily along the beach and is federally endangered, often falls victim to these predators, whose abundance has increased directly in response to human activities.

Suddenly the stillness is shattered, and in unison the skimmers rise silently from their nests, fly low over the dunes, and disappear beyond the Beach Grass. When they are well away from the colony they begin to "bark." Just as suddenly, the Least Terns fly up in a noisy, chaotic mob, shrieking loudly and circling overhead. A Peregrine Falcon swoops low over the colony, its dark cigar-shaped body moving with unbelievable speed straight at the milling terns. While the skimmers course low over the grass, watching the proceedings, the falcon strikes straight through the flock of terns, misses its unsuspecting target, and zooms high up in the air, changing directions. The terns fly up as well, swirling around the predator, diving down, some almost hitting the dark shape, which seems disoriented by the numerous terns. The terns are mobbing the Peregrine, their usual defense against predatory birds and small mammals. Without warning, but with unerring timing, the Peregrine flips over on its back without breaking its speed, and with its talons it snatches a bold Least Tern in the throes of making a dive. Turning again and clutching its prey, the Peregrine streaks over the Beach Grass to its nesting tower in the marsh, far beyond our view.

The Least Terns continue to circle and call for a few minutes, and then gradually the survivors settle, resuming their incubation activities. They remain alert, their heads raised, peering anxiously around. The skimmers, who have maintained a respectable distance from the ruckus, now swoop down over the colony, still maintaining their loose formation, still barking loudly. Sometimes one lands, flops along the ground with its wings outstretched in a distraction display (fig. 35), but usually the birds remain in the air. Again and again they

35. Black Skimmer giving a distraction display. (Photo by J. Burger)

circle out over the dunes in the direction the Peregrine flew, as if to verify its departure, only to return and continue circling. It is several more minutes before, confidence restored, they start to land. The skimmers remain alert, but now nearly all of the nests are attended by both members of the pair, as if the mates had materialized out of thin air when danger was near. Finally, twenty minutes later, the colony is calm again, and most birds return to sleeping, incubating, courting, or defending territories.

The peace between the Least Terns and skimmers is an uneasy one, but both derive certain benefits from nesting with the other. The terns benefit is that they are nesting with a larger species that can deter some predators and adds more eyes to look for them. The skimmers benefit from extra defense, for when a predator actually does enter a colony, they usually fly away, leaving the smaller and more scrappy terns to drive off the intruders. It is clear that the skimmers derive the most benefits since they almost never nest alone, but rather in colonies with other species.

On salt marsh islands, the skimmers in New Jersey always nest in colonies with Common Terns, and it is the Common Terns that conduct the noisiest and most aggressive defense, risking their own necks to chase away intruders. The skimmers typically fly low out over the bay, coming back now and then to check if it is safe, but they never return until the danger has passed. In areas south of New Jersey, such as the Carolinas or Texas, the skimmers nest with Gull-billed Terns. Only when they nest in very large and massive colonies do they dare nest alone, and then they are more aggressive themselves and sometimes fly menacingly at approaching predators. In all our work in tern and skimmer colonies, we have only been physically struck twice by a defensive skimmer, compared to dozens of strikes by Least Terns and thousands by Common Terns.

Least Terns and Black Skimmers arrive from their southern wintering grounds in late April. They are some of the last colonial birds to start breeding in New Jersey, months after the Herring and Great Black-backed Gulls, and the herons and egrets, and a few weeks after the Laughing Gulls. Their arrival depends on the weather, on ocean temperatures, and on fish availability. Both species are dependent upon small baitfish, and their reproductive cycles are timed so that small fish are abundant when their young hatch.

Least Terns and Black Skimmers usually return to the traditional colony sites they have used for many years. If these sites become unfavorable because of new predators or excessive human disturbance, the birds will abandon them and seek new habitats. Then they course up and down the coast, looking for other suitable spots, sometimes joining existing colonies. When people allowed the natural coastal processes to shape the beaches as they had for millennia, there were always plenty of places to nest. For when the high tides and severe storms removed the sand from one nesting beach it was deposited elsewhere, creating new habitat. And so the birds moved, finding many new colony sites that were equally suitable and available. Now we have developed much of the shoreline with houses and parking lots, and we have built jetties and groins for the express purpose of thwarting the normal shore processes. We no longer want the storms to remove the sand from in front of our beach houses or to cut new inlets through barrier islands. We want the sand to stay just where it is. But it is touch and go, requiring extremely expensive beach nourishment programs, and, even with all of our tinkering, the winter storm tides are rough on the beaches.

While stabilizing the beaches may be fine for people, it is not so for birds because the process of succession continues, with more and more Beach Grass moving in, followed by bushy vegetation that renders the beach unsuitable for these birds. Habitat management today requires making decisions about whether we manage for people or for the birds. If the remaining habitat is not protected, we will see our Least Terns and Black Skimmers decline and disappear from the barrier islands. Protection of colony sites will give these birds, so much a part of our beach experience, a chance at survival. So far, they are holding their own, but their situation requires our constant vigilance.

Once the terns and skimmers reoccupy a former colony site or find a new one, they set about claiming territories. Many of the birds return to the same nest site they used last year, and there they wait for their mates to reappear. After a few days of reestablishing the pair bond and some carefree days of courtship, they lay eggs and begin to incubate. For both Least Tern and skimmer males, courtship involves bringing fish to their mates. Males bring fish to their females many times a day, and present their prize to her delicately as she stands on the territory. Fish presentation is often followed by copulation, and then the male goes out to find another fish. By feeding the female the male contributes significantly to her nutrition, enabling her to lay larger eggs that produce healthier chicks that carry his genes. Fed by the male, the female is able to remain on the territory and defend it against intruders. There are always a few unmated males around that are searching for territories and possible mates, and the female must fend them off. Sometimes a young male tries to court the resident female with a fish, which she sometimes eats but chases him off anyway.

While the Least Terns court during the day, making it possible to watch their activities, the Black Skimmers court mainly at night, with only sporadic courtship during the day. Mostly they sit or stand, and sleep, waiting patiently for nightfall. When the sun goes down, the males begin to leave the colony to skim across the shallow creeks to catch fish for their mates.

The skimmer's beak is uniquely designed. It is a very thin, knifelike blade with the lower mandible extending beyond the upper. The birds fly low over the water, cruising into the winds, with the lower mandible slicing the water's surface. When they contact an object, hopefully a fish, the upper mandible clamps down and the skimmer rises from the surface to swallow its prize or to carry it back to the colony. This difficult feeding skill can also be hazardous if the skimmer contacts a rigid object. Many have chips missing from their bill tip, evidence of these unpleasant encounters.

Egg laying usually begins in mid to late May, or even early June in a particularly late year. Skimmers lay in nests that are merely a depression in the sand, hollowed out by vigorous sand kicking. Least Terns usually lay two but occasionally three eggs, but Black Skimmers lay up to four or occasionally more, depending on the food supply. When the weather is rainy and cold, or when the small bait fish populations are low, the clutch size is smaller. Incubation usually begins with the first egg in the Least Terns, and with the second or third egg in the skimmers.

Both parents incubate, changing off at intervals of two to five hours, with incubation taking over three weeks. Since the eggs were laid on successive days, the chicks generally hatch on successive days. While the two or three Least Tern chicks are usually the same size, there is greater size discrepancy in the chicks of Black Skimmers, since as many as six days may pass between the hatching of the first and last chick. This asynchrony in hatching is advantageous. If food is very abundant, all the chicks obtain enough food, grow well, and survive. However, if the food supply is low, or there is a run of rainy weather when it is difficult to forage, only the largest chicks in a brood will successfully compete for food, grow, and survive. Thus the asynchrony ensures that some strong and healthy young are raised in most years. If all the chicks hatched on the same

36. Black Skimmer adult and its gray chick. (Photo by J. Burger)

day, competition might result with all the chicks sharing the food in a desperate effort to survive. All the chicks would then grow slowly and fledge at a suboptimal weight, which would most likely result in their dying as soon as they left the colony on their own. This result has been shown experimentally by providing parents with artificial broods of chicks of the same size.

One parent always remains on the territory to protect the chicks, particularly when they are small and vulnerable (fig. 36). As the chicks grow, the parents bring back larger and larger fish, and they do so by choice. It is not just that the fish are growing larger in the estuaries, but that the parents select the right size fish for their chicks. We have demonstrated this by comparing the size of fish that parents bring back to their small chicks with the size of fish that courting males bring back to their mates at the same time of the year. Thus fish of a wide range of sizes are available in the creeks, and the skimmers select the correct size, partly by where they feed and partly by swallowing fish that are too big or too small. Sometimes there are comical errors. For example, when an adult tries to feed a chick an oversized fish, the chick dutifully tries to swallow it and ends up with a hefty tail protruding from its beak. It may take hours for digestion to proceed enough for the chick to swallow its giant meal.

The prefledging period takes about three weeks in the Least Tern and four weeks in Black Skimmer. Usually one parent remains with the chicks until they are nearly full grown; they protect the chick from neighbors and from predators. If predators enter the colony, parents give alarm calls to the chicks,

37. Least Tern with chick, nesting next to a clamshell for protection from the wind. (Photo by J. Burger)

which scatter and then crouch down in the sand to wait out the danger. The young downy chicks of both species are off-white or gray with fine speckling and blend into the sand (fig. 37). Older skimmer chicks are marked with brown and black, and blend well with blackened twigs and straw at the edge of the vegetation. The camouflage or cryptic coloration is remarkable when the chicks remain motionless, and most people walk right by the chicks without seeing them. Their cryptic coloration has served them well over time, and the vigorous activities of their parents usually draws the predators away from the colony before they can find the chicks.

Unless the colony is disturbed, both species continue to use their original nest site, returning to feed the chicks there. If the colony is disturbed, the parents move the chicks, sometimes several hundred yards by standing a short distance away and calling to them. Sometimes the chicks scatter during the move, and this makes it harder for parents to find them. Once the chicks can fly, they continue to use the nest and colony site, and to be fed by their parents. Learning to be independent for terns and skimmers is a difficult task, and the parents have to continue provisioning them until they learn to forage on their own.

By early July the parents are spending most of their time away from the colony, fishing. The chicks are big enough to defend themselves and their territory, and they begin to pick up and manipulate twigs and grass, learning skills they will use later in foraging. At this point the chicks are able to fly from predators or intruders. Gradually the chicks spend more and more time away from the colony, learning to forage on their own, but they still rely on their parents for several months. By August the colony is generally deserted, the barren beach giving little hint of its recent activity. Only a few weathered eggshells and some molted feathers remain.

FOR MORE INFORMATION: Call the Endangered and Nongame Species Program; the coordinator for monitoring colonial waterbirds is at Tuckahoe Wildlife Management Area (609-628-2436). Or call the main office at Trenton (609-292-9400) for more information on colonial waterbirds.

CAUTION: Any observations of bird colonies should be made from a sufficient distance (at least 100 yards or one football field) so that the birds show no sign of disturbance. Use binoculars to see more details. If the birds are disturbed and do not return to their nests after a short time, visitors should back away.

38. Fiddler Crabs on a recently exposed mudflat on the road to East Point on Delaware Bayshore. The large visible claws identify most as males. (Photo by J. Burger)

10

Fiddler Crabs
at Low Tide

The sleek black mud is alive with hundreds of quarter-sized, tan bodies moving in all directions, some busily stuffing algae in their tiny mouths with their front legs, others scurrying across the mud, males chasing males, still others sparring with neighbors. A large dark shadow moves across the mud, and every Fiddler Crab in its path dashes madly for a tiny burrow entrance, like so many schoolchildren playing musical chairs. The heron jabs quickly, seizing and swallowing a hapless crab in a single motion.

KEY LOCATIONS: Cheesequake State Park (Monmouth County), Seven Bridges Road (Ocean), Stone Harbor marshes, and along the road to East Point on Delaware Bay (Cape May).

DIRECTIONS: For Cheesequake State Park, take the Garden State Parkway to exit 120, follow directions to Cheesequake State Park. Once in the park, pass the guardhouse, make the first angular left down a dirt road, and make a right into the Nature Center. There you can ask directions to the most accessible marsh.

For Seven Bridges Road, take Garden State Parkway to exit 58; take Route 539 south about 4 miles to Route 9. Turn right on Route 9 for about one block and south on Great Bay Boulevard. Drive to the end through the Great Bay Boulevard Wildlife Management Area.

For Stone Harbor, take Garden State Parkway to exit 10 and drive east on Stone Harbor Boulevard. The Wetlands Institute is on the right before the bridge over the Intercoastal Waterway. Trails lead through marsh habitat.

For East Point (Delaware Bay), go north from Delmont on Route 47 and take Glades Road west (the turnoff is about 200 yards south of milepost 27). Go 3.9 miles and park near the small wooden bridge. Both Mud and Brackish-water Fiddler Crabs are common here. One can continue to the scenic East Point Lighthouse on the bay shore.

BEST TIME TO VISIT: Fiddler Crabs spend the winter underground in burrows, but are active above ground from May to early November, when the air temperatures are above about 60 degrees Fahrenheit. They are active any time of day when the tide is low and the mud banks along creeks are exposed. Sexual activity occurs only in the warmer months of summer.

PRIME HABITAT: Mud banks along creeks and mudflats in salt marshes; burrows are concentrated between the low and high tide lines.

Tide waters lap the base of the swaying Cord Grass, still brown after the snows of winter, as a slight breeze blows across the marsh. The sun is high overhead; its rays are warm, the marsh is just awakening, and the new green Cord Grass is nearly a foot high. As the tide slowly recedes, the mud along the banks is covered with a sheen of water that glistens like chocolate marble and then begins to dry, revealing a paper-thin layer of green algae. Still, the marsh is quiet, the silence broken only by a male Red-winged Blackbird perching on a Marsh Elder bush growing on a high spot not far away. His melodious "O-ka-lee O-ka-lee" goes on and on, as he sings from his territory.

The tide falls lower, and small openings, not much bigger than a pinky finger, appear in the mud. The holes are regular in size and shape. There are no piles of dirt around the holes; they simply materialize. After a few minutes, there is slight movement as a tiny claw appears, and slowly the first Fiddler Crab comes into view. It peers over the rim, and then retreats into its burrow. A crab appears in another hole, and then one emerges, moving slowly over the rim, keeping one leg in the burrow. Finally, the first brave one emerges completely, walking slowly across the wet mud, stuffing algae into its mouth.

Within minutes, the mudflat is alive with tan and brown Fiddler Crabs, moving in all directions. They have been underground during the high tide for more than nine hours, and most are hungry and anxious to feed before the tide turns and covers their burrows once more in its inexorable rhythm. At first, most are watchful, peering around for any danger, assessing the level of the tidewaters, but then they begin to feed. Although their flattened bodies are nearly circular, with legs along two sides and eyes facing forward, they move sideways across the marsh. Most feed, but some males, identifiable by one huge claw, spar with others. Some merely sit partially upright as if to absorb the warm sunlight.

Fiddler Crabs resemble most shore crabs, with a smooth shell or carapace that is convex. The shell has six sides, and the carapace is covered with a variety of ridges, furrows, and serration, giving it a rough texture. Although they have eight legs, the front pair are used as shovels to push food into their mouths nearly continuously. Here the males are at a disadvantage, for one of their front claws is greatly enlarged for use in combat and sexual interactions (fig. 39). It is useless for feeding, so they use only one claw to stuff food into their mouths. The females, however, use both, and alternate one after the other in rapid succession.

39. Male Fiddler Crab facing forward. (Photo by Robert Loveland)

They feed by rhythmically bringing bits of algae and mud to their mouth, where they separate the food from the minerals and mud. The mud clings to their mouth, and every few moments they wipe their mouth with the claw, then continue stuffing in more mud. They must feed rapidly while the tide is low, for in only a few hours it will return, forcing them back into their burrows to wait out the high tide.

Fiddler Crabs are mainly diurnal, active at low tide, and highly gregarious. You never find just a few Fiddler Crabs, you find hundreds upon hundreds. They are part of the invertebrate phylum known as crustaceans. There are over sixty different species of Fiddler Crabs all over the world, living in temperate and tropical waters in marshes and mudflats, although they are more common in the tropics. Since they are adapted to warm climates, their activity depends on temperatures. They are active in the tropics all year, but in more temperate climates they are active only in the warmer months. The world's foremost authority on Fiddler Crabs, Jocelyn Crane, lives in New Jersey.

Different parts of a marsh may have a different tidal reach, depending on their slope. The salinity may also vary, for example, where freshwater creeks enter a marsh. The greater the variation in tidal ranges and salinity in a marsh, the more species there are likely to be. In New Jersey, three species of Fiddler Crabs live on the mudflats, and their distribution depends on tidal conditions. The Mud Fiddler Crab lives in the vegetated areas, venturing to the edge of the marsh only where the vegetation is dense. The Sand Fiddler Crab prefers mud mixed with sand, and competes with the Mud Fiddler Crab where there is very little sand in the mud.

The Brackish-water Fiddler Crab prefers a muddy substrate and brackish water, and can be found nearer uplands than the other two species. Under the cover of vegetation, it sometimes continues feeding even when high tides spill a film of water over the mud. Although Brackish-water Fiddler Crabs are active, they are difficult to see because of the dense vegetation. Since the Mud Fiddler Crab is more aggressive in defense of its burrows, it often forces the Brackish-water Fiddler Crab still higher on the marsh. The behavior of the three species is remarkably similar. All spend most of their time feeding, at least when the tide is out.

A nearby Fiddler Crab feeds voraciously, moving slowly across the mud. Suddenly she raises her body and prances quickly across the mud, only to stop abruptly and begin feeding anew. Over and over this pattern is repeated until it is clear that when a Fiddler Crab strays too far from a burrow while feeding, it dashes quickly across the mud so it is again close to another burrow.

Fiddler Crabs do not seem to own burrows, they simply use the one they are closest to. It is a matter of survival, since they use these burrows both to escape predators and to wait out the high tides. Some even avoid territorial or sexual aggression by running quickly into a burrow. When there is slight movement, an unexplained shadow, or an approaching Clapper Rail, they scramble to safety.

Clapper Rails sneak slowly among the marsh grasses, searching the ground for unwary Fiddler Crabs, their main prey item. Since they are streaked in many shades of brown, the Clapper Rails blend with the marsh muds and fade into the shadows, although from a crab's-eye view, they may appear menacing. They can disappear among the marsh grasses in seconds, and just as quickly reappear to snatch an unwary crab. The crabs' only defense is to dash to a nearby burrow or hide in the water and wait for danger to pass. Sometimes they misjudge and enter a burrow that is already occupied. A scuffle ensues and one leaves, perhaps to be snatched up by the waiting Clapper Rail.

By day, the Fiddler Crabs must watch for Clapper Rails and crows, but when the sun begins to sink in the west and light levels decrease, Black-crowned Night Herons fly into the marshes and stalk along the creeks, searching for the crabs. Black-crowns feed from dusk until about midnight, and they take Fiddler Crabs mainly in the last light of dusk when the tide is rising and the Fiddler Crabs are furiously feeding before going into their burrows. The Black-crowns forage again at dawn, and again the Fiddler Crabs must be vigilant. Full darkness of night does not provide protection, however, for Raccoons sometimes prowl the marsh, feeding on the crabs. Although only a few Fiddlers come out to feed during low tide at night because Raccoons stalk them in the shadows, the crabs are easy prey. Natural predators are not their only enemy, for some local fishermen dig down in the burrows for Fiddler Crabs to use as bait for fish.

While the activities of the Fiddlers are modified by the appearance of predators, they are absolutely ruled by the tides. As the tide begins to turn and the water rises slowly, the crabs watch carefully, moving closer and closer to the burrows. With rising water, they repair their burrows, flinging dirt in every direction. When the water is a few inches from their burrow and begins to fill in the bottom, they dash in, pulling in a mud plug behind them. As the rising tide reaches the burrow, the crabs apply finishing touches, smoothing out the plug and trapping air in the burrow. The crabs will use the air until the next low tide frees them to again go aboveground.

Sometimes the crabs dig new burrows by pulling out mud with the legs on one side. They curl their legs around the mud, creating a basket to move the dirt away. On and on they dig, scraping mud from the burrow until it is deep enough so they can disappear within. Only bits of mud being pushed out of the burrow are evidence of the industrious activity below. As the burrow gets deeper and deeper, the mud literally rolls out of the burrow as the circular action required for the crabs to shove out the mud with their legs creates tight mudballs. When there is no danger about, the crabs alternate digging a burrow with feeding.

Many of the new burrows are dug by females who do not spend any time defending themselves from other females or fighting for territories. While females spend almost no time in aggression, males spend a lot of time in aggressive encounters with other males. Sometimes, however, a female is aggressive too (fig. 40). As summer approaches and the temperature becomes warmer, the interests of the males turn to courtship, and they spend long hours sitting in one place, waving their enlarged claw, or cheliped, around, trying to ward off other males and attract females. The frenzy of courtship increases with increasing temperatures, and the males wave their chelipeds higher and higher, tilting their bodies upward, as if trying to stand out in the crowd.

Eventually an interested female makes contact; the male slowly climbs on her carapace from the rear, and the female bends down, nearly touching the soil. The male daintily strokes her carapace for several minutes, and then delicately turns her over on her back, and inserts the tips of his gonopods into her gonopore. They remain in contact for nearly an hour, and the male passes a small packet of sperm, in a spermatophore, into the genital opening of the female.

After her eggs are fertilized, the female carries the developing eggs, and just before they hatch, the female makes her way to the water's edge, where they are released. The young larvae float away with the tidal currents and are carried to

40. Female Fiddler Crab on the bottom has just knocked over the one at the top in a laboratory experiment. (Photo by J. Burger)

other mudflats and mud banks, sometimes far removed from a parental home they have never known. Mortality is high because the tiny larvae are food for small fish and other predators, but eventually a few find a safe haven where they mature.

Not only do the adults and young larvae have to escape predation, but they also face the more recent threat of environmental contamination. Because Fiddler Crabs feed on bacteria, algae, and decaying vegetation on the mud surface, they are very vulnerable to waterborne contaminants. Any contamination on the mud layer affects them. They are used as indicators to assess the damage from pollution, especially chronic oil pollution or the catastrophic effects of a massive oil spill. They are useful not only because they feed in the intertidal zone, but because they are so numerous and occur in nearly all coastal areas with mudflats.

Our studies following the Exxon oil spill in the Arthur Kill on January 2, 1990, show that even during the winter, Fiddler Crabs far below the surface are vulnerable to oil spills. Although this oil spill was relatively small compared to others, such as the *Exxon Valdez* spill in Alaska, the damage was still catastrophic. Within hours, as oil penetrated the upper layers of mud, Fiddler Crabs began emerging on the surface covered with oil. They remained on the surface, lying in pools of oil, exposed to the cold stress of winter, helpless to avoid predators and vulnerable to desiccation. As the tides spread the oil over the mudflats, more oil slowly seeped down through the pores in the soil, around the mud plugs, and into their burrows. The oiled crabs struggled to survive, pushing out their plugs to emerge on the surface. Everywhere we looked, hundreds of crabs had emerged; all had died, some within minutes, others within hours. More still died below the surface, some having climbed halfway up, some still in the bottom of their burrows. It was impossible to estimate the extent of the death below the soil, but the following spring, we found far fewer crabs in several oiled creeks that entered the Arthur Kill than in those that had escaped oil.

Shortly after the spill, we dug crabs up from their underground burrows. We also went down to Cheesequake State Park to dig up crabs there for comparison. As we expected, in the absence of oil no crabs were evident on the surface at Cheesequake. We had to dig to find them to take back to the laboratory, where we compared their behavior and survival with those from the Arthur Kill. We washed all the oil off the crabs we dug up from the Arthur Kill, but this effort still did not ensure their survival. When housed in the laboratory, the oiled crabs moved more slowly, were less aggressive, could not climb up a simple incline, and spent more time just standing about than the crabs from Cheesequake. With time, they failed to dig burrows, while those from Cheesequake constructed burrows in our aquaria, flinging mud in every direction and quickly disappearing from view. Since the oiled crabs remained on the surface, they would have desiccated if we had not moistened them. Eventually the oiled crabs died. Those from Cheesequake continued to feed happily and periodically returned to their burrows even though we provided no tides to cover them.

In the spring, when it was time for the Fiddler Crabs to emerge from the oiled creeks in the Arthur Kill, there were far fewer than in unoiled creeks. Those from the oiled creeks spent more time being aggressive and less time feeding and digging burrows than their neighbors from nearby pristine creeks. These crabs were more vulnerable to predators because they moved less quickly and often lacked nearby burrows for escape.

The crabs were not the only ones affected. Snowy Egrets and Glossy Ibis nesting on nearby Prall's Island normally feed on Fiddler Crabs. They experienced lower reproductive success in the first summer after the spill. Although the birds laid typical clutches and hatching success was normal, few chicks survived to fledging; most starved. These two species feed primarily in the intertidal zone, the area most hard-hit by the oil spill. Unable to find the expected abundance of crabs in the creeks near the colonies, the parents had to fly long distances to forage and were unable to provision their young adequately.

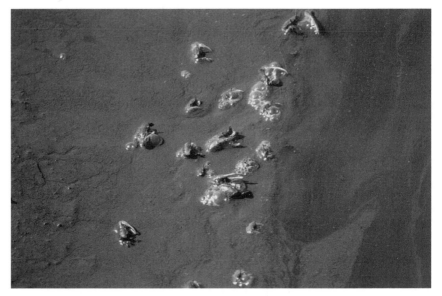

41. Following high tide, Fiddler Crabs emerge from their burrows in the sand. (Photo by J. Burger)

Our data on Fiddler Crabs, egrets, and ibises were interesting because they showed that even an oil spill in the winter can be devastating. The oil spill occurred when the egrets and ibises were on wintering grounds hundreds of miles away, and when the crabs were eight to twenty inches below the surface of the mud. Yet thousands of crabs died immediately, and the crabs that survived the initial spill were affected when they emerged from their winter inactivity several months later. The egrets and ibises that arrived in April and May were affected by an oil spill that had happened many months earlier. The Fiddler Crabs play a key role in the salt marsh ecosystem, and any harm that befalls them affects a web of other organisms as well (fig. 41).

Fiddler Crabs are not only delightful to watch, but they are extremely important to the ecology of marshes worldwide. In a year, the population of Fiddler Crabs in a square yard of marsh or mudflat, which can range as high as forty to fifty crabs, can turn over 20 percent of the upper six inches of soil. When Fiddler Crabs disappear from the marsh, either because of oil spills or other pollution, the productivity of Cord Grass can decrease by nearly 50 percent. And, as noted, the populations of other animals that rely on the crabs can be severely affected as well.

The Fiddler Crabs along the Jersey shore are active until early November, when cold winds blow across the marsh. In the winter it is even more important that they have a deep burrow well below the frost line. They devote even more time to burrow construction, digging them deeper and deeper. When the temperature dips below about 58 degrees Fahrenheit, they go into their burrows for the winter, pulling in and constructing a solid mud plug. There they will stay for the winter, waiting for the warm temperatures of spring to heat the air in their burrows, signaling that it is time to emerge.

FOR MORE INFORMATION: Call Cheesequake State Park (732-566-2161) for tide information. Or call your local park or check tide charts obtainable from bait shops along the shore.

42. Eastern Tiger Swallowtail is one of our showiest butterflies. (Photo by J. Burger)

11

Butterflies in Gardens

As far as the eye can see, specks of yellow and white dance above the Alfalfa field. Somber-dressed Buckeyes with subtle orange markings flutter ahead of us, while their spiky black-and-orange caterpillars munch on the nearby Purple Gerardia. Yellow-and-black Tiger Swallowtails and black-and-green Spicebush Swallowtails flit among the flower heads, while tiny Skippers, their identity disguised in orange-and-brown patterns, nectar at the roadside flowers.

KEY LOCATIONS: Scherman-Hoffman Sanctuaries in Bernardsville (Somerset); Frelinghuysen Arboretum in Morristown (Morris County); Rutgers Display Gardens in New Brunswick (Middlesex County); New Jersey Audubon's Owl Haven Sanctuary near Freehold (Monmouth County); Edwin B. Forsythe (Brigantine) National Wildlife Refuge (Atlantic); and Pavilion Circle in Cape May Point (Cape May). Many new butterfly gardens are being planted in parks throughout the state.

DIRECTIONS: Scherman-Hoffman Sanctuary: Take I-287 to exit 30B for Hardscrabble Road (there is no sanctuary sign at the exit). At the exit, go west on Childs Road for a quarter mile, and bear right onto Hardscrabble Road for about 2 miles to the entrance on the right.

Frelinghuysen Arboretum: Take I-287 to exit 36. Go east on Morris Avenue (Route 510), and after a half mile bear left onto Whippany Road (Route 511) for about a mile to the second traffic light (you will pass the one-way exit from the arboretum). Turn left (west) on Hanover Road (Route 650) and go a quarter mile. The arboretum entrance is on the left. Follow entry road uphill to visitor's center. Butterfly Bushes and other flowers are planted around the buildings. There are also woods and meadows to explore.

Rutgers Display Gardens: Take Route 1 to Ryders Lane exit. Go east on Ryders Lane to the first driveway on the left. Immediately make a left onto the entry road, and follow it as it curves to the left. Turn left at the first T junction and right at the second T junction. The display gardens include perennial gardens and bushes (several types of Butterfly Bush), as well as an annual garden that is planted and tended each year by numerous volunteers.

New Jersey Audubon Society's Owl Haven Sanctuary: In Tennent, take Route 9 to Route 522 (near Freehold). Go west 1.4 miles. Address is 520 Route 522. Call for hours and days they are open, because access is restricted.

Edwin B. Forsythe National Wildlife Refuge: From the Garden State, take exit 48 to Route 9 south. Go about 6 miles, turn east onto Great Creek Road and follow sign to the refuge entrance (0.6 miles).

Pavilion Circle in Cape May: Take the Garden State Parkway to its south terminus and continue straight ahead on Lafayette Street (Route 633) into Cape May. Turn right on Sunset Boulevard (Route 606) and continue west about 2 miles to Cape May Point. Pass Lighthouse Avenue and turn left on Lake Drive. Bear right at the fork which leads to the circle. Migrating Monarchs can also be observed from the Hawk Watch platform in Cape May Point State Park, which is accessible near the east end of Lighthouse Avenue (see chapter 17 for directions).

BEST TIME TO VISIT: May to September, with a peak in July–August.

PRIME HABITAT: Butterfly gardens, weedy fields with wildflowers such as Common Milkweed, and roadside plantings of wildflowers.

The brilliant colors of Daisies and Coneflowers, Butterfly Bushes, and Butterfly Weed, whites and pinks, purples and oranges, capture our attention. It takes moments to focus on the fluttering wings of the many butterflies attending the flowers. Butterflies are often a subtle spectacle because few are in evidence at any one time, but sometimes they occur in the hundreds or thousands, and these collections are truly spectacular.

Butterflies have long captivated the imagination. How can anything so frail and ephemeral have such intricate beauty? There is a poster where every letter of the alphabet is portrayed by the pattern on some butterfly's wing. The few large, colorful species such as the Swallowtails and Monarchs are conspicuous and easily recognized, so it is hard to realize that nearly 150 species of butterflies occur in New Jersey, many of them tiny and plain brown in color. Butterflies are intimately connected in our minds with flowers, and a field of summer flowers is a place where many butterflies can be found. Finding such a field has grown increasingly difficult. After all, a field full of summer flowers is better known as a field of weeds or, worse, a vacant or abandoned lot.

Left alone for fifteen or twenty years, an abandoned field undergoes succession into a woodland. We know how to protect woods. We can designate them state forests and manage them for recreational enjoyment and timber harvest, but when it comes to fields of weeds it seems that we only know how to bulldoze and pave them into housing developments and malls. Farmers used to rotate their crops, and each year there would be some weedy fields of fragrant flowers blooming summer and fall, offering havens for butterflies and like-minded creatures, but the suburban pressure on farmlands reduces the acreage year by year.

To find butterflies today, it is easiest to seek an organized butterfly garden. Fortunately many have caught the gardening "bug" and the number of such gardens is rapidly expanding. In the past, only a few enthusiasts cared about attracting butterflies, but increasingly communities and nature groups have begun planting flowers specifically to attract them. Some of the gardens are quite respectable in size, others are hardly more than a single Butterfly Bush.

Butterflies have a classic four-stage metamorphic cycle: egg-larva-pupa-adult. After mating, females lay eggs on host plants; the tiny eggs hatch into tiny caterpillars which eat voraciously, grow rapidly, and shed their skins repeatedly. Finally the full-grown caterpillar enters the pupal stage by forming a chrysalis, and undergoes striking anatomical and biochemical changes to emerge a few weeks later as a fully formed adult. In some species the adult females are ready to mate as soon as they emerge, whereas in others, mating is delayed for a few days.

There are about seven hundred species of butterflies and about seven hundred species of birds in North America, yet in any state there are far more birds than butterflies. New Jersey, for example, has recorded over four hundred birds, yet barely one hundred and fifty species of butterflies. Many butterfly species have very restricted ranges and are confined to a single mountain range or habitat. Often the main determinant of their local distribution is the occurrence of the host plant for their caterpillars. Some species are entirely host specific; their caterpillars consume only a single species of plant. The Monarchs are slightly less host-specific, but their larvae eat only Milkweeds. Cabbage Butterflies devour any of the plants in the cabbage family including lettuce and kale. Still other species can thrive on a wide range of host plants. The variation in host specificity is enormous, and naturally those species with wide-ranging appetites are likely to be much more widespread in distribution.

There is a temporal difference between birds and butterflies as well. Since adult butterflies live only a few weeks, they appear in waves. Spring-breeding adults produce a generation of summer-breeding adults, which may produce a generation of fall-breeding adults. The offspring of the last group of adults hibernates in the egg, larva, or pupa stage, until the following spring when the cycle begins anew. Butterflies such as the Cabbage Butterfly breed almost continuously, and there are always adults in evidence from April to October. Some, such as the Spring Azure, have but a single brood of adults that emerge early each spring. They breed, but when their caterpillars enter the pupal stage, development is suspended, and they remain in the chrysalis throughout the summer, autumn, and winter until the following March, when they finally complete their maturation, and emerge as pale blue waifs on fine spring mornings.

Some of the best-known butterfly gardens in New Jersey are on New Jersey Audubon, university, or public lands, but many new ones are being developed, for a butterfly garden can be created easily in a private yard, a community park, or an industrial site. Flowers particularly suitable for attracting butterflies include the Butterfly Bush (Buddleia), Common Milkweed, Orange Milkweed (also known as Butterfly Weed), Daisies, Mints, Liatris, and Purple Coneflower. There are several nurseries that supply plants suitable for assembling a butterfly garden. The plantings should be extensive, for single flowers do not produce enough nectar to sustain butterfly visitations. It is better to have a garden with a large patch of just three or four species rather than a few plants of many species. It is important to have a selection of plants that will assure some blossoms throughout the season. Persuading neighbors to join in the process enhances the attractiveness of a local area.

Attracting butterflies to your garden requires planting an appropriate selection of flowering plants as well as some of the host species suitable for common butterflies. Some purists use only native New Jersey species, of which there are many. However, that would mean doing without a Butterfly Bush, since that species is native to Asia, but is a very attractive centerpiece for any butterfly garden. The five most common butterfly species observed in gardens are Cabbage White, Monarch, Tiger Swallowtail, Black Swallowtail, and Silver-spotted Skipper.

To complete their life cycle, adult butterflies need abundant sources of nectar and their caterpillars require suitable host plants (fig. 43). Since many of

43. Northern Broken-dash Skipper nectaring at a Black Knapweed. Note the long black tongue dipping into the flower. (Photo by J. Burger)

the butterflies use trees as host plants for their caterpillars, it is not practical to plant hosts especially for them. One exception would be the Hackberry Tree, which is easy to grow and on which three species—Hackberry Emperor, Tawny Emperor, and Snout—depend. If you can set aside part of the yard as a natural meadow, then plant Bluestem Grass, a host for several species of skippers.

Butterfly Bush, also called Buddleia, has become increasingly available at nurseries. Even a single large Buddleia can be a sufficient lure in a small yard, while several with flowers of various colors serve as a major magnet for many species of butterflies. Buddleia blooms from mid-July until late September, with long, slender, lilaclike spikes. The main colors range from pale pink to deep purple, but there are also white and yellow varieties. We were surprised to discover that there are times when the white variety is favored over the pink, but the yellow always seems to be a poor relation. In late summer, the branches of our Buddleia are cloaked with the dancing forms of swallowtails and Monarchs, American Ladies and skippers.

Milkweeds are a valuable addition to a butterfly garden. There are more than one hundred species of milkweeds in North America, not to mention fourteen species in New Jersey alone. The Orange Milkweed or Butterfly Weed is commonly sold in nurseries for butterfly gardens and is very attractive to fritillaries, Pearl Crescents, and Coral Hairstreaks. The Common Milkweed, however, with its large globular heads of pinkish white flowers, attracts a great diversity of butterflies, and we once counted six species of butterflies on one flowering head. Its cotton-fluff seeds are a familiar part of our autumn landscape, but unfortunately most people consider this a weed species and pay little regard to protecting stands of it. The Common Milkweed is famous as the host plant for the Monarch, but the nectar is an important food source for many other butterflies as well as bees, wasps, moths, and beetles. In stores and fruit stands you can buy orange blossom honey, and clover honey; we have never seen a bottle labeled "Milkweed Honey," even though it is probably an important contributor to many kinds of honey marketed under other names. If there are damp spots in the yard, plant Swamp Milkweed, which flowers profusely and is very attractive to butterflies.

There are many other floral choices. For example, a large bed of Zinnias attracts swallowtails, but the Zinnias must be the old-fashioned kind that look like a colored daisy with a yellow central disk. The double-flowers prized by horticulturalists produce no nectar and are generally worthless for butterflies. Purple Coneflowers and Cosmos are also often appealing, both as flowers and as a butterfly attractant.

It is easy and immensely satisfying to develop a butterfly garden. It requires a change in traditions to accept some of the weeds as flowers, but the butterflies value them highly. The combination of frailty and beauty dancing in our garden on a summer afternoon can be enormously thrilling. Several useful books on butterflies and gardens are listed among the Suggested Readings at the back of this book.

The main relatives of the butterflies, sometimes found in butterfly gardens, are the moths, a few of which are colorful and active during the day. The Hummingbird Clearwing and Snowberry Clearwing are two of the Hawk Moths frequently seen in butterfly gardens. However, most moths are small and somberly dressed in grays and browns, and they are active mostly at night. They include some of the most destructive of all insects since their caterpillars eat a wide variety of vegetable matter including books, clothes, crops, and trees. A single species, the introduced Gypsy Moth, has been the target of very extensive and expensive pesticide spray campaigns, which have seriously harmed a number of butterfly species, such as Giant Swallowtail and Aphrodite Fritillary, without eliminating the Gypsy Moth.

Once you start to look at butterflies, it is natural to try to identify them. A few butterflies are easy to identify, but many others are subtle in hue and pattern and require experience and guidebooks. There are several guidebooks for identifying butterflies, of which the most useful in our area is Jeff Glassberg's *Butterflies through Binoculars*. Many of our butterflies are easily identified, but there are quite a few look-alikes that are challenging. Below we briefly describe the seven main families or kinds of butterflies and some of their commonest members.

The largest and showiest of our butterflies are the *swallowtails,* so called because they have long, black projections on their hind wings. There are four species of swallowtails in New Jersey. The most familiar of these is the Tiger Swallowtail which is mainly yellow with heavy black lines. Individuals are commonly seen sailing high over roadways, and they are frequent garden visitors throughout the state. The Spicebush Swallowtail is mainly black with a bluish green wash on the hind wing. It too is a common visitor to gardens, and its host species are the Spicebush and Sassafras. Similar, but smaller, the Black Swallowtail is particularly common in the coastal part of the state, and the male is readily recognizable by a broad yellow band across the hind wing. Its hosts are Parsley, Carrots, Dill, and Fennel. One of the most interesting, however, is the Pipevine Swallowtail, a handsome black species with bluish green iridescence, which uses the Pipevine or Dutchman's Pipe as its host plant. Like the Monarch, it stores toxic chemicals extracted from its host plant which render it toxic to birds. The palatable Black and Spicebush Swallowtails are considered as possible mimics of the distasteful Pipevine Swallowtail. This species is rare in most of New Jersey, because its host plant is rare. The easiest way to find it is along the Palisades, which are covered with luxuriant growths of Pipevine.

We have followed the "plant it and they will come" philosophy for our garden by planting several Pipevines and waiting for the day when they are discovered by an errant pair of Pipevine Swallowtails which tarry and raise a family, establishing a new colony of this brilliant green-and-black butterfly.

Our Pipevine is quite successful, sending its large, rounded leaves high into the nearby apple trees. Each spring it bears yellowish, U-shaped flowers, which imaginative botanists have likened to oriental Turkish pipes; but alas, no Pipevine Butterflies have found it yet.

The most numerous butterflies in New Jersey are the family of *sulfurs* and *whites.* Although they are only half the size of swallowtails, they are very conspicuous. The most abundant of these butterflies are the omnipresent Cabbage Whites and the Orange Sulfurs. In the 1800s both were rare in New Jersey. The Cabbage White was introduced accidentally from Europe in the late 1800s, and within thirty years it had spread so dramatically that it was, and remains, our most numerous butterfly. Many people assume that since it is white, it must be a moth, and they are incredulous when we explain that it is really a butterfly. Farmers call it the Cabbage Moth or Cabbage Worm. Here in New Jersey, the Cabbage White is common in gardens where any plants of the cabbage family are sown. It often occurs by the dozens or hundreds. Not surprisingly, however, it does not usually occur in forests since there are few suitable host plants.

One of our most spectacular butterfly experiences anywhere occurred at a wildlife refuge in Utah where we estimated a million Cabbage Whites busily nectaring at American Licorice and Tamarisk flowers. Some of the plants had more than a hundred butterflies jostling for position on the floral heads. Such spectacles can occur any place with a superabundant food source, but cannot be predicted.

A century ago the Orange Sulfur was mainly a species of the southwestern United States, but during the early twentieth century it spread rapidly eastward, aided by the increasing cultivation of Alfalfa, its favorite host. It is now common and widespread in New Jersey, and it is not unusual to see thousands of Sulfurs coursing lazily over a field in quest of mates.

There are several other species of whites and sulfurs in New Jersey. The large, lemon-colored Cloudless Sulfur is a southern species that spreads northward during some summers, and in late summer it can often be seen bouncing along roadsides in the coastal part of the state.

A large family of small butterflies includes the *blues, coppers,* and *hairstreaks.* There are about twenty species of these small, plainly colored but elegantly designed butterflies. They are quaintly subtle, never spectacular, and only the inveterate butterfly enthusiast is likely to even see them, much less identify them. The exception is the Spring Azure, a delightful, small, pale-blue wisp that flutters across our paths in the early springtime. Hairstreaks are among our favorite butterflies. They are smaller than Cabbage Whites and are as subtle in hue as the former are bold and conspicuous. Hairstreak wings are varying shades of gray, green, or brown, crossed by streaks or circles of red, black, and white. Most have small tails at the corner of the hind wing, with a black or black-and-orange eyespot at the base. These appear to resemble an eye and antenna combination, which deceives predators into harmlessly attacking the hind end and sparing the vital head. We often see hairstreaks that are missing the eyespot and tail, suggesting that it does indeed function in predator deception.

Some of the blues or azures are unusual because their caterpillars are captured by ants and taken into dens. There the caterpillars secrete a sweet substance called honeydew, which the ants eat; the ants in turn protect the caterpillar from minute parasitic insects. This is one of the most unusual relationships among insects; because both species benefit, it is called "commensalism." The blues in our area, however, do not benefit from this association.

Another unique member of this family is called the Harvester. Whereas all other butterfly caterpillars are vegetarians, the Harvester caterpillar is a carnivore, specializing in Wooly Aphids, which form a cottony coating on the branches of trees such as Alders and Beech. This rare species has been found at Scherman-Hoffman Sanctuary and at Frelinghuysen Arboretum.

Our largest family of butterflies is called the *nymphalids*. These include many of the boldly marked orange butterflies ranging in size from the small Pearl Crescent with its complex pattern of black spots, to the large Great Spangled Fritillary, whose underwings are bedecked with shiny silver spots. This is the family that contains many of the "pretty" butterflies. They are mostly medium-sized butterflies, such as fritillaries, anglewings, emperors, admirals, ladies, and buckeyes (fig. 44).

44. Two Common Buckeyes nectaring on Sedum. (Photo by M. Gochfeld)

One of the earliest spring nymphalid butterflies is the Mourning Cloak, a black butterfly with a conspicuous yellow band around the edge of the wings. One of the latest autumn butterflies is the Comma, another nymphalid of the anglewing group, orange with black dots and deeply indented wings. The Painted Lady is probably the most widespread butterfly in the world. It occurs in both the Old World and the New World, as well as on remote islands. It cannot survive our harsh winters, however. In the early springtime, Painted Ladies in the southwestern United States breed, and their offspring, also quite prolific, breed a few weeks later. In some years they produce such a superabundance of Painted Ladies that they emigrate from the southwestern deserts into the northwestern and northeastern states, migrating by the tens of thousands and sometimes millions. In some summers, Painted Ladies can be quite numerous in New Jersey, whereas in other years they are absent. The American Lady is very similar to the Painted Lady but is seen here every year, although not usually in great numbers. Some of the nymphalids, such as the stunning Baltimore Checkerspot, black with orange and yellow spots, are threatened by loss of habitat. The Baltimore needs marshy fields with Turtlehead, and this habitat is in short supply in New Jersey.

Another group of butterflies, the *satyrs*, includes species that are medium-sized butterflies, mainly brown, with various combinations of eyespots (black dots surrounded by yellow or white circles). Some taxonomists consider these part of the nymphalid family. These species tend to be woodland butterflies, and they seldom come to nectar in gardens. Two of these, the brownish tan Little Wood Satyr and the blackish Common Wood Nymph are common and widespread and can be found almost anywhere in the state. Their brownish shapes dance through forest undergrowth, and since they seldom pause to nectar, they seem never to stop. Others such as the Eyed Brown and the Northern Pearly Eye are quite rare and are confined to specialized habitats. The Plain Ringlet is a remarkable species which has been spreading southward from Canada since about 1980. It invaded New Jersey for the first time in 1994 and has already become fairly common in the northwestern parts of the state.

Along with the swallowtail, the *Monarch* (see chapter 15) is one of our largest and best-known butterflies. It is our sole representative of the family of Milkweed Butterflies. Some taxonomists consider that it, too, is a nymphalid. Its overall orange coloration with bold black lines is distinctive, although the slightly smaller Viceroy, a nymphalid, is a mimic of the Monarch (fig. 45). A common summer and fall butterfly, particularly in coastal regions of New Jersey, it engages in impressive southward migrations to central Mexico (see chapter 15). Its caterpillars eat milkweed plants and incorporate some of the toxic alkaloids of the milkweed into their tissue. Thus both the caterpillars and adult Monarchs are distasteful and toxic to birds, while its mimic, the Viceroy, is generally quite palatable. Viceroys benefit from being confused

45. Mangled Viceroy, which resembles a Monarch. It got eaten because it may not have been as good a mimic as was once thought. (Photo by J. Burger)

with Monarchs: birds that have once tasted a Monarch will reject both species. In some places, however, both species are eaten by birds.

Finally, there is a large family of small butterflies called *skippers*. Until recently, most specialists considered skippers not to be butterflies at all, and because they are difficult to identify, many butterfly enthusiasts continue to ignore them. Except for the familiar Silver-spotted Skipper, which has a conspicuous white square on its wings, most of the skippers are small blackish or brownish with various combinations of orange, yellow, or black marks. Many are weak fliers that spend their time among the grasses on which they lay their eggs.

The diversity of butterflies is impressive, but we must be continually vigilant to protect old abandoned fields, with a wide range of wildflowers in our midst; formal and beautiful butterfly gardens can never substitute for natural habitats. The spectacle of brightly colored waifs dancing over flower heads in midsummer is part of our Jersey landscape, and one to be treasured.

FOR MORE INFORMATION: Information can be obtained from Scherman-Hoffman Sanctuaries (908-766-5787), Forsythe National Wildlife Refuge (609-652-1665; http://bluegoose.arw.r9.fws.gov/), Owl Haven Sanctuary (732-780-7007), and Cape May Bird Observatory (609-861-0700). Cape May Bird Observatory sponsors butterfly/dragonfly walks during the summer. For N.J. Audubon: www.nj.com/audubon/.

The North American Butterfly Association produces several leaflets and a newsletter on butterfly gardens, called *Butterfly Garden News* (North American Butterfly Association, 4 Delaware Road, Morristown, NJ 07960). Access the North Jersey chapter of the North American Butterfly Association through http://www.naba.org/.

There is a native plant society that sells native plants for butterfly gardens (Native Plant Society of New Jersey, Inc., Cook College: Office of Continuing Education, P.O. Box 231, New Brunswick, NJ 08903-0231).

46. Grass Pink Orchid. (Photo by J. Burger)

12

Grass Pink and Other Orchids at Webb's Mill

Suddenly the Atlantic White Cedars give way to an open bog, a wonderland of miniature shrubs, tiny flowering plants, and open areas of water. Stunning patches of magenta, rising several inches in the air on hundreds of straight spikes, are scattered in a sea of subtle hues.

KEY LOCATIONS: Webb's Mill Bog or Swamp is part of the Webb's Mill Branch in Greenwood Forest Wildlife Management Area (Ocean County).

DIRECTIONS: Located on the east side of Route 539, about 5 miles south of Route 70. The bog is located 6.5 miles north of the intersection of Routes 72 and 539.

BEST TIME TO VISIT: For Grass Pink, visit in June to early July. However, the bog is worth a visit anytime between April and September because there is a succession of bog flowers, and the small insect-eating bog plants are visible most of the year.

PRIME HABITAT: Grass Pink and the other plants described below usually occur in marshes or wet bogs with acid conditions.

The pinelands stretch endlessly, with scraggly, misshapen Pitch Pines and oaks bordering winding sand roads. Here and there a two-lane paved road makes traveling quicker but no less enjoyable. In some places the pines rise to a height of forty or fifty feet, sometimes even sixty, and in others barely eight. Their reddish brown trunks bear gnarled branches tipped with green, and a thick mat of brown needles and oak leaves covers the ground. With only a slight drop in elevation, the surface intersects the water table, and the pines give way to Atlantic White Cedars, tall straight trees that are a darker green, their small compressed scales forming frondlike leaves. They grow mainly where the ground is wet and boggy, for they can tolerate getting their roots wet.

The path leading through the Atlantic White Cedars to Webb's Mill Bog is dark, for the young cedars are so dense that little light penetrates, making it energetically wasteful to maintain these lower branches. Most have died long ago. It is always possible to tell for how long a road has invaded the pinelands, for when trees adjacent to the road have shed their branches, it indicates that the road is recent; trees that always had open space do not shed their lower branches but spread out to form a nice round pattern. Where there are openings in the canopy and light can penetrate through the White Cedars, a lush undergrowth of Sweet Pepperbush, Highbush Blueberry, Dangleberry, and other heaths has grown. Should you visit in early summer, you can pick blueberries on your way in, assuming the birds did not get them first.

Before the 1800s, White Cedar forests extended for many miles, and even the Meadowlands of northern New Jersey had White Cedar forests. But the wood was so highly prized for making boats and shingles for houses that the trees were cut as rapidly as possible. In the early 1900s, over twenty million cedar shingles (669,000 board feet) were cut each year in New Jersey. Even as late as 1982, 250,000 board feet of Atlantic White Cedar were cut from southern Jersey. Today, only about 26,000 acres of forest contain at least half White Cedar. Once cut, White Cedar rarely regenerates, for the young seedlings require full sunlight. When disturbed, hardwoods outcompete the slow-growing cedars. Then, too, White-tailed Deer are particularly fond of the young seedlings and can eliminate new growth.

Although Webb's Mill Bog is a wonderful place to visit and see some of the bog plants, it is important to remember that the site has been disturbed for many, many years, as have most of the Pine Barrens. It has been cut over several times, burned, and had bale upon bale of Sphagnum Moss removed. It is thus much more open, with more light penetration to the ground, than an undisturbed White Cedar bog. A truly undisturbed bog would be far darker, with denser trees and no shrubs and a complete Sphagnum cover, but with its boardwalk, Webb's Mill is far easier to enter than typical bogs that are miles from the nearest road. Here one can experience the ambiance and unique bog plants (fig. 47).

There is an opening in the Atlantic White Cedars, revealing a large shallow bog encircled by cedars on one side and pine woods on the other. A narrow wooden boardwalk meanders through the bog only inches above the water, providing endless opportunities to examine and photograph the rare plants. Most bogs in New Jersey are not accessible, or when they are, the visitor can get only a glimpse from the edge. But here it is possible to walk slowly and dryly along the boardwalk, appreciating intimate views of some of New Jersey's rarer bog plants.

While there are many bog plants worth searching for, one of the loveliest is Golden Club. In late April the bog is festooned with yellow spikes rising on short stems. The Golden Club is in full flower, and what it lacks in size it makes up for in brilliance. The yellow to orange-yellow flowers form a compact spike, called a club, and are borne atop a white, fleshy stem. They rise above most other plants, emerge from the shallow puddles, and grow from the open expanses of water. In some places the elongate leaves lie half in the water, but in

47. View of Webb's Mill from the boardwalk. The beginning section of the boardwalk is visible on the left. (Photo by J. Burger)

others they curve out of the water, framing the yellow spikes. On closer inspection, the leaves have a grayish film that repels water. Another wonderful place to see Golden Club is Whites Bog (see chapter 25 for directions), the best place for these in New Jersey.

Along the boardwalk are clumps of Pitcher-plants, no less interesting but a bit less exciting in early May. They are aptly named, for their leaves form odd-shaped pitchers that open upward, with a partial roof. The old leaves that form a fringe around the bottom are a dark purple, while new red-streaked green leaves are beginning to sprout. Pitcher-plants are carnivorous, and their pitcher-shaped leaves are well adapted to their task of catching insects.

Small glands on the outside of the leaves and the pitcher rim produce a sugar which attracts little insects that crawl in to partake of the food. Once inside, they cannot crawl back out because the inside of the pitcher is covered with tiny hairs that point downward. The entrapped insects eventually fall to the bottom of the pitcher, drowning in the water that has collected there. The plant slowly digests the insects and absorbs the nutrients. Actually, bacteria and fungi that live in the water accumulated in the pitcher do most of the digestion, but they are aided by digestive enzymes of the Pitcher-plant. Usually some insects are visible in the pitchers. The plants derive nitrogen from the bodies of the insects to supplement nutrients in these acidic, nutrient-poor soils. In late May to early June the Pitcher-plant flowers—wonderful dark red disks about the size of a silver dollar—bloom atop a stalk. Most are about a foot high, but they can grow to three or four feet. The flowers remain visible for several months. Although they produce seeds, Pitcher-plants spread mainly by rhizomes.

Pitcher-plants are conspicuous, but one must take a closer look to see some of the smaller carnivorous plants, such as the sundews. The Thread-leaved Sundews have very narrow leaves, up to four inches long. The Round-leaved and Spatulate-leaved Sundews are very similar with their tiny disks surrounded by short reddish filaments. As the names imply, one has round leaves while the other has spoon-shaped leaves. They nestle down in the Sphagnum Moss, but their basal rosettes are a giveaway. The small flowers appearing in July and August are usually white tinged with pink. They trap their insects by exuding a sweet sticky substance on the tips of reddish hairs on the outer edges of the leaves. The insects land, becoming trapped on the surface. The plant eventually absorbs them, after digesting them with the surface enzymes secreted from inner glands. Early settlers used these digestive juices to remove warts and corns, but we would not recommend it.

June is a wonderful time to visit, particularly toward the end of the month, for the wild Blueberries begin to ripen. Out on the open bog in full sun, the Grass Pink is in flower, casting a delicate magenta-pink across the water. Although the plant can be over a foot tall, the pink flower is only about an inch long and is borne on a grasslike stalk. Each stalk can have as many as three or four flowers. Each flower is more lovely than the last, each a more delicate pink or a more brilliant magenta. It is the overall effect of hundreds of pink flowers that is so captivating.

Should you decide to visit Webb's Mill in July, when a few Grass Pinks are still in flower, you will find three other wonderful plants: White Fringed Orchid, Golden Crest, and a very rare plant, the Bog Asphodel, another brilliant yellow flower also called Bog Candle. It is a New Jersey endemic, meaning that it occurs only in New Jersey, in the heart of the Pine Barrens. It once occurred near Lewes (Delaware) and in several mountain bogs in the Carolinas, but these sites have disappeared, along with the flower. The Bog Asphodel is in the lily family, but it has no close relatives in the eastern United States. It is not more than a foot high, but its bright yellow flowers dot the bog in profusion from late June through much of July. Since it requires full sun to flower, it does not grow on the edges of the bog, under the shade of the cedars, but flowers in abundance in the middle.

If a bog fills in, or the canopy closes over, the Bog Asphodel puts all its energy into plant growth and does not flower. It waits for many years until a bad storm blows down the cedars, or a fire clears the bog, and then it flowers once again. Many of the Pine Barrens plants employ this strategy—they simply wait out the years without bright sunlight.

Golden Crest flowers with the Bog Asphodel, at least in the New Jersey pinelands, forming yet another carpet of yellow flowers. It is a member of the

Amaryllis family. Its multiple flowers are borne on stalks, and each resembles a miniature Amaryllis. An even more wonderful flower, however, is the White Fringed Orchid, which flowers from mid-July to August. It is also small, as are many of the flowers in the White Cedar bogs, but it is beautiful, with its exquisite, creamy-white flowers borne on a short, slightly twisted stem. The flowers are small, but very delicate, with a long fringed lip at the bottom; each one is more photogenic than the next.

Another treasure to watch for in Webb's Mill is the rare Curly Grass Fern. This fern's normal range is highly restricted: it occurs in one small population on the Long Island Barrens, one in Sussex County in Delaware, and in the bogs of Nova Scotia and Newfoundland, but there are scattered populations in the Pine Barrens, no doubt isolated here when the last glaciers retreated. It is only about two inches tall, but the tiny green curls of its leaves are easy to identify. It actually looks more like a grass than a fern, and although it grows in Webb's Mill, it does not normally grow in the close shade of an undisturbed White Cedar forest or where there are dense mats of Sphagnum.

Webb's Mill is unusual; bare white sand is visible in places beneath the shallow water. Unlike most bogs in New Jersey that have a deep layer of spongy peat, Webb's Mill has lost its peat, perhaps due to a raging fire that burned the peat in a particularly dry year, and also due to historic harvesting. The conditions are still right, however, and the bog persists. In most places it is extremely shallow, only a few inches deep. Interestingly, some areas of the bog contain peat, making it possible to see the different successional stages of a bog. As the slow-growing Sphagnum Moss creeps across the marsh, it invades some of the sandy areas, providing habitats for other plants such as Sundews.

Sphagnum crowds together, forming dense mats that provide places for other plants to root, and the water-conserving properties of the moss create moist conditions for plants in the event that part of the bog dries up in a drought year. Clusters of stems, with the leaves arising from them, give the moss a star-shaped appearance. As valuable as the moss is for the bog, it is also valued for preventing soil erosion, as a packing material, as a mulch, and for other horticultural purposes. When older plants die and fall to the bottom, they become compacted, and blocks of this peat were cut and used for fuel by the early settlers. Peat is still harvested for fuel in some parts of the world. And of course, the American Indians used Sphagnum as an absorbent diaper material for their infants and for menstruating women.

Webb's Mill is famous as a laboratory for botanists and ecologists anxious to learn the plants of the bogs. In addition to Golden Club, Pitcher-plants, Sundews, Golden Crest, and Bog Asphodel, described above, it is also home to Bog Clubmoss, Turkey Beard, St. Peter's Wort, and a number of bladderworts, a peculiar aquatic carnivorous plant. Horned Bladderwort, a submerged carnivorous plant, is one of several bladderworts that grows profusely in New Jersey

48. Horned Bladderwort grows in profusion on Webb's Mill.
(Photo by J. Burger)

waters. This species sends up slender spikes topped by small, brilliant yellow flowers (fig. 48). The bladders, which are borne underwater on underwater stem and leaf networks, entrap minute aquatic insects.

As exciting as the bog is from a botanical viewpoint, it is equally interesting for its rare animals. The Pine Barrens Treefrog, discussed in the spring section, can be heard here at night. Other bog species include the Four-toed Salamander and a number of unusual insects. At any time of the year, Webb's Mill is fascinating, for many of the typical bog plants are there, the Sundews and Pitcher-plants wait for insects, scattered clumps of Sphagnum Moss shield many of the other plants, and the low shrubs and bushes add yet another dimension. The somber Atlantic White Cedars guard the entrance to the bog. The bogs of the Pine Barrens date to the end of the last Ice Age, and they are gradually filling in; some bogs may remain relatively unchanged for many millennia, or they may disappear.

FOR MORE INFORMATION: Call the New Jersey Division of Fish, Game and Wildlife (609-292-9400) (www.state.nj.us/dep/fgw). You can also call your local Nature Conservancy for information about bogs that may be on its nearby preserves.

49. American Lotus flower amid a sea of leaves. (Photo by Mary Leck)

13

American Lotus at Mannington Marsh

The air is calm; only a slight rustling of the towering Phragmites breaks the silence, framing the vista dotted by the huge yellowish white flowers and the broad green leaves of the American Lotus that blanket the surface of Mannington Creek, fringed by patches of White and Rose Mallow. The Lotus are in full bloom, their pale yellow flowers facing the sun, extending as far as the eye can see in a lake of interlocking Lotus leaves, each straining to grow taller than the next.

KEY LOCATIONS: Mannington Marsh on the upper reach of the Salem River (Salem County) is an excellent place to view Lotuses; some are found in a few other marshes in Sussex and Salem Counties. Mallows can be seen in many parts of New Jersey, including Barnegat Bay, Cape May, and along Route 1 in Trenton.

DIRECTIONS: Very visible near Mannington Creek, on the Salem-Woodstown Highway (Route 45). Several other roads (Route 540 and Route 620) also cross the marsh. Take the N.J. Turnpike south to exit 1; go south on Route 540 across the marsh and north on Route 45 toward Woodstown.

BEST TIME TO VISIT: End of July and into early September for both Lotus and Mallow.

PRIME HABITAT: Freshwater marsh.

In May, well after our native white Water Lily has burst forth with a profusion of leaves covering the marshes and ponds in south Jersey, the American Lotus tentatively begins putting up its leaves. The earliest leaves lie flat on the water, but later leaves extend skyward for a foot or more. At first these leaves are tightly rolled, with small sharp edges on their undersurface. Gradually they unfurl, forming nearly perfect circles atop stout stems that barely sway in the late spring breezes. First one leaf, and then another, until five or six leaves spread out above the water. The leaves are a rich lime green rather than the darker forest green of Water Lilies.

The leaves are giant shields, up to about a foot and a half in diameter. They rise on rough, prickly erect stems from an underground stem, called a rhizome, buried below the mud and muck of the marsh. The edges of the leaves are curled up slightly, giving the leaf a saucerlike appearance. When it rains gently, water beads up and accumulates in shimmering pools on the leaf surface. If these beads persist when the sun bursts forth, the water magnifies the rays, which burn small holes in the leaf surface.

Several plants emerge from each long, white, fleshy rhizome, sometimes forming curly lines of leaves that trace the course of the partially buried stem and rhizome system. In most of the marsh the Lotus plants are so dense it is impossible to identify which aboveground leaves are connected to one another. The leaves, crowded together, are vying for the sunlight.

American Indians and the early settlers baked the rich white rhizomes, which are said to taste a bit like sweet potatoes. Although some of the rootstock is near the surface, much of it goes far deeper, and it is difficult to dislodge the plant from the sucking, cloying mud. The Indians also collected the green seeds from the pods and roasted, baked, or dried them for later use, including bread making. The roasted seeds taste like chestnuts and are highly nutritious. The Sacred Lotus of Japan and China was actually grown extensively for food, and some scientists argue that our American Lotus is just a variety of the Asian Sacred Lotus, which has a pink flower. In the fall, when the fruit pods dried, American Indians used them for rattles and as body ornaments. Today we often see them in dried flower arrangements.

The American Lotus grows from the Gulf States north to the Great Lakes region, but it is relatively rare in the northern states, and in New Jersey it grows in only a few marshes, such as the Mannington Marsh in Salem County. This highly localized distribution is surprising, because the Lotus is abundant in the marsh. Farther south and in the Mississippi Valley, the American Lotus forms very large stands that extend for miles and is considered a weedy pest.

In early summer, a stalk appears tipped with a light green conical bud, the sepals and petals tightly fused. Day after day the stalks get taller and the buds enlarge, until they finally burst and the pale yellow petals gradually open. Row upon row of petals form a magnificent flower cup framing a swollen, flattened, pale yellow receptacle, with about a dozen pits, each with a single imbedded pistil, the female flower part. The stamens, or male organs, are shed early. Across the marsh, flower after flower opens until there is a sea of color.

At first the flower petals remain fairly upright, a cup facing the sun, but in the middle of the day, the petals move down, and are nearly horizontal. By evening the petals have ascended, for the flower closes at night, to open again the next day, slightly wider than the day before. For three or four days the flower opens, and then, on the last day, even a slight breeze blows the petals from the flower, until all that is left is the inch-wide, funnel-shaped receptacle. By now, the seeds, in small pits in the receptacle, are beginning to appear as little dots. The fruit ripens over a period of weeks; the receptacle gets wider and the pits expand to accommodate the growing seeds, each encased in its small cup. The whole receptacle enlarges until it is over four inches across and a rich lime green, with similarly colored seeds.

With time, the receptacle, which now resembles half of a large orange up-turned to the sun, turns a brownish black. The fruits, each slightly larger than a pistachio nut, darken and harden. The flower stalk weakens, and the receptacle bends under its own weight, nearly facing the water. As the receptacle dies, it shrivels, releasing the seeds into the water, where they float for a few days, then sink to the bottom. Few actually sprout, however, and most reproduction is by the underground stems, which are quite prolific. The seeds, however, can wait a long time before germinating. On several occasions we have tried to sprout American Lotus seeds in our pond. We abraded the seed coat vigorously with a file and soaked the seeds for days, and finally one of about twelve seeds sprouted, grew for a couple of weeks, and then died. Other people have had better luck. The low sprouting success of the seeds is not a problem because they produce so many plants from the long underground rhizomes.

While the earliest seed pods ripen, several other buds appear on stalks; sometimes three or four buds are present at the same time, although usually only one is in full bloom at any one time. Flowering continues through most of August, when the last flowers are slightly smaller than earlier ones. By this time the plants have almost exhausted the energy stored in the underground stems, and it is time for the plant to put its energy into restoring the stems for the long winter, energy that will be needed for growth in the next spring.

Although the marsh may beckon at this time, and the avid photographer will want to wander among the Lotus flowers, it is treacherous to try walking on the soft mud near the edge, which is saturated with water. You can sink up over your knees rather quickly. The mud makes it difficult to walk, even to retreat. Once beyond the edge of the marsh, the mud hardens up and it is easier to walk. Here and there a pale stem bud rises from the muddy bottom, and it will soon put up a leaf or two. The Lotus leaves are nearly waist high, and the flowering stalks or ripening pods are nearly shoulder high.

In the fall the leaves gradually die and fall into the water, where the rhizomes become dormant, awaiting the cold of winter. Only a few black fruit pods, scattered across the marsh, are visible above the waves. The rhizomes are quiescent, waiting until the next spring.

Mannington Marsh has a long history. At one time, American Indians wandered the marshes in search of ducks or to dig the Lotus tubers for food. The early colonists did likewise, and, with time, the marshes became famous for "railbirding." Gunners in the 1800s and early 1990s gathered at the marshes to shoot the migrating "railbirds" in the fall. A good migration of Soras, Virginias, Clappers, and even King Rails moved through the marshes. One person acted as a "pusher," sloshing through the marsh with a twelve-foot pole to push the reeds at the edge of the marsh, scaring up the rails for the hunters hidden at the marsh edge. The rails have all but disappeared today, and local residents report almost no rail migration.

In the late 1800s and early 1900s, considerable attention was devoted to draining marshes for agricultural purposes. Articles in the *American Farmer*, published in Baltimore, gave directions on how to ditch the marshes and when

50. Mary Leck standing among the American Lotus at Mannington Marsh (*top*). (Photo by Charlie Leck) Rose Mallows growing at the edge of Mannington Creek and marshes (*bottom*). (Photo by J. Burger)

to plant seeds (before the marsh had dried down completely). It was important not to have the marsh dry out too much, or the soil would become compact and unusable for agriculture. The Mannington Marshes were also destroyed, but the Lotuses turned up within a year or two in a nearby lake in Woodstown. The draining practices continued in many marshes and were reversed only in the early to mid-1900s. These marshes are one of the few places in New Jersey where these magnificent American Lotuses can be easily observed.

Freshwater marshes, such as Mannington Marsh, were particularly vulnerable to draining because water already drained from the marsh with some regularity. Because the water was fresh, many different kinds of crops could be grown, while tilling salt marshes was constrained by the high salt content in the soil, since few plants can withstand the salinity.

Tidal freshwater marshes are rare because they occur at the interface between true salt marshes and the upriver marshes with no salt intrusion. They arise mostly where there are expansive estuaries associated with large rivers, such as the Hudson and Delaware. The mighty strength of the tides forces the water back and forth, but at some point upstream from the river mouth, they are not sufficient to drive tidal waters. All the tides succeed in doing is moving the freshwater back and forth, back and forth, so the freshwater marsh experiences a tidal swing, but salt water from the sea does not actually reach as far as the marsh.

Another tall, large, flowered plant is the Rose Mallow (fig. 50). It grows in large stands along the drier edges of the creeks and marshes, and towers over the Lotuses, guarding them from intrusions. The flowers are enormous, measuring up to seven inches across. At Mannington, most are pure white, pinkish at the base of each petal, with bright yellow stamens; a few are pale pink. In other places the pink form predominates. The leaves are large and triangular, and are one of the food plants of the Painted Lady Buterfly, as well as a number of moth species. Not only butterflies and moths find the leaves inviting, for tea was once made from the leaves to treat mild digestive disorders.

While the pale yellow Lotuses are spectacular for New Jersey, in more southern parts of their range they can be a pest. In some places the Lotuses stretch for miles and miles, unbroken. They can clog up small meandering rivers and lakes, and are exceedingly difficult to eradicate because some of the rootstock grows far below the mud surface and it is impossible to remove them. What is a pest in one place, however, is a jewel in another, and the massive expanse of pale yellow American Lotuses and White and Rose Mallow gleaming in the sun on a warm August day is truly breathtaking.

FOR MORE INFORMATION: Call the Salem County Historical Society (856-935-5004).

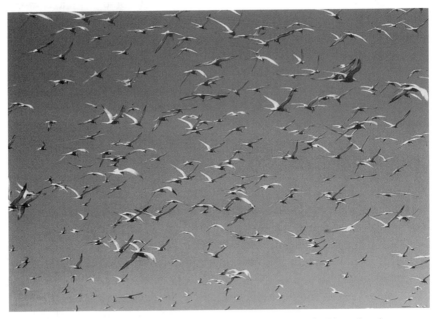

51. A mass of Common Terns rising from a sandbar, spooked by a hawk or other predator. (Photo by J. Burger)

14

Coalescing Terns and Skimmers at Hereford Inlet

In the fading light of dusk, a dense flock takes wing, flying low over the sandbar, out over the inlet, away from an immature Bald Eagle migrating southward. Plunging toward the water near the island, in a vain attempt to capture a Black Duck, the eagle has unwittingly scared up a thousand terns and Black Skimmers that circle out over the water and land on the sandbar once more. The barking and squawking notes finally diminish as the birds settle into their nightly roost, the eagle long gone.

KEY LOCATIONS: Champagne Island or other sandbars in Hereford Inlet (the exact location is not constant because the islands are reshaped by severe winter storms).

DIRECTIONS: Take Garden State Parkway to exit 6 and Route 147 east toward North Wildwood; take Ocean Boulevard (Route 61) left (north) across Nummy Island toward Stone Harbor. Look for the flocks anywhere between North Wildwood and Stone Harbor.

BEST TIME TO VISIT: Late July to early September.

PRIME HABITAT: Sandbars and sandy islands surrounded by water, where the birds can rest undisturbed by predators.

The sea rages all around, sending waves high on the beaches, over breakwaters, onto jetties, and into marinas. The strong winds continue, day after day, night after night. A flock of Brown Pelicans sails along the coast; the birds fly low over the waves, hardly moving their wings, sailing on the updrafts from each wave.

In the middle of Hereford Inlet sits a small sandy island protected from the full brunt of the storm. Like all sandy islands along the Atlantic Coast, this island changes shape, sculpted by winter storms. Some years it is larger, sometimes it is smaller, sometimes it is barely above sea level, and at other times it is sufficiently high for Black Skimmers and Least Terns to nest successfully, and well over one thousand pairs have nested there on occasion, their nest sites far removed from mammalian predators. When the sands are piled high, they provide suitable nesting sites beyond the reach of flood tides. Skimmers claim the higher places, and the Least Terns nest on the edges of the colony, where they are exposed to the greatest potential for high tides. Both species avoid heavily vegetated areas.

The fate of this island is a matter of curiosity to many people living along the shore and a subject of gossip and comment each spring. But to Least Terns and Black Skimmers it is critical, not only because it can provide crucial nesting space, but because it provides essential resting and roosting places where the birds coalesce into large flocks at the end of the breeding season, prior to migration. In late July or August, there may be over two thousand Black Skimmers and various terns (including Common, Forster's, and Least, as well as a few Royal and Caspian) roosting on this island. Facing into the wind, the birds look like so many decoys placed there by design. Usually the Black Skimmers are in one dense flock, the Least Terns in another, and the other terns are intermingled among them. For this assemblage is not one of choice, but of necessity, for the birds need a safe place to spend the night.

While nesting, the Black Skimmers seek out Least Terns on sandy beaches or Common Terns on the salt marshes. They do not nest by themselves because they rely on the early warning system and effective defense of the terns to deter predators. If all else fails, the terns are far more likely to be the ones taken by predators because they pursue and dive-bomb them, while the skimmers usually circle at a safe distance (fig. 52). On the nesting colonies, however, they have nests, eggs, and chicks that are vulnerable and not very movable.

While roosting, birds are concerned for their own safety and are quite mobile. They can leave the sandbar when predators are close, circle out over the bay toward the ocean, and return only when the island is again free of predators. There is still an advantage in roosting close to the terns because they provide more eyes to watch for danger. But the advantage is simply a matter of having more eyes, not that the Least Terns themselves are necessary. It is just as useful to have one thousand Black Skimmers roosting together, or five hundred each of skimmers and terns.

Birds roost and migrate in flocks because they derive benefits from being in the group. A solitary bird must spend a great deal of time watching for predators (called "vigilance"), regardless of whether it is foraging, nesting, roosting, or migrating. Time spent watching for predators is time that cannot be spent feeding or resting. Thus, birds that flock together can decrease the time each one spends watching for predators because other members of the flock are also looking for predators.

Research with a number of species, including Common and Least Terns and Black Skimmers, indicates that the time an individual spends watching for predators while in a flock is related to the number of birds in that flock. Birds in larger flocks spend less time watching for predators than those in a small flock. Thus a bird in a large flock has a better chance of deriving an "early warning" benefit than one alone or in a small flock.

52. Common Terns usually dive-bomb predators, such as this Red-tailed Hawk (*top*), while Black Skimmers fly away from the disturbance, leaving the terns to attack (*bottom*). (Photos by J. Burger)

Having an early warning system, however, is not the only advantage of being in a flock. A member of a flock has a smaller chance of being the one targeted for predation than a solitary bird or one in a small flock. This is called the "selfish herd" pattern, where an animal remaining in a herd or flock benefits because the chance that it will be the one captured by the predator is greatly reduced. Moreover, predators sometimes find it difficult to pick out one animal to capture from a dense flock. For example, a Peregrine Falcon might have trouble isolating one tern to pursue out of a thousand, particularly if the birds maintain formation and no one individual gets too far from the flock. Such lone individuals are easy to pick out and attack.

The congregation of Black Skimmers and Terns on Champagne Island at Hereford Inlet, however, is there because it is the end of the breeding season. The terns and skimmers are no longer tied to their traditional colony sites, and they can find a safe place to gather. Terns from many other colonies join the roosting flock. Finding a safe place is particularly critical at this time because the young of the year, which fledged only a few weeks ago, are still dependent on their parents for food. Having a known place to return to ensures that parents and young can find each other if they have become separated during a day of foraging.

It is not uncommon to see a full-grown young Least Tern or Black Skimmer begging from a parent. This behavior pattern is easily recognized because the chicks draw in their head, lower it, and hold their body to appear as small and vulnerable as possible. They give low, begging sounds, rather than the loud, raucous calls they may have used only a few minutes before. They are eliciting provisioning behavior on the part of parents that have cared for them for over two months, and it is best to be submissive.

This extended parental care is critical for both species because their foraging techniques require substantial skills and are difficult for the young birds to learn. It is not easy to learn to plunge-dive for fish, as the Least Terns must, or to learn to skim across the water of salt marsh creeks with lower mandibles submerged, as the Black Skimmers do (fig. 53). Mastering the technique is not the only problem; the young birds also have to learn where and when to feed. Schools of fish are patchily distributed, and tides and winds determine where skimmers can feed successfully.

While hawk-watching is fast paced, observing the roosting Black Skimmers and Least Terns is casual. For the most part, the birds just stand there, facing into the wind, their feathers sleeked and their heads held low. Since skimmers are partly nocturnal in their foraging activities, they remain on the sandbars and sandy islands for much of the day. Now and then one goes out to skim for a fish, but mostly they just stand about.

The Least Terns all leave the sandbar in the early morning to go feed, either on nearby inland lakes, in the estuaries, or in the larger bays and inlets. A flock of feeding terns is fascinating to watch as they circle over the water ten to

53. Black Skimmer just about to put its lower mandible in water to skim for fish. (Photo by J. Burger)

twenty feet up, selecting a target, quickly changing directions, and diving at full speed. They are not always successful and often emerge without a fish, but more often than not they surface with a shimmering silver shape flopping in their beak. After barely a second's pause, they rise from the surface and, with a head toss, quickly swallow the fish.

Terns continue to feed their young for several weeks after they leave the breeding colony. It is easier to watch tern parents feed young because this often occurs on the sandbars and is visible with binoculars or a telescope. The parent returns with a fish in its mouth, and before it can even land, the young tern is running back and forth on the sand, trying to get to the parent before its sibling does, for competition for food is still strong. When the parent lands, the young tern grabs the fish and, with a few head tosses, swallows quickly to prevent neighboring chicks from stealing it. Its duty performed, the adult settles in for a rest and begins to preen, working its bill carefully over its feathers to clean them, applying oil from a gland at the base of the tail to waterproof them. Some parents leave immediately to find another fish. For much of the day, however, the terns and skimmers remain quietly resting.

There are other more industrious birds on these same sandbars or sandy islands, however. Piping Plovers, a federally endangered species that nests in New Jersey, run up and down the beaches and sandbars, pecking at invertebrates at the water's edge, or catching insects in the mass of decaying vegetation at the tide line (fig. 54).

54. Piping Plover normally occur solitarily or in pairs along the Jersey shore. (Photo by J. Burger)

American Oystercatchers, quite large for a shorebird, also gather on these sandbars. Forty years ago, Oystercatchers were quite rare on the Jersey shore, particularly as breeding birds, and the sighting of one was an event that bird watchers waited for. Now they are quite common. Nearly every salt marsh has a pair or two that nest on the highest salt marsh wrack or on a small patch of sand high on the marsh. They are particularly fond of nesting on wrack with Black Skimmers and Common Terns, deriving an early warning advantage from them. Moreover, the terns are very aggressive in defending their own nests, and thereby defend the Oystercatchers as well. If food is particularly scarce, the Oystercatchers simply begin eating the tern eggs, and we have seen them completely destroy large tern and skimmer colonies in less than a week.

Small flocks of Sanderlings feed along the edges of the islands and bars, particularly where the surf makes prey available. Their tiny pale gray bodies are a delight to watch as they run up and down with each advancing wave. Once in a while they stop to probe deeper in the sand just above the waves, but usually they run back and forth. Just as suddenly, the whole flock takes off, flies a short way around the island, and begins anew; with each wave they run up and down, up and down, probing up and down like a sewing machine.

Occasionally flocks of Semipalmated Sandpipers, Semipalmated Plovers, Dowitchers, Black-bellied Plovers, and Knots land on the mudflats or sandbars, either to rest or to feed. They also rest high up on the sandy islands, where they can have a good view of approaching danger, but they feed on the mudflats or along the shoreline. This gathering of shorebirds from breeding grounds farther north predicts the coming of fall, for they are migrating to warmer climes in South America. While the pressure to reach their Arctic nesting grounds was strong because of the short breeding season, once they leave the Arctic their journey is not nearly so harried or rapid. They need only head for warmer regions before the cold weather comes to New Jersey. Some of these species will remain in New Jersey into December, and even into January in a warm year. Our research with shorebirds in the laboratory has indicated that the birds that remain in New Jersey are physiologically adapted and can adjust more easily to changes in temperature than birds of the same species that fly immediately to Texas and farther south.

The terns and Black Skimmers that are sitting on the sandbar also have few immediate pressures. Their only task is to obtain enough food to lay down fat sufficient to migrate southward. The Black Skimmers skim along salt marsh creeks in the late afternoon and evening, while the Common Tern hover over schools of fish and plunge-dive into the water in search of small fish (fig. 55). The skimmers and Forster's Terns will likely linger into November and then move south along the coast of the Carolinas, as far as Florida. The Least Terns will migrate to northern South America, and the Common Terns will fly to Brazil, with some continuing as far south as Patagonia. Their journey, however, can be piecemeal. They are not required to fly nonstop to Florida. Instead, they can remain here as long as the weather is warm and food is abundant, and then leisurely make their way south to warmer climes.

55. Common Tern hovering just prior to plunge-diving for fish. (Photo by J. Burger)

Like the weather they must endure, the terns and skimmers have experienced stormy times over the past 150 years, with great swings in populations. Early accounts indicate that they nested in great numbers along the New Jersey shore in the early nineteenth century, a time when the shore was hardly inhabited and largely inaccessible. As more and more people invaded their habitat after the 1850s, eggs were harvested and birds slaughtered by commercial hunters for sale in the markets in Philadelphia and New York. In the 1870s feathers became highly prized for ornamentation and even whole terns were mounted on women's hats. The European tern, heron, and egret populations had already been depleted, and attention was turned to the abundant bird populations of our Atlantic Coast. From eastern Canada to Texas, birds were shot in huge numbers, year after year, until by 1890, only tiny remnant populations persisted on remote islands.

Bird conservation did not begin until the early 1900s, when the Audubon Society had its beginnings and purchased sanctuaries to protect nesting birds. This was a dangerous task, and more than one warden was shot by bird poachers. Vigorous media campaigns gradually swayed public and then political opinion, and by 1913 it looked like protective laws might be passed. However, the Migratory Bird Treaty Act with Canada was not signed until 1918.

Remarkably, birds began making a comeback shortly thereafter. By the 1930s quite a few colonies of terns and skimmers, as well as egrets and herons, were scattered along the New Jersey shore. Populations swelled into the 1950s and then began to stabilize as various adversities came into play. Pesticides began to take a toll, and many of the nesting beaches were subject to development or direct human disturbance. Common Terns and Black Skimmers sought alternative nesting habitat on salt marshes, but Least Terns did not adapt to this change and their beach-dwelling colonies were subject to harassment and displacement at a rate that continues to increase even today. Today the Black Skimmer and Least Tern are endangered in New Jersey, and the Common Tern is listed as a species of "special concern."

Vigilant management by conservation groups, both from the Department of Environmental Protection and from nongovernmental agencies, is required if the future of these bird populations is to be secured. Public support and funding are required to achieve success. While breeding populations of Least Terns and Black Skimmers have remained relatively constant for the last twenty years, they seem to be declining again, which is cause for concern. Still, large flocks coalesce in the late summer and fall on the sandbars at Hereford Inlet, where adults and their young gather in small family groups to exploit good fishing areas.

FOR MORE INFORMATION: Call the Endangered and Nongame Species Program. Its biologist in charge of colonial waterbirds is based at the Tuckahoe Office (609-628-2436).

Fall

56. Migrating Monarchs on the top of a bush in Cape May. (Photo by J. Burger)

15

Migrating Monarchs at Cape May

Brilliant orange-and-black wings flutter vigorously at the white and violet sprays of flowers on the Butterfly Bushes. At the same time, high above, a fragile waif sails ahead of the brisk autumn wind, helping it on its way to the Mexican mountains two thousand miles away where it will pass the winter among millions of its kind.

KEY LOCATIONS: Anywhere along the New Jersey coast, but especially at the Pavilion Circle garden and the Hawk Watch platform in Cape May Point (Cape May County).

DIRECTIONS: To reach Pavilion Circle, take the Garden State Parkway to its south terminus and continue straight ahead on Lafayette Street (Route 633) into Cape May. Turn right on Sunset Boulevard (Route 606) and continue west about 2 miles to Cape May Point. Pass Lighthouse Avenue and turn left on Lake Drive. Bear right at the fork onto Cape Avenue, which leads to the circle. Migrating Monarchs can also be watched from the Hawk Watch platform in Cape May Point State Park, which is accessible near the east end of Lighthouse Avenue (see chapter 17 for directions).

BEST TIME TO VISIT: Monarchs occur throughout New Jersey in summer and early autumn. In September–October they migrate, mainly along the coast. Mid-September to mid-October is the main concentration period at Cape May. Monarch migration occurs mainly on northerly and northwestern winds.

PRIME HABITAT: Gardens and beachfronts. Monarchs can be seen throughout Cape May Point, since people there have planted Butterfly Bushes and other flowers especially attractive to butterflies. One can simply walk up and down any road and see Monarchs and other species of butterflies. The best garden is in Pavilion Circle, where sometimes hundreds can be seen at once. Monarchs also nectar on Seaside Goldenrod, which begins flowering in October.

The brilliant purple, pale rose, and ivory white flowers of Butterfly Bushes form a bank of color that gleams in the sunlight. These spikes are like Victorian lace, wound loosely around a gently arching stem. The spikes are made up of hundreds of tiny florets, each yielding precious nectar for their frolicking visitors. The dancing movement is dazzling, the effect so riveting that it is difficult to isolate one butterfly from the next. Slowly, however, the shapes dissolve into Monarch butterflies, each trying to find just the right floret with the most nectar. Each flower spike is like a miniature lilac but more slender and elongated, and there are many Monarchs probing for the nectar or waiting as the sunlight warms their wings. Each butterfly clings to a flower, probing with its long proboscis.

Dozens of butterflies swirl around the bushes. Some advance systematically along a spike, probing, and stepping sideways to probe the next floret. Others flutter frivolously, sipping at one spike and flying to the next. Although most are Monarchs, other butterflies feed among the bushes as well, flitting freely from flower to flower. There are Red Admirals, American Ladies, and Black Swallowtails, all brightly colored and equally lovely. Here and there is a smaller brown butterfly, a Buckeye, and a real rarity from the South, the Long-tailed Skipper.

The fall migration of Monarchs at Cape May Point's Pavilion Gardens is one of the most exciting events we have witnessed anywhere in the butterfly world. Cape May is rightly famous for its migrating Monarch Butterflies as well as its migrating birds. On a warm September day, with northwest winds after a few days of bad weather, several hundred Monarchs can dance among the Butterfly Bushes that are in full bloom. They are fueling up for their long migration, much as songbirds and hawks do during their stopover in Cape May.

Monarchs capture our imagination because of their long migrations and their ability to survive for many months. They are also our best example of protective mimicry. These large, orange butterflies, their wings etched by black veins, are members of the Milkweed Butterfly family (Danaidae). Several species of Milkweed Butterflies occur in the Americas, and many others occur in Africa and Asia.

One can see Monarchs at Cape May in three ways: dozens of fluttering wings amid the blooms of Butterfly Bushes, single individuals, tilting from side to side seemingly at the whim of the brisk northerly winds as they sail southward alone, and masses of butterflies clinging closely together, often one hanging upon another in their nightly roosts. How many Monarchs one can find at Cape May depends on the year, the season, and the weather. Some years Monarchs are superabundant with up to 1,500 per hour passing the Hawk Watch, while the next year they may be inexplicably rare, as in 1992. Their numbers increase during the summer, peak during September and early October, and then decline. By early December they are only a memory. Although today it seems obvious that the Monarch is a long-distance migrant, no less an observer than W. H. Edwards wrote in his life history of the Monarch in 1878 that it hibernated for the winter.

Whenever we visit the American Museum of Natural History in New York, we stop to marvel at the exhibit of a Monarch roost enclosed in a glass case. It remains a favorite memory of our childhood visits to the museum, and we never tire of gazing at the thousands of butterflies that festoon every aspect of a small bush. What patience it must have taken to assemble the exhibit. Although we have never been fortunate enough to find a roost as large as that one in the wild, they do occur. Indeed, one has to be extremely lucky to chance upon one of their roosts, but once found, if the roost is not disturbed, it is possible to see the Monarchs assemble there night after night, until the last has departed for Mexico.

Butterflies symbolize fragile beauty, and children sometimes hear that butterflies live for only a day. Actually, most butterflies live for a few weeks, but the Monarch is special among our butterflies—some Monarchs live for more than six months, even as they make an arduous and perilous journey all the way to southern Mexico. There our Monarchs pass the winter. Why Monarchs that migrate along the coast of New Jersey end up in the high mountains of Mexico, while those from the Rocky Mountains pass the winter along the California coast, is certainly a puzzle.

Butterflies have a typical insect life cycle, egg-larva-pupa-adult, which in the Monarch requires about a month to complete. After mating, the female lays her eggs on tender young leaves of Milkweed plants. The eggs hatch after about a week, and the tiny caterpillars begin to munch; these are called the *first instar larvae*. As a caterpillar grows, it soon outgrows its tight "skin," which it then sheds or crawls out of. During the course of two weeks, it does this trick four times, each instar larger than its predecessor.

During this period the Monarch caterpillar is brilliantly banded with yellow, white, and black (fig. 57). Although they usually hide on the undersurface of leaves, their striking coloration is another adaptation to avoid predators. They are distasteful to birds, which can connect bad taste and brilliant colors, so this has been called *warning coloration*. The color pattern is believed to aid birds in learning to leave alone such conspicuous objects, for once tasted the bird experiences severe ill effects. Once a bird has tasted a Monarch, it spits it out or even vomits it up, and thereafter avoids such unsavory prey. The sickening taste is actually due to certain chemicals, called *cardenolides*, which are in the Milkweed leaves that the caterpillar consumes. The caterpillar stores these noxious chemicals in its tissues, and these are then passed on to the adult butterfly, which is also distasteful.

This is not a clear-cut matter, however. Not all Milkweed species or plants have the same concentration of the chemicals, so not all Monarch caterpillars are bad-tasting or sickening. Also, some birds can apparently tolerate even distasteful Monarchs, because orioles and grosbeaks regularly dine on the Monarchs at their Mexican wintering roosts. In any case, most of the Monarch

57. Caterpillars of Monarchs are strikingly colored. This one is rolled in a ball for protection. (Photo by J. Burger)

caterpillars, like the caterpillars of most butterflies, get killed before they are old enough to enter the third stage of life. This stage, the *pupa* or *chrysalis,* is one of the most fascinating events in nature.

The full-grown caterpillar, sensing that its time has come, seeks a sheltered place where it will pupate. It spins a cocoon of pale green silk, which it suspends from a branch or wooden structure. There, over the course of nearly two weeks, it gets nature's equivalent of a "makeover." It develops reproductive organs, and its digestive track is drastically altered from one suitable for digesting coarse leaves to one suited only for sipping nectar. The wings, the signature structure of a butterfly, slowly develop all shriveled up inside the confines of the cocoon.

Finally, the cocoon splits, and a fragile adult butterfly, or *imago,* emerges tentatively, crawls a few steps, and begins the difficult but crucial task of inflating its wings. The veins on a butterfly wing are not merely structural supports but are hollow tubes into which the newly emerged butterfly pumps fluid to expand the wings. A failure at this stage results in deformed wings and is likely to be fatal.

After a few hours, the Monarch can test its wings and take its first flight, heading toward a nectar source and a mate. The females of some species of butterflies are ready to mate as soon as they emerge from the chrysalis, but the Monarch requires a few days for its eggs to mature. Then it begins to mate and lay eggs to start the cycle anew. So far, the cycle as described above is typical of almost all butterflies, but the Monarch's yearly cycle has a unique twist, which we can follow through the year.

In midwinter there are no Monarchs in New Jersey. At this time most of the Monarchs from eastern North America have gathered in several huge roosts in the fir forests at elevations of about 10,000 feet in the mountains of Michoacan in southern Mexico. Some of these roosts have been estimated to contain more than thirty million Monarchs. They spend the chilly nights in a torpid state, sleeping with minimum use of energy so they have no need to feed. On sunny mornings, they warm up enough to flutter and take flight; some may even sip moisture, while others rest on the ground (fig. 58). The vision of millions of black-and-orange wings is an unforgettable sight for those who have made the journey to see the wintering Monarchs. Each year more and more tourists flock to the Mexican mountains to see them, and this ecotourism brings much-needed revenue to the poor villagers—sufficient, one hopes, to discourage them from chopping down all the fir trees for firewood or lumber.

Around late February or early March, when the days are warmer, the Monarchs begin to respond to new signals from some internally programmed clock. No longer content to roost and bask, they begin to migrate northward from their winter quarters. Journey North, an Internet-based program that allows schoolchildren to follow the arrival of spring, and migrating Monarchs, across North America through reports of "first sightings," is now in its sixth year. About four hundred classrooms in Canada and the USA make use of the

58. Millions of Monarchs gather at an overwintering site in Mexico. (Photo by Patti Murray)

data provided by generous observers. Enthusiastic schoolchildren throughout Mexico also keep track of the Monarchs' progress.

The first Monarch wave reaches the southern United States in March. There the adults begin to mate, and soon their caterpillars are munching Milkweed leaves. By early April, one cycle is complete (egg-larva-pupa-adult), and the new generation of adults migrates northward, while most of their parents who hatched the preceding September decline and die. This second brood spreads out over the eastern United States, breeds somewhere in the latitude of the Carolinas, and produces a brood that migrates northward and repeats the event.

Depending on how early the butterflies leave Mexico and how far they migrate before breeding, New Jersey may be invaded by the third brood of Monarchs (late May–early June), or in some years by the fourth brood (July). Here they breed again, producing yet another northward-bound brood. We get additional waves of visitors from the south late in summer, until we begin to see a reversal with the southbound migrants in early autumn. At this time, Monarchs are most numerous from New England to Minnesota and south to North Carolina and Arkansas. There is also a western population that occurs from western Canada to California. Those western Monarchs winter mainly along the Pacific Coast in California, and protecting their winter roosts from development and commercial exploitation has become a major challenge.

Each brood that emerges is sexually mature and ready to mate and is driven by some program, not yet understood, to migrate northward and breed. But there comes a time in late summer, probably related to a shortening daylength, when the newly hatched Monarchs respond to a different program. They enter a state of reproductive diapause. Their sexual organs do not mature, and they are programmed to migrate southward. Not until late winter, when they are in their Mexican roosts, will their "go north and breed" programming take over.

There has been a nationwide program to study the Monarchs by putting small numbered plastic tags on their wings (fig. 59). This tagging program has provided the information that we now have about the Monarch cycle. The Cape May Bird Observatory has been censusing and tagging migrating Monarchs since 1990. Dick Walton directs this marking project. It is likely you will see one of the observatory's interns at the Pavilion Circle gardens, carefully netting Monarchs, attaching the tags, and releasing them to continue on their way. About five thousand Monarchs are tagged in a typical fall migration period, of which only a handful are ever encountered again. But from these few recoveries we know that butterflies that leave the northern states in September do get all the way to the Mexican roosts. Monarchs are also tagged in Mexico, and, very rarely, one actually makes it all the way back north the next spring, which means that it had to live nearly ten months—not bad for a paper-thin creature.

59. Banded Monarch at Cape May, nectaring on a Butterfly Bush. (Photo by J. Burger)

The number of Monarchs varies dramatically from year to year. For example, 1991 was a bumper year and Monarchs were abundant over most of eastern North America. In 1992, however, the Monarch population declined 75 percent from its 1991 level, and the decline was 90 percent along the Atlantic Coast. Parasites can kill thousands of caterpilliars in some years, contributing to fewer migrating Monarchs. Unusually cold winters or severe storms in Mexico can kill millions of Monarchs at a time, reducing their population the following year. The severe snowstorm of December 30, 1995, killed about 30 percent of all Monarchs, and the following year the Monarch migration at Cape May was much slower than average, yet a year later the population had rebounded to a record high. Monarchs have had to live with snowstorms for many millennia and have developed a boom-or-bust economy. Even in a poor year it is easy to find at least a few Monarchs at Cape May. Numbers were the highest ever in 1999.

Discovering the wintering quarters of Monarchs in Mexico was not a simple task. It took years of sleuthing and hard work. Fred Urquhart was the Canadian scientist who directed the search beginning in the 1940s. He spent many years tracking the butterflies southward, following up rumors of their occurrence. Kenneth Brugger, who had retired to Mexico, began to correspond with Urquhart, and on January 2, 1975, he found the wintering roost site. The quest is immortalized in Urquhart's book, *Monarch: International Traveller.* Imagine the excitement, after years of frustration, of climbing through a mountain shrouded in morning mist and coming on a scene with millions of black-and-orange wings, just beginning to stir after a night of torpid inactivity.

The marvelous Monarchs migrate more than 2,500 miles, navigating by an internal sun compass, a combination of daylight and the position of the sun in the sky. In 1999 researchers discovered that Monarchs can orient on cloudy days using the Earth's magnetic field.

Today, like habitats everywhere, the Monarch roosts are in jeopardy. Those on the Pacific Coast of California are threatened by development, while the fir forests of Mexico are being assaulted by timber companies, and their future is grim. Small towns like Angangueo, gateway to the El Rosario roost site, stand to gain more money in the long run from tourism than from timber. The timber and its revenue will surely be exhausted after a few years, while the Monarchs will return year after year, a quickly renewable and lucrative resource.

In 1986 the Mexican government declared six of the wintering sites as ecological preserves, but enforcement is difficult. A Mexican group known as Monarcha is trying to encourage tourism in an effort to halt, or at least slow, the lumbering that threatens the Monarchs. Because the Monarchs migrate from Mexico to Canada and back again, it is a natural resource shared among the three countries. There are networks of Monarch watchers in all three countries, and, as already noted, schoolchildren can plot the northward and southward movement of the Monarchs using Internet communication. An encouraging sign is that more than 250 elementary schools in Mexico alone are participating in documenting not only the migration of the Monarchs, but their behavior as they pass through northern Mexico.

Monarchs are not yet endangered, but the mass roosting of the Monarchs in Mexico is considered an *endangered phenomenon.* International conservation groups are making an effort to encourage preservation of the Monarch mountain roosts, only eight of which are known to exist in Mexico. Future generations of Monarchs not just in Mexico, but throughout eastern North America, depend on their success.

In Cape May, the flight of the Monarchs is enchanting. When the sun goes down and cool fall breezes rush in from the ocean, they are defenseless. It is up to us to protect their foraging bushes as well as their roosting sites. When the sun once again rises, the Monarchs take flight, either in search of nectar or to head south. It is hard to believe that this erratic, fluttering, and soaring flight of the Monarchs will carry them across Delaware Bay and over thousands of miles to Mexico. The sunlight glancing off hundreds of Monarchs flitting among the Butterfly Bushes at Pavilion Circle is breathtaking and enthralling.

FOR MORE INFORMATION: Call the Cape May Bird Observatory (609-884-2736 or 609-861-0700). The observatory runs a Monarch Monitoring Project, with information at http://www.concord.org/%7Edick/. For more information, contact the North American Butterfly Association, 4 Delaware Road, Morristown, NJ 07960; http://www.naba.org/.

60. Black Vulture (*top*) and Turkey Vulture (*bottom*) flying over Chimney Rock. (Photos by Chris Williams and J. Burger)

16

Migrant Hawks on the Inland Ridges

Gliding effortlessly on rising air currents, the migrant hawks trace lovely arcs against the blue sky as they swirl past the eager watchers. Some streak by at eye level, while others circle effortlessly in large kettles.

KEY LOCATIONS: There are hawk lookouts at Montclair (Essex County) and Chimney Rock (Somerset County) on the Watchung Mountains; and at Sunset Mountain (Sussex County) and Raccoon Ridge (Warren County) on the Kittatinny Mountains.

DIRECTIONS: Montclair (in the Watchungs): Take Garden State Parkway to Watchung Avenue (exit 151). Drive west to the end of Watchung Avenue (about 2.1 miles), and turn right on Upper Mountain Road. Go north 0.7 mile and turn left on Bradford Avenue. Go about 0.1 mile and take the second right onto Edgecliff Road. Go 0.3 mile to parking lot on the right. Just before the parking lot you will see a staircase to the observation platform.

Chimney Rock (in the Watchungs): Take I-287 to the exit for Route 22 east. Follow Route 22 east (actually northeast) for 1 mile to the Vosseler Avenue exit. Take the jughandle and turn left (west) on Vosseler Avenue to cross Route 22. Go uphill about 0.6 mile to the summit. About 100 yards after the summit there is a small road on the left, Miller Lane. It is not well marked and is easy to miss the first time. Turn left on Miller Lane and go about 0.5 mile to the parking lot. The trail to the hawk-watching platform begins at the parking lot.

Sunrise Mountain (Kittatinnies): Go toward Stokes State Forest in extreme northwestern New Jersey. At Culver's Gap, look for sign to Sunrise Mountain. Turn right onto Upper North Shore Road (Route 636) for 0.2 mile and left onto the Sunrise Mountain Road for about 4 miles, bearing right at the sign for the mountain. At the parking lot, walk right (south) on the Appalachian Trail for about 200 yards to the lookout point on the top of the mountain.

Raccoon Ridge (Kittatinnies): This is an excellent site, but access is difficult. Take I-80 to exit 12, and follow Route 521 north about 5 miles. Turn left on Route 94 and go 3.8 miles. Turn right on Walnut Valley Road and go for 2.6 miles. Stop at gate to notify the guard that you want to go to the Hawk Watch. Drive past gate for 1.1 miles, bearing right at first fork, left at second fork, and right at third fork into the Boy Scout camp. Park and walk straight ahead. Then turn left and hike up the old steep road for about 0.75 mile (bearing right at the fork). Turn left on the Appalachian Trail, which runs along the ridge top. Continue about 0.25 mile to the main lookout on a rock outcropping. The hike goes from 700 feet elevation at the Boy Scout camp to 1,500+ feet at the ridge line and takes about half an hour.

BEST TIME TO VISIT: Mid-September to late October. About September 20 for the peak Broad-winged Hawk migration, October for Red-tailed and Sharp-shinned Hawks, and late October for Golden Eagles, Goshawks, and Ravens (not a hawk).

The optimum time for a New Jersey hawk watch is a day with brisk northwest winds, after several days of southerly winds. Fair weather is good, but on a hot day, the thermals rise so strongly that the hawks ride high overhead, affording less satisfactory viewing.

PRIME HABITAT: Lookout points on the Watchung and Kittatinny Mountains.

In mid-September we follow a poorly marked road past houses to a gravel parking lot, then a narrow trail that leads to a fenced balcony perched precariously on the western lip of the Watchung Mountains, next to the graffiti-splattered Chimney Rock from which this hawk lookout derives its name. A visitor from the West would marvel at the nerve of New Jerseyans, calling this range a mountain, but it rises several hundred feet above the valley floor. A mile to the north of the lookout is a series of ridges and promontories, each with a name such as "the knob" and "the notch" that helps the official hawk counter point out incoming birds to the less-experienced visitors. Below is a gravel quarry, with trucks rumbling back and forth, unaware of the hawks flying overhead, or of the watchers on the ridge (fig. 61). "Hawk over the Peak," comes a voice, and we search in unison for a tiny dot at the limit of vision. The counter swings his scope, finds the dot, and shortly announces, "Broad-winged, wait, several, here they come, there's a dozen at least."

Although the ambience is marred by the churning dust and the noisy machinery and trucks in the gravel quarry well below us, our eyes are focused on the hawks. Soon they are in view, a dozen indeed, and more behind them. Rather than beat a steady path from north to south, the hawks are circling upward, riding the warm air updrafts, called thermals. As the sun rises above the horizon, it begins to warm the air over the land. Along mountain sides, the air rises in an upward, counterclockwise spiral, and the hawks coast into these updrafts and circle upward effortlessly on their broad, outstretched wings. No need for them to expend energy flapping when the winds give them a free ride. As the hawks enter the vortex, they swirl upward, mere dots before our eyes, and then at great altitude they coast downward, out of the gyre, ahead of the

61. The view from Chimney Rock, with the gravel quarry below and the Watchungs on the right. (Photo by J. Burger)

northwest winds, until they reach the next ridgetop, much closer to us, where they catch the next updraft and swirl upward again. For them it is an endless amusement park, swirling and gliding for hundreds of miles along the mountain ridges that funnel them past our vantage point. Broad-winged Hawks from all over eastern Canada, New England, and New York are moving past us.

Remarkably they seem to be in no hurry, despite the long journey to South America that lies ahead. In the next week or so their path will take them along the Appalachians, through the Ozarks, through the Texas coastal plain, across the Sierra Oriental of Mexico, and along the mountain spine of Central America. Observers in Panama, the ultimate funnel, may witness tens of thousands of hawks on a single day, before the birds enter South America and divide their path, some going east along the coastal range into Venezuela, while others soar south along the eastern slope of the Andes.

This is both an old and a new phenomenon. The mountains have been here for a hundred million years, and the hawks for some tens of millions of years. However, during the first half of the twentieth century, the ridgetops became a very different kind of amusement park. The hawks faced a murderous onslaught as they migrated southward, for the ridgetops were favorite gathering places for gunners that slaughtered the hawks for sport. Then hawks were viewed as evil pests, as murderers of songbirds and small game, and gunning was conducted with an air of self-righteousness. Maurice Broun, first curator of the renowned Hawk Mountain Sanctuary, described the carnage in his book *Hawks Aloft.* On a fine October day, hundreds of hunters (up to four hundred were counted) would gather at a favorable lookout to shoot the hawks as they passed close by. They used blinded pigeons and tethered hawks as lures, and the unsuspecting hawks would be shot as they came to capture the pigeons. Hundreds of hawks were shot in a day; tens of thousands in a season, year after year after year. Hawk numbers declined drastically.

In 1934 the first refuge for migrating hawks was set up by Mrs. Rosalie Edge of the Linnaean Society of New York at Hawk Mountain on the Kittatinny Ridge in eastern Pennsylvania. But Hawk Mountain was only a minute point where hawks had safe passage. There were gunners waiting for them both to the north and south, and indeed, the Brouns' own safety at the sanctuary was sometimes in jeopardy. Police officers who might be needed to protect the sanctuary turned out to be hawk gunners themselves. The main contribution of Hawk Mountain was to focus the nation's attention on the tragic destruction of valuable birds of prey. It provided an alternative recreational value to hawks, as watcher rather than the shooter. Tourists from far and wide flocked to the Pennsylvania Dutch country near Drehersville to visit the famous hawk lookout, and hundreds of people crowded the rocks on favorable autumn days. The local economy received an infusion, and after a few years, hawk watching gained acceptance.

When we visited Hawk Mountain in Pennsylvania in the mid-1950s it was already world famous. Late in the afternoon we drove to another well-known lookout called Bake Oven Knob. While Hawk Mountain was a hawk preserve, Bake Oven was still a gunning site. It was late afternoon and the gunners were leaving. They were not at all happy to see us with our binoculars rather than guns and tried to frighten us away. We gazed nevertheless at the scene spread out on the rocks before us, and then, like undertakers, we began our count. We counted 147 dead Sharp-shinned Hawks and 7 Cooper's Hawks. At that time these species were not protected. There were also protected species, including a dead Osprey, a Marsh Hawk, a Red-shouldered Hawk, and three Red-tailed Hawks. We also found a live Red-tail with a hideously broken wing. It crouched in fear in a rock crevice, where it had been left to die. When we tried to extract it, it uttered a piercing scream, slashing wildly with its beak, and tightening its claws in the leather jacket we used as a shield. There were other dead birds as well. Several Robins, quite a few Blue Jays, and even a Myrtle Warbler. It was hard to imagine anyone thinking of this as recreation.

We took the Red-tailed Hawk back with us, hoping to restore its wings and its flight. One of the naturalists nursed it back to health, and it lived out its life playing a very useful educational role, traveling from fairs to schools, encouraging the public to support hawk protection.

Although virtually all songbirds had been protected by the Migratory Bird Treaty Act signed by the United States and Canada in 1918 (and by Mexico in 1936), quite a few birds were excluded. Some fish eaters like Double-crested

Cormorants, Belted Kingfishers, and Great Blue Herons were not protected because they competed for fish or had a propensity to dine at fish hatcheries. Hawks and owls were likewise excluded. By the mid-1950s some states began to extend protection to most hawks and owls, but the three bird-eating hawks or accipiters—Sharp-shinned, Cooper's, and Goshawk—were still not protected. Because it remained legal to shoot these hawks, and it was a popular sport, many of the protected hawks that migrated along the ridges were killed as well, just as we saw that day at Bake Oven Knob. In the very rare instances when a hunter was charged for shooting a protected species, he could argue, disingenuously, that he had made a mistake in identification, and judges were loath to impose fines.

It was a serious conservation issue, and when we were in high school, one of the prime conservation objectives was the passage of model hawk laws to protect all species. For more than twenty years, Rosalie Edge, one of the early environmental activists, made this her cause célèbre, and eventually those she recruited to her cause prevailed. It was she who surprised the Pennsylvania gunners by leasing their favorite shooting site, which became the Hawk Mountain Sanctuary. As high school students, we wrote impassioned letters to state and federal legislators urging the protection of all birds of prey. Not until 1972 did all hawks and owls gain federal protection—a conservation success for a society still rooted in the frontier mentality of destroying predators and claiming the land. Prior to that, the impact on all hawks was disastrous, particularly on the Sharp-shinned and Cooper's Hawks. These species all but disappeared from many parts of New England, and the numbers counted on migration were perilously low.

After twenty years of protection, the hawk numbers rebounded substantially, and it became possible to count a thousand Sharp-shinned Hawks in a single day. This protection, coupled with environmental education, has popularized hawk watching and lookouts such as Chimney Rock. Ironically, today the Pennsylvania Game Commission is considering making a request to the federal government to allow hawk shooting in order to encourage Pheasant populations for hunting.

Chimney Rock is on the easternmost ridge of the Watchung range, which parallels the Kittatinnies. The range, comprising three parallel ridges, extends from Ramapos in northern New Jersey to central New Jersey. One of the strong points of Chimney Rock is that two of the Watchung ridges converge here, serving as a hawk funnel.

By 10 A.M. there are fifteen people crowded onto the Chimney Rock platform. As we watch an approaching kettle of Broad-wings, thirty-five birds in the air at one time, a Sharp-shinned Hawk beats its way southward just below eye level. It is a beautiful dark gray, with three dark bands in its tail. This is a male, not much larger than a Blue Jay. Every few minutes one or two Sharp-shins pass the lookout, some below us, some above. Most pass close to the ridge, but a few fly high over the valley to the next ridge. Some of the Sharp-shins are moving in steady flight while others are circling upward on the thermal currents.

The kettle of Broad-wings is high overhead as it moves southward, almost in unison. The origin of the word "kettle" as it applies to hawks is obscure, but the phenomenon is spectacular, nonetheless. The birds are swirling still, but losing altitude slightly, until they pick up the next thermals on the ridge behind us. But more Broad-wings are coming—dozens more. By 10:30 we have counted over three hundred. The counter explains that there have been six days of southerly winds with very little movement, and the hawks are backed up somewhere to the north of us. "Today's the day," he announces expectantly. Each year produces a few days of spectacular migration intermixed with many "slower" days. Some species such as the Broad-wings are famous for migrating in great numbers, while others, like Ospreys, drift through in small numbers each day throughout the season. In some years, half the Broad-wings for the entire season come through in a single day.

Our attention is called to another approaching dot, "adult Bald Eagle" is announced, and we are thrilled as this huge bird, with its white head and tail, flies past at very close range. It is a magnificent bird, certainly deserving of being our national emblem. Not too long ago, however, Bald Eagles were also very rare, the victims of pesticides (see chapter 26). Before the day is over, we will see three more eagles—another adult and two immatures. Seeing the immatures is especially gratifying because it signifies successful reproduction and a glowing recovery for this species. Indeed, in 1999, the Bald Eagle, which was one of the first species to be declared endangered, was taken off the federal endangered list with great fanfare, because of the great success of its recovery, but is still listed as endangered in New Jersey. The Bald Eagles we see today may travel a long way, perhaps to Florida, before they find suitable wintering quarters. But there is both a breeding and a wintering population in New Jersey.

Quite a few Bald Eagles spend the winter in New Jersey, with a peak of 176 in the winter of 1996–1997. The numbers have been lower in recent years, and whether this is merely a fluctuation or indicative of a reverse trend needs to be watched closely. These eagles winter mainly along the coast, particularly along the Delaware Bayshore, but also on the inland reservoirs such as Round Valley.

Back at Chimney Rock, the most spectacular event begins at about 11:30 A.M. It starts as just another Broad-wing kettle, but as we stare at the dots, more and more materialize behind them. It seems never to end: it's not dozens, not even hundreds, but eventually there are more than a thousand birds in the air at one time, all of them Broad-winged Hawks. For forty minutes it is hard to know where to look. There are hawks everywhere, almost all well above eye level. Some rise so high that they disappear from view. The flight must extend east of our ridge, out of our field of view, and it extends west to the next parallel ridge. As the hawks disappear southward, more emerge from the north. No longer is it a kettle, but a mass movement, so many hawks that even the experienced counter finds it hard to count. The estimate is that 1,800 Broad-wings pass by in this mass movement. This is indeed a spectacle. But the counter tells us that in 1993, over 8,400 Broad-wings were counted in a two-day period, and on September 20, 1996, more than 12,500 Broad-wings passed by in a one-hour period, and 17,490 were counted for the day.

This is what Maurice Broun, founder of the Hawk Mountain Sanctuary, called a red-letter day. By the time our flight ends, there are about thirty people packed onto the narrow platform and the surrounding slope who have shared in this spectacle. Some of the regulars remark how dull it was in recent days, and others cannot wait until they will come back again tomorrow, knowing that such a spectacle cannot be repeated soon. Indeed, there are many days when the hawk watches are dull because the wind is "wrong."

Meanwhile, the scene is repeated at several other lookouts in New Jersey as well as in adjacent New York and Pennsylvania. Sunrise Mountain, Raccoon Ridge, Montclair, and several other lookouts attract visitors. Some people are regulars, some come once a season, and others are only curious and may never get hooked, but all take part in the exciting pastime of hawk watching. We take this enthusiasm for granted now, but when Hawk Mountain Sanctuary was set up more than sixty years ago, the enthusiastic tourists flocking to see the hawks were as much of a spectacle to the local communities as the birds themselves.

Later we check the Chimney Rock Web page (see below) and find that there are more than 160 hawk-watch sites in eastern North America. For the three falcon species (Kestrel, Merlin, Peregrine), which are mainly coastal migrants, Chimney Rock is often in the top ten of the inland sites.

Chimney Rock has been known locally as a hawk lookout for more than fifty years, but it did not gain national prominence until Chris Aquila and colleagues began the serious business of counting the hawks in 1990. This requires experienced volunteers who can identify the hawks—often a challenge when the birds are far away—and who count them with confidence. You have to be careful not to let any get by, and not to count them twice. There is a counter at each of the lookouts, and they will tally all the species and numbers and compare notes. The best year ever at Chimney Rock was 1996, when over 31,000 hawks were counted. More typical are results for 1997 and 1998, when over 18,000 hawks of thirteen species were counted, including about 10,000 Broad-wings and over 4,000 Sharp-shins. The number of hawks counted each year at the different lookouts naturally depends on the number of days that counters are present during the migration period (September 1 to November 30), but also on wind and weather conditions. In some years, Chimney Rock has had the highest count of any of the lookouts, including Hawk Mountain. And there are fascinating species differences. For example, there are far more Red-tails counted at the Kittatinny sites than in the Watchungs, while the reverse is true for Kestrels. Not only hawks get counted; the Common Loon, a declining species, and geese and swans are conspicuous migrants that are tallied as well. Songbirds, too, are counted at the lookout. Some autumns, Evening Grosbeaks, a species that has been quite rare in New Jersey in the past twenty years, turn up at several of the lookouts, an exciting event for birders. One of the attractive features of Chimney Rock is that many of the birds pass quite close. Since this is the end of the Watchung Ridge, the birds descend in anticipation of changing their flight course.

What will happen to the Broad-wings that headed south today? Where will they spend the winter? Although they are concentrated in the hundreds or thousands as they pass the lookouts, in winter they will be spread out over large areas of South America, where there have been virtually no studies of their behavior. Deforestation is, of course, rampant in South America where these forest-dwelling hawks pass half their lives (October to March).

Where agriculture supplants forests, pesticides are used in abundance, including many chlorinated compounds, now banned in the U.S., which almost sealed the fate of so many birds of prey a generation ago. Because of aggressive marketing, the use of chemical pesticides in South America is actually on the rise. Some species, such as Bald Eagles, Ospreys, and Peregrines, are again experiencing an increase in pesticide residues in their tissues. Some species are showing a long-term decline, according to the Hawk Migration Association of North America data network, which collects data from over three hundred hawk-watching sites nationwide. Yet 1998 was a bountiful year for most hawks at Chimney Rock. Maybe the two consecutive mild winters allowed for a buildup of the prey species on which the hawks rely to feed themselves and their offspring.

That seems like a good explanation for the record numbers of Red-tailed and Red-shouldered Hawks, which eat primarily rodents; but it is not adequate to explain the success of eagles, or of the Sharp-shinned Hawks which eat mainly other birds, nor of the Broad-wings which are especially fond of snakes (fig. 62). The study of population biology is complex indeed, and there are always many factors that influence the numbers of birds in a given year. That is why people focus on long-term trends rather than on short-term fluctuations. A continuous decline over several years is much more meaningful than a very large decline from one year to the next.

After the peak of the Broad-wing migration, things settle down at the inland hawk lookouts, where counts only occasionally reach a total of one thousand hawks a day in October. By November, most of the hawks have passed, although a few Red-tails and Golden Eagles are still moving southward. After the first week of November, hawk watching slows down, with just a few birds each day, mainly Sharp-shins and Red-tails; there may still be a few Goshawks, only a few of which are counted each year. There could be other surprises as well,

62. Cooper's Hawk migrating past Chimney Rock. (Photo by D. H. Guston)

including perhaps some day a Gyrfalcon, but we're not holding our breath for that.

Many of the hawk themes mentioned above apply equally to the Cape May hawk watch, but the patterns of movement, and to some extent the species composition, are different. The hawks at Cape May have taken a coastal route on their way to South America. Many of the birds counted there are immatures that have not learned to exploit the updrafts along the ridges, and falcons, which do not seem to use the updrafts.

Another small kettle of Broad-winged Hawks glides into view, just barely at the limit of observation. We strain to pick out the tiny black specks against the clear blue sky. They sail out of sight without affording us a closer look, the equivalent of the big fish that got away. Our disappointment fades, however, when a pair of Cooper's Hawks glide majestically below us, providing us with a spectacular sight.

FOR MORE INFORMATION: Contact the New Jersey Audubon Society (908-204-8998). For Chimney Rock information, check http://www.rci.rutgers.edu/~magarell/chimney__rock/. For information on Hawk Mountain, check Hawk Migration Association of North America at http://www.hmana.org/.

63. Adult Peregrine Falcon migrating past Cape May Point. (Photo by Sherry Meyer)

17

Migrant Hawks
at Cape May

Under the shadow of a stately white and red lighthouse on a cool October day when the winds are just right, a hundred watchers gather to view the procession of Peregrine Falcons, Merlins, Ospreys, and other hawks, some drifting low, others circling high, some so high they are hard to identify against the brilliant autumn sky.

KEY LOCATIONS: Cape May peninsula (Cape May County), chiefly Cape May Point State Park. Also Higbee Beach.

DIRECTIONS: Once in Cape May, take Sunset Boulevard (Route 606) west toward Cape May Point. Turn left on Lighthouse Avenue and follow signs to the state park entrance by the lighthouse. The hawk-watch platform is across the parking lot (see next chapter for additional directions).

BEST TIME TO VISIT: Last half of September and first half of October for the peak of migration. Hawk migration lasts from September through November.

PRIME HABITAT: Any open vista with associated forest edges along the coast.

A slightly chilly autumn breeze rustles the tops of the Phragmites just below us, but the mass of birders all face in the same direction, their binoculars trained on a tiny spot in the brilliant blue sky. As at hundreds of migratory hawk lookouts scattered across North America, there is an official counter, an intern from the Cape May bird observatory, who must decide whether this is a large Sharp-shinned Hawk or a small Cooper's Hawk. Hawks, also known as raptors for their "plundering" ways, elicit rapture in the thousands of hawk-watching devotees who gather to watch their passage.

The distant hawk circles lazily, in no apparent hurry to reach its faraway wintering grounds. It is a mere silhouette, and the watchers wait patiently for it to approach. With a shout, one watcher calls people's attention to a flash of brown as a young female Sharp-shinned Hawk sails into view over the reeds, heading south on rapidly beating wings. This bird passes by so close that binoculars are not necessary. It is followed a few minutes later by another.

Turning back to the sky, the distant dot has finally reached the zenith, where, based on the relative proportions of wing and slightly rounded tail, it can be identified as a Cooper's Hawk. But meanwhile several other spots come into view. Two are Sharpies, one is an Osprey, and one, with sharp-pointed wings, is a Peregrine Falcon. The Peregrine is wasting no time as it flies at tree-top level, on wingbeats so powerful that experienced hawk watchers can identify it at the limit of vision. They call this the "jizz," a term that originated with the plane spotters of World War II; the mere appearance of a bird, its shape or flight behavior, reveals its identity.

The thrill comes moments later when the Peregrine accelerates its wingbeats and dips down almost to the water's surface, scattering a small flock of Gadwall. The Peregrine comes up empty clawed, but it leaves the spectators, and the Gadwall, breathless. The Peregrine used to be called a Duck Hawk, and it is clear why. John James Audubon painted an unlikely scene with a pair of Peregrines facing each other, each tearing apart its own duck prey with bloodstained beaks.

Both hawks and birders are engaged in a ritual. The hawks are migrating from their summer breeding grounds in Canada to faraway wintering grounds and have followed the coastline southward from New England, until they concentrate in Cape May. The birders likewise have migrated from far and wide, concentrating in Cape May to see the spectacular hawk migrations. Watchers have been gathering at Cape May for decades, and before them it was gunners who gathered for autumn hawk shoots.

Cape May peninsula is one of the most significant stopover sites for fall migrants on the Atlantic Flyway. It is a funnel point for birds coming down from much of the Northeast, as well as for migrating butterflies and dragonflies. Monarchs and Red Admirals move through in the thousands, and several species of migratory dragonflies—Globe Trotters, Green Darners, Saddlebags, and Shadow Darners—pass through, largely unnoticed. Thousands upon thousands of birds and insects migrate through Cape May Point, head out across Delaware Bay, or turn northward to cross the bay at a narrower point. This brings them to Higbee Beach, another favorite site for watching migrants.

Cape May is an important stopover for over 130 Neotropical migrants, a term for birds that spend the winter in Central and South America (see next chapter), and many short-distance migrants bound only for the southern United States. Over four hundred species of birds have been recorded in Cape May peninsula during fall migration. Cape May's reputation, however, is intimately connected with its hawk migration, which was already well known over a century ago. Each fall at least fifteen species of hawks pass through Cape May Point, and each year there are a few surprises, a rare hawk such as a Swainson's Hawk, or a Sandhill Crane perhaps. Data from the hundreds of hawk watches conducted across North America reveal that more birds of prey pass through

New Jersey in migration than through any other state except Texas. Texas excels because it is the ultimate funnel, receiving migrants from all across North America.

The Hawk Watch at Cape May Point State Park is a spectacular place to observe hawks, for both the novice and the experienced hawk watcher. Since it is monitored during the migration period, there is always someone who can identify the hawks and point them out when they are only dark specks in a pale blue sky. There are also a number of information presentations, many given right at the Hawk Watch. On a good day with northerly or northwest winds, it is impossible not to become excited by the passage of hundreds of hawks visible from the platform. There are slow days as well. When the winds are wrong or the temperature is hot, only a few hawks pass. Then one must turn attention to the other natural sights, ducks on the Lighthouse Pond, butterflies such as the rare Little Yellow, dragonflies, and marsh plants labeled along the boardwalk nature trails.

Among all of the North American hawk watches, New Jersey has the greatest concentration of several species, including American Kestrel, Cooper's Hawk, Northern Harrier, Osprey, Peregrine Falcon, Merlin, Red-shouldered Hawk, and Sharp-shinned Hawk. Over 90 percent of these species at Cape May are immatures who have had little experience with optimal foraging in unfamiliar surroundings, and no experience with migration. Preserving suitable habitat for these inexperienced birds is particularly critical, because this is the next generation of hawks.

The counting of hawks at Cape May is an extremely important task because it provides quantitative data on migration, which is then combined in a centralized database with counts from the other hawk watches. Analyses of these data reveal seasonal and yearly trends in numbers of each species. It is data from such hawk watches that has led to the concern for declines of Kestrels and other species that have been recorded at many hawk watches throughout the Northeast. In fact, there were over 11,000 Kestrels at the hawk watch in 1976, but in 1996 there were only 8,000. The decline in New Jersey's breeding Kestrel is noticeable as well. It has gone from being a familiar shape on a utility line to a rare treat. Other species that are declining include the Golden Eagle and the Red-shouldered Hawk. There is some cause for optimism for the species that are increasing, including Peregrine Falcon, Merlin, Harrier, Osprey, and Bald Eagles, all species that were severely affected by DDT in the 1960s, and whose populations seem to be rebounding.

A large whiteboard near the stairs to the wooden hawk watch platform tells you the tally for the previous day, the seasonal tally, and the peak flight and date for the year—providing a quick overview of what to expect. Peak daily counts on a good day can be incredibly exciting. Imagine seeing 11,000 Sharp-shinned Hawks pass overhead in one day, or over 9,000 Broad-winged Hawks. Gone are the days when you could see over 24,000 Kestrels in one day, as were

64. Cape May Hawkwatch, with tallies for the day. (Photo by
J. Burger)

observed on October 16, 1970, or even the fifty Goshawks seen on November 7, 1973. But the hawks passing by the lookout are still impressive (fig. 64).

The hawks at Cape May are on the wing shortly after dawn, searching for appropriate habitat and pursuing prey, their acrobatic flights a delight to watch. Kestrels and Merlins may begin their migration flights shortly after dawn, or if the winds are not right or they are still underweight, they search for places to feed. Some species of hawks are relatively easy to see, including the Sharp-shinned, Red-tailed, Broad-winged, Osprey, and American Kestrel. Others,

TABLE 3. Temporal Patterns of Common Hawks

American Kestrel	Mid-September to mid-October
Bald Eagle	Mid-September to early November
Broad-winged Hawk	Mid-September to mid-October
Cooper's Hawk	Mid-September to mid-October
Marsh Hawk	September through November
Merlin	September to mid-October
Osprey	September through mid-October
Red-tailed Hawk	October and November
Red-shouldered Hawk	October to November
Sharp-shinned Hawk	Mid-September through October
Turkey Vulture	October through November

such as the Turkey Vulture, are seen only with strong northerly winds. Still others, such as the Goshawk, occur late in the season and mainly during invasion years, when foraging or weather conditions force them farther south. The hawks do not all come through at the same time, there are seasonal differences (see table 3).

Like many other regions of New Jersey, the Cape May Peninsula has lost 30 to 40 percent of its wild habitats in the last twenty-five years, and remaining open country including farmland is a ripe target for development. This has had a profound effect on the available habitat for spring and fall migrants. The plight is particularly critical for migrant hawks because so many of them are young, and their survival is critical to the continuation of many species. It is not too late to preserve forests and fields in Cape May County, but it will take vigilance, planning, and extreme patience in dealing with a wide range of public interests. One of the most lucrative interests in Cape May County is ecotourism, and birding is certainly the most important (for a further discussion, see the chapters on shorebirds and passerine migrants). The three main events these ecotourists come to see are Neotropical songbirds, migrant hawks, and the thousands of shorebirds in the springtime.

Unlike the shorebirds that fly several thousand miles non-stop to reach the beaches of Delaware Bay, some migrant hawks make relatively short flights, stopping along the way to replenish food reserves. This makes the availability of food at stopover or staging areas extremely important. Several factors, including physical factors, food availability, and geography, influence where hawks and other birds stopover. Birds follow certain landmarks during migration, such as coastlines, and this effort needs their concentration. As the birds move down the coast, they reach funnel points such as Cape May, where they are channeled through a single point. This results from the gradual reduction in land area caused by the convergence of the Atlantic Ocean and Delaware Bay until there is only the point of land left, jutting out into the bay. When birds reach the point, they are faced with the broad expanse of Delaware Bay. Although from their vantage point high above us, the birds must be able to see the Delaware shore in the distance, many species seem perturbed and drop out of the sky to rest and refuel. They may even wait a few days for favorable winds to help them across or to aid them in flying north along the shore to a point where the bay narrows.

Food availability and migration conditions are the factors that determine whether birds stop along the way or fly non-stop. Once they have stopped, however, the behavior of hawks is influenced by both the available habitat and by prey. Our research, in collaboration with Larry Niles of the Endangered and Nongame Species Program, shows that hawks do not occur in similar densities all over Cape May Point; they concentrate in habitats that are similar to their breeding or wintering habitats. Sharp-shinned Hawks that breed in dense forests are most common in forests while stopping over at Cape May. Northern Harriers, also called Marsh Hawks, which breed in open fields and wetlands, are found most commonly in marshes during migration. Red-tailed Hawks, one of the commonest migrants at Cape May, prefer the edge between open fields and woodlots, an environment similar to their preferred breeding habitat.

The hawks are clearly selecting foraging habitat on Cape May that is similar to habitats they use throughout the year. This is not surprising, particularly since the majority of hawks that migrate through Cape May are young birds whose brief experience foraging on their own was in the habitat around their nest.

The finding that hawks, like migrant passerines and shorebirds, require a range of habitats during their migratory stopover helps our understanding of the differences in age of the birds in hawk migration routes. For many years it has been clear that adult hawks usually migrate down the inland mountain ridges, following the updrafts, and do not concentrate along the coasts (see previous chapter). By contrast, a relatively high percentage of young hawks migrate along the coasts, through Cape May. Up to 95 percent of the hawks captured at Cape May in the several banding stations are immatures. This is much, much higher than at any other hawk-banding station in this region.

The reason for this age-related difference in migration pattern is unclear, although most students of hawk behavior believe that the inexperienced birds are simply funneled along the coast. However, it is more likely that they are also searching for familiar habitat that they recognize because it occurred around their nests. They learned how to forage in those habitats, and have the most success foraging there. They might thus avoid the inland ridges, where the dense trees and mountains provide the wrong visual image.

Adult hawks, on the other hand, have had several years of migration to improve both their migratory behavior and their foraging while on migration. The oldest known hawks, based on banding data, are Red-tailed Hawks and Ospreys, which reached twenty-three years of age. But many other species, such as the Red-shouldered Hawk, Broad-winged Hawk, Rough-legged Hawk, and Marsh Hawk reach about twenty years of age. Given the difficulties of finding banded hawks, and the potential problems of band loss, it is amazing that such old hawks have been recovered.

The realization that a diversity of habitats is required by migrating hawks, as well as by passerines, increases the importance of habitat preservation. It also makes it imperative to look at habitat on a landscape scale. Not only is the overall amount of each habitat important, but their relative placement may be critical in providing foraging and roosting sites for the migrant hawks.

It is not easy to migrate along the coasts because, without the benefit of rising thermals, energy costs are high. The young hawks must fly in a generally southwesterly direction, while the prevailing northwesterly winds threaten to push them out to sea. The birds must use energy to compensate, and they can also encounter periods of fog, which may ground them for several days.

The difficulties of migrating along the coasts, however, are offset by the high numbers of prey available at Cape May, particularly for the bird-eating Sharp-shinned and Cooper's Hawks, and the Merlin and Peregrine Falcon. Not only are small passerines funneled down the Cape May peninsula toward the point, but many of these birds are immatures as well, inexperienced both in foraging and in avoiding predators. The inexperience in foraging of young passerines means that they usually spend more time each day foraging, increasing their own vulnerability to hawks.

A fall weekend in Cape May is spectacular for the sheer number of migrating birds and birders that converge on the place. As well as being a sensational place to watch birds, it is a wonderful place to watch people. They descend on the place as if to a mecca. They come alone, in small groups, and in large caravans of cars, all bent on seeing the most species over the two-day weekend. The road to Higbee Beach is lined with cars, each pulled precariously off the road, each birder too excited to park neatly for every second might mean the loss of a bird. The pathways are filled with people, their binoculars trained on bushes and trees, or to the sky in search of hawks.

Old-timers swear that it is nothing like it used to be, when weary warblers wobbled out of the sky to pitch into tiny woodlots, and thousands of Sharp-shinned Hawks careened around. Still, the sight of an Osprey sailing overhead with a small Tuna or Pompano dangling from its claws is quite a sight. Magically, the Osprey lands on a dead snag above our heads and proceeds to tear apart the flesh, glancing only now and again at the hordes of birders with their binoculars trained on its every move.

The fall spectacle of migrants at Cape May is still a magnet, and people come in droves to watch hawks from the platform in the shadow of the magnificent lighthouse or to look for passerines among the fields and forests of Higbee Beach. The ecotourists are no longer taken for granted in Cape May, for bird watchers are attracted from all over the world. Paul Kerlinger has determined that ecotourism is a $31 million a year business in Cape May; ten years ago it was only $10 million. Most of the expenditures are for accommodations, meals, programs, and tours. Birding is a major component of Cape May's economy. A generation ago, most tourist facilities closed down after Labor Day, but now they remain open to serve the bird watchers and others who continue to arrive into mid-October.

Not only are the birds an incredible treat, but the town of Cape May is just beginning to wake up when the hawks stop migrating by late afternoon. A few hawks are still foraging, but most are roosting under cover. Fishing, farming, and catering to tourists of all kinds are the principal occupations of Cape May, and they do it up in style. The brilliant sun glances off the old stately buildings that line the ocean beach. With their fresh paint, the gingerbread houses are large and magnificent and are well worth an evening of leisurely strolling about town. The eighteenth- and nineteenth-century hotels are charming, and it is still possible to stay in one for a night or two. In Cape May there is a wealth of Victorian architecture in pink, pale blue, and lavender lace, revitalized by a federal urban renewal grant of $3.2 million in 1966. Legend has it that there are more descendants of the *Mayflower* in Cape May County than in Plymouth County, Massachusetts. Across the road, rimmed by sand dunes, is the broad beach which made Cape May famous with Philadelphian vacationers in the late 1800s. The Atlantic and Delaware Bay meet at Cape May Point. From ground level, it looks boundless in both directions, and the open water must seem daunting to tiny songbirds, already low on fuel after an all-night flight from somewhere in New England. It is no wonder the birds pitch from the sky into the forests of Cape May, searching for food and shelter before continuing their journey. Some of these tiny warblers, weighing barely a quarter of an ounce, will end up a month from now in South America, where, we hope, they will find that their traditional wintering habitat has not been destroyed. They will pass this way again next fall, and again will be dependent on habitat that is equally vulnerable here. Other small warblers, however, will end up in the mouths of Sharp-shinned Hawks that assimilate the small passerines to fuel their own migrations to distant lands.

FOR MORE INFORMATION: Cape May Bird Observatory (609-861-0700) is always a good source of information about the fall migrants at Cape May. You can also call the Higbee Beach Wildlife Management Area (609-292-2965) for information about Higbee Beach. Your local Audubon Sanctuary office is also a good bet for local information on migration. At Hawk Mountain Sanctuary, the Hawk Migration Association of North America maintains a database summarizing all hawk-watching data; their Web page is http://www.hmana.org/.

65. Massive flocks of Tree Swallows course over the ocean at Cape May in the fall. (Photo by Sherry Meyer)

18

Migrant Songbirds at Cape May

Before the first orange-red rays rise over the ocean above the distant horizon, before darkness gives way to dawn, the sky is filled with chirps, chips, and twillicks as unseen warblers, vireos, and thrushes wing southward, maintaining vocal contact with their own kind. Massive flocks of Tree Swallows dip over the ocean. With the first light, the birds drop out of the sky, some from the northwest and some coming in off the ocean. Dozens of different species land in the trees, shrubs, and on the ground, until it is almost impossible to decide where to look, what to listen to, or what to identify.

KEY LOCATIONS: Cape May Point (Cape May County), including Higbee Beach.

DIRECTIONS: For Higbee Beach, take the Garden State Parkway south to the end, take Route 109 west to Route 9; turn left onto Route 9, at first traffic light turn left onto Seashore Road (Route 626), turn right onto New England Road, and follow to the end. Arrive early; the parking lot fills quickly.

BEST TIME TO VISIT: Last half of September and first week of October for the peak of fall migration.

PRIME HABITAT: Any forest with associated open fields and streams nearby, preferably along the coast of the migratory pathway. Birds are easiest to see in edge habitats, between the fields and forests.

In the pale light of dawn, the trees are filled with chirps and twitters as tiny songbirds search for a much-needed meal after a long night of migration. Some pitch out of the sky, a few sit exhausted in the open, one even falls at our feet. Most scramble amid the branches, searching for food. The rows of bushes shelter elusive insectivores and bold berry eaters.

In the early morning, the migrant songbirds are searching for suitable habitat for foraging, for they must eat enough to store sufficient fat reserves for the next leg of their journey southward. Hawks, such as Sharp-shinned Hawks, also materialize from the skies, to land and search for their prey. They too are hungry, and are anxious to take advantage of the abundance of small birds.

By midmorning, bird activity has diminished. Foraging slows down, and the birds rest, hidden in the branches. The Sharp-shinned Hawks still zip along the woodland edges in pursuit of unwary songbirds, and overhead more hawks are visible as they follow the coastline (see chapter 17). When they reach Cape May Point, some will start across Delaware Bay if the winds are right and they have enough fat reserves, while others turn and find resting places or move north-ward along the Delaware Bayshore.

Cape May peninsula is one of the most significant stopover sites for fall mi-grants on the Atlantic Flyway. It is a funnel point for birds coming down from much of the Northeast, as well as for migrating butterflies and dragonflies. Throughout the northeastern states and eastern Canada, any landbirds travel-ing southeast or south ultimately hit the coast and follow the coastline south, eventually passing through Cape May. Others arrive over the ocean. The Cape May peninsula, extending eighteen miles into Delaware Bay and the sea, is one of the world's great migration bottlenecks. Birds must face the hurdle of a Delaware Bay crossing. Cape May is the avian hub on the migration highway, and Higbee Beach Wildlife Management Area is a favorite place to view this migration.

While it is still dark, one may hear numerous chips of unseen birds passing overhead. The two-note call of Swainson's Thrush stands out from the other voices, but even experienced birders have trouble identifying most of the calls. By dawn the birds are calling from the trees and bushes, and for the next hour they are joined by newly arriving birds. On a rare morning when a brisk north-west wind follows several days of poor weather, there may be a true fall-out with thousands of birds landing in the first hour of light.

One must arrive early, for the parking lot at Higbee fills up quickly, at least by 8 A.M. on a fair, autumn weekend. The number of people that bird watch increases yearly, and in 1995 over fifty-four million people did so. The best way to see Higbee's birds is to follow the paths that lead from the parking lot around the fields. The paths begin at a tiny butterfly garden and continue around the edge of several fields, along a row of tall bushes and then along the edge of a beautiful Dune Woodland forest, the best remaining example of this habitat which once covered much of the peninsula. American Holly, several oaks, Red Cedar, and Hackberry trees are some of the dominant species.

Beyond the dune forest is Delaware Bay. Thousands of swirling wings fly low over the water, course above the land, and wheel back over the water in an end-less cascade of small Tree Swallows, alternating flashes of white underparts with their dark green backs.

In September the warblers are the main attraction, and on good days, with northwest winds the night before, one can see twenty-five species of these in-sectivorous songbirds. Unlike their brightly colored spring plumage, these fall migrants wear duller and streakier colors. Occasionally, a bird seems to forget that it is fall rather than spring, and one might hear the loud "cher-tee cher-tee"

66. Yellow-rumped (Myrtle) Warbler during fall migration at Cape May. (Photo by Sherry Meyer)

of an Ovenbird. Usually, however, it is the single-call notes that attract attention; the "chuk" of a Yellowthroat, its black mask peering at us from the tall grass, or the "chip" of a Black-and-white Warbler working its way up a tree trunk, searching for insects in the bark crevices.

In early October the sparrows and Myrtle Warblers (now called Yellow-rumped) appear in great numbers (fig. 66). As one walks the edge of the field, flocks of dozens of Chipping Sparrows and a few Field and Song Sparrows fly up, offering clear views as they perch in the bushes. Among them, one could spot a rare Clay-colored Sparrow. Overhead flock after flock of Blue Jays are passing, some flying southeastward toward the point, and some heading back northward, searching for the right place to cross the bay. Flickers are often numerous, and unlike most woodpeckers, they feed on the ground. Occasionally a Sharp-shinned Hawk careens into a flock of Flickers, apparently scattering them for amusement since this large woodpecker is almost the size of the hawk. On a typical autumn day it is not unusual to find forty or fifty species at Higbee, although there are absolutely dead days, as well as some "fall-outs" when a hundred species have been counted in a morning.

Higbee Beach is maintained for migrating birds and butterflies, with a diversity of habitats, including open fields, woods, and Phragmite marshes. The greatest diversity of migrants is at the edge of the woods and in the rows of bushes. Many resident bird species are typically found in only one habitat, for example Alder Flycatcher and Yellow-breasted Chats in brushy fields, and

Red-winged Blackbird and Marsh Wrens in marshes. During migration the habitat preferences are sometimes cast aside, and woodland and open country birds are found side by side. However, most species still show typical habitat preferences. Some species such as House Wrens occur anywhere, but others, such as sparrows, are found in open fields. Since so many species occur typically in only one habitat, it is crucial to maintain a wide range of habitats at Higbee Beach. The birds concentrate at Higbee Beach not only because of its location, but because of its diversity of habitats.

Since 1972 over 40 percent of the suitable habitat for migrant landbirds on the lower six miles of the Cape May peninsula has been lost. Like many parts of New Jersey, there has been a lot of residential development, and the patches of open space that are set aside under well-intentioned "open space" plans are small, fragmented, and often inadequate for foraging. These remnant patches are separated from more continuous habitat. For us, habitat loss is very heartbreaking, for it removes some beautiful places from our world. But for migrants passing through Cape May it may spell death of individuals and decline of species. We are losing the marshes, fields, and forests that North America's birds need to survive. We are replacing them with pavement and suburbia. Some species such as Crows, Robins, Mockingbirds, and Starlings can survive in suburbia, but most species cannot. It is not that we care less for the birds that can survive around our homes, but that the loss of the birds of the forests and fields decreases our overall biodiversity. When we convert a forest into suburbia, we may trade sixty-five species of breeding forest birds for five species of suburban birds. Once they had somewhere else to move, but this is no longer the case—much of that habitat is already gone.

As bad as it is for resident birds, the situation is even more dire for the migrants that come to Cape May each spring and fall. They have a limited time in which to forage. They cannot wander aimlessly over the landscape searching for appropriate habitat; their foraging days are numbered because they must continue onward. Young birds, the bulk of the fall migrants at Cape May in the fall and the future of their species, are particularly at risk because their knowledge of appropriate foraging sites is more limited and their foraging skills are fewer.

Most migrant landbirds make a series of short night flights, starting shortly after dusk. Some land around midnight, while others continue until daybreak. From midnight on, birds drop out of the sky, landing wherever they can. With the first light, they may reevaluate their position, looking for higher-quality habitat nearby. Some land, exhausted from their long journeys (fig. 67). This mass movement of migrants trying to find suitable, high-quality habitat is called the "morning flight." In searching for prime habitat, birds need to balance nutritional and immediate energy needs with the risk from predators. Many stopover sites, such as Cape May, feature a high concentration of prey

67. An exhausted Rose-breasted Grosbeak that overshot the coast on a brisk
northwesterly wind and had to struggle back to land. (Photo by J. Burger)

and predators, and all require large amounts of food to put on enough fat to
fuel their southward migration.

Food availability is clearly key, although some songbirds eat a greater range
of foods on migration than while breeding or overwintering. Birds that normally eat mainly insects often eat a bit of fruit. Those birds that have more flexible diets during migration show faster rates of weight gain, allowing them to
be on their way more quickly. Since most land birds show strong habitat preferences, it is challenging for us to learn their choices and find their preferred
habitats.

There is tremendous concern for the plight of Neotropical migrants because they seem to be decreasing at an alarming rate. Unlike most ecological
disasters, there are reliable counts on the number of Neotropical migrants that
date back to the early 1960s and 1970s. Studies of Neotropical migrants in
places like the Rutgers University Hutcheson Memorial Forest, by B. Murray
and his colleagues, provide critical data for evaluating population trends. The
major problem seems to be habitat loss, both in quantity and quality, both in
North America and the tropics. Not only has development resulted in loss of
habitat and fragmentation, but development itself seems to impact the birds
in nearby forests and fields. For many years, biologists believed that habitat
loss and degradation were the primary causes of the declines. Recently, however, the quality of development appears to affect the diversity and number of

Neotropical songbirds in forest patches. Forest patches of the same size have fewer songbirds when there are more houses on the perimeter. Woodlots of the same size that are not surrounded by houses have consistently more Neotropical species, and more individuals, than do urban woodlots. This suggests that it may be necessary to create a buffer around forests if we want to continue to have Neotropical migrants breeding within them.

Species that are adapted to breed in forest interiors are the most affected by development because development results in smaller and smaller forest patches, and the forest patches are often separated by greater and greater distances. With decreasing forest size, there is more edge in proportion to the amount of interior. Edges affect forest birds in many ways: there are changes in vegetation structure, there are changes in vegetation species, there are changes in the kinds and numbers of predators, there are changes in the kinds and numbers of competitors for food and nest sites, and non-native and highly invasive species of plants succeed in establishing themselves in edge areas. These species choke out the native plants and alter the habitats, rendering them unsuitable for many birds.

The increased amount of edge relative to the forest area on the breeding grounds results in another hazard. Many of our songbirds are hosts to Brown-headed Cowbirds, a brood parasite that makes no nest of its own but lays its eggs in the nests of other small birds such as wrens, vireos, warblers, and sparrows, as well as medium-sized birds like thrushes and tanagers. The Cowbirds may throw out a host egg prior to laying their own. More seriously, however, the baby Cowbirds are more aggressive than their nest mates and monopolize the food, growing and surviving at the expense of their foster siblings. Occasionally one can actually see a warbler or sparrow feeding a baby Cowbird, twice its own size.

The Kirtland's Warbler, a species that nests only in the Jack Pine forests of Michigan, teeters on the verge of extinction. Its numbers were already depleted by the loss and fragmentation of its habitat, which allowed the Cowbirds access to their nests. Only massive Cowbird control programs have saved the Warbler from extinction thus far. Cowbirds have a serious impact on many other songbirds, especially where habitats are fragmented.

Added to the loss of breeding and migratory habitat is the loss of wintering habitat. The cutting of the rain forest is highly popularized, but other forests are being destroyed as well. Many of the migrants are mainly forest species that spend their winters in the undergrowth or canopy of forests. In Central America, for example, new breeds of coffee have been developed that can tolerate full sun. The traditional "shade-grown" coffee required a canopy of mature trees under which the coffee trees grew to about ten to fifteen feet in height, flowered, and produced their berries. With "sun-tolerant" coffee available, the fincas can dispense with the larger trees, effectively eliminating populations of many of our migrants, as well as many of their own native species.

Some people have proposed solving the problem of habitat loss and degradation by connecting isolated forest patches with corridors of similar habitat —for example, maintaining a narrow belt of forest along a highway or stream to connect two small woodlots. While this may be suitable for species that thrive in edge areas, it may actually be detrimental to interior-nesting species because it increases the number of edge species (both competitors and predators) in both woodlots. Furthermore, the presence of a corridor forest may entice interior-nesting species into an otherwise unsuitable habitat. While corridors serve very useful functions, particularly for mammals, they are not the answer to protection of interior-nesting Neotropical migrants. Maintaining habitat areas of adequate size is crucial, for they must be wide enough to provide interior habitat.

New Jersey's Endangered and Nongame Species Program is working very hard to understand the patterns of habitat use and migratory behavior of a wide range of migrants in Cape May through their Landscape Project. Unlike most previous management efforts, this is a multispecies approach and, we feel, the wave of the future. Its goal is to maximize protection for the rare species by combining this multispecies, habitat-based approach with a new Geographic Information System (GIS) to produce habitat maps, so that local and state planners, as well as landowners, can see what habitats are critical and make wise future land use decisions. Increasingly, in small states like New Jersey, as well as in any highly developed coastal state, land use conflicts are at the root of most of the problems wildlife face. Learning to resolve these conflicts to the benefit of both people and wildlife is one of the most important tasks of the twenty-first century. The hard work and dedication of a wide range of people will result in the protection of even more forests and fields for these magnificent migrants, and the monumental migration that occurs each fall will continue to be one of our state's ecological highlights.

The anticipation of hundreds of migrant songbirds dropping from the sky in the early dawn, anxiously searching for food amid the low shrubs and fields, is delicious. The chips, clicks, and chirps of unseen migrants that waft down from the darkness above are nearly impossible to identify, but the challenge remains. As dawn breaks over the nearby ocean, shallow shafts of light penetrate the forest, providing the first fleeting glimpses of the fall migration at Cape May. Within the first hour of dawn, the number of species falling from the sky is amazing, providing a unique and stunning spectacle.

FOR MORE INFORMATION: Cape May Bird Observatory (609-861-0700) is always a good source of information about the fall migrants at Cape May. You can also call the New Jersey Endangered and Nongame Species Program (609-628-2103) for information about Higbee Beach. Your local Audubon Sanctuary office is also a good bet for local information on migration. The Cape May Rare Bird Alert (609-861-0466) provides additional information.

68. A mass of blood-red Cranberries float to the water surface, the beginning stage in their harvest. (Photo by Mark Robson)

19

Cranberries in the Pine Barrens

A shimmering carpet of vibrant red glistens in the warm autumn sun. A sea of small red spheres, a bit larger than peas, undulates slightly in the light fall breezes, hiding the delicate green Cranberry foliage below the water. This managed bog, surrounded and protected by Pitch Pines and Scrub Oak, is an important part of New Jersey's history and economy.

KEY LOCATIONS: There are many commercial Cranberry operations in the Pine Barrens, but two of the easiest to see are located at Double Trouble State Park (Ocean County), and at Whites Bog in Lebanon State Forest (Burlington County).

DIRECTIONS: For Double Trouble, take the Garden State Parkway south to exit 80 and bear left just off the exit ramp. Turn left onto Double Trouble Road and drive about 4 miles to the park entrance. Or from the Garden State Parkway north, take exit 74, make a left onto Lacey Road, a right onto Dover Road, and another right onto Pinewald-Keswick Road. Go about 3 miles to the Double Trouble park entrance.

For Whites Bog Village, go to the junction of Route 70 and Route 530, and take Route 530 west toward Brown Mills. After 1.2 miles turn right at the entrance to Whites Bog Village.

BEST TIME TO VISIT: While bogs are interesting and peaceful at all times of the year, they are particularly worth visiting in late summer when they are fairly dry and it is possible to see the Cranberry bushes with their lime-green berries, and in late September and early October when the Cranberries are being harvested.

PRIME HABITAT: Bogs in the Pine Barrens.

Small ditches run in parallel lines through the sunken fields, bringing water to the dense growth of deep-green Cranberries, laden with bright vermilion berries. Each stem bears two rows of tiny, oval-shaped, leathery leaves, which curtail water loss when the bog dries down. The plants are barely visible beneath the vibrant red berries. A lever is pulled, damming the outflow, and slowly the water floods the field, rising higher and higher until the Cranberries disappear. As the water level rises, the chilly autumn wind raises tiny whitecaps.

Noisily, a giant green mechanized harvester rumbles out onto the bog and moves slowly back and forth, rolling and shaking the vines to dislodge the buoyant Cranberries that bob to the surface. Back and forth the harvester moves, like a giant reaper, leaving behind a colorful wake. Within hours the entire gray water is covered with a vibrant tapestry of red berries. Workers descend into the bog, walking waist deep in water; using mechanical "beaters," they slowly guide the Cranberries onto giant conveyer belts, which lift them out into large crates waiting in truckbeds. The task is slow, for the berries must not be damaged.

The American Cranberry is native to the Pine Barrens, where it is but one of many different kinds of herbs, vines, and even orchids that grow in the shallow, acid bogs. The leaves are green throughout the year, and their small threadlike vines creep over and among the other plants. The thin woody stems trail along the ground, sending up erect branches that are covered with small, elliptical leaves. The tiny flowers are borne on four- to six-inch stalks, and look like little shooting stars, with four pinkish white petals pointing backward from a yellow pointed cone. The early settlers thought the downward-pointed stamens looked like the bill of a Crane and named them "Crane Berries," from which the more familiar name derives. Cranberries flower from early June to mid-July, and soon after the small, pale green berries appear (fig. 69). The fruit ripens in late September to early October.

Cranberry cultivation began in New Jersey in the 1840s when "Old Peg-Leg" John Webb undertook to grow Cranberries in an old bog he had started to drain. His venture was a success, and he got fifty dollars a barrel for his crop the first year. Ship chandlers in Philadelphia sold them to whalers, who used the berries, rich in Vitamin C, as an antiscorbutic to prevent scurvy. The Cranberry craze was born. This was followed by land speculation as people bought land to invest in Cranberries, and some land brought one hundred dollars an acre, an outrageous sum in those days, although by the late 1800s these wild land prices dropped.

Today about thirty-five families work the Cranberry bogs in New Jersey, but Cranberries are New Jersey's fifth most important agricultural crop. New Jersey produces enough to be the third largest producer in the world, after Massachusetts and Wisconsin. Cranberries are truly one of New Jersey's traditional industries, started soon after European settlement, although the Lenapé Indians had already been eating the berries and used them for medicine and to make a red dye. All of New Jersey's commercial Cranberry bogs are in the Pine Barrens, and most are part of the Ocean-Spray cooperative.

69. In late summer the diminutive shrubs are laden with pale green berries. (Photo by J. Burger)

Commercial Cranberry farming began in New Jersey before the Civil War, and by the late 1800s the Double Trouble Cranberry Company was producing some of the largest harvests in New Jersey. Although Double Trouble is a state park today, the Cranberry bogs are still active and are leased by a private grower. This provides one the unique opportunity to watch Cranberries growing throughout the year, while being in a state park. There is a delightful and informative nature trail that takes you through pine woods and alongside the Cranberry bogs.

In addition to the Cranberry bogs themselves, there is a self-contained Cranberry production village, with a sorting and packing house that dates from the early 1900s. The buildings contain intact Hayden Cranberry sorters, which used a series of perforated conveyer belts to sort the berries. Then the hand-scooped berries were brought by conveyer belts to the second floor, where women seated on both sides manually separated the ripe berries from the green ones and from twigs and leaves. These clean berries were moved to another area for packing and shipping. In addition to the packing house, there are pickers' cottages and the foreman's house. The workers were seasonal, and were housed two families to a cottage. Other buildings include a general store, bunkhouse, schoolhouse, and sawmill.

Double Trouble gets its name from the difficulty early Cranberry growers had in maintaining the dams necessary to provide water for growing and harvesting the Cranberries. One legend holds that the "double trouble" name comes from heavy spring rains that washed out the dam, making it necessary to repair it under difficult conditions. Another story claims that the dam was repeatedly broken by Beavers who gnawed at it, causing leaks that always had to be repaired. One day two breaks were discovered, and the owner shouted, "Here's double trouble!" and the name stuck. Whatever the origin, the name clearly dates to the beginning of Cranberry farming in the region.

Before Double Trouble became a commercial Cranberry bog, it was a thriving sawmill community employing 2,500 people, producing shingles, laths, and timbers for sailing ships, effectively removing all of the native Atlantic White Cedars from low-lying land. Once they removed the cedars, they cleared the native understory of Blueberries and Huckleberries and planted Cranberries.

Although Cranberry farmers frequently started with cleared White Cedar bogs to create commercial bogs, others were formed by draining low-lying wet areas that had rich soil. Nearby streams were diverted to provide the constant supply of water needed during the growing season. Water is essential even during the winter, for bogs are flooded when there is the threat of frost, and some Cranberry bogs are kept flooded throughout the winter. The area to be "bogged" is cleared of all remaining vegetation, leveled, and ditched for irrigation. A main ditch runs through the center of the bog, flanked by side ditches; another main ditch runs around the entire edge of the bog. This extensive irrigation system allows workers to maintain the correct moisture for the root system of the Cranberries. When the beds are ready, small Cranberry cuttings are planted, and it takes three to five years for the vines to produce a profitable crop. With care, a Cranberry bog can produce berries forever (fig. 70).

While Cranberry farming at Double Trouble State Park causes little problems for the Pine Barrens ecosystem, there is an uneasy truce between federal advocates for Pine Barrens protection and Cranberry farmers. Cranberry farmers would like to expand the total holdings, now amounting to about 3,800 acres of fields, into surrounding wetlands and bogs, requiring removal of dense stands of stately American White Cedars. It is a question not only of the loss of Pine Barrens wetlands, but whether continued expansion will damage the sensitive ecology of the Pinelands. The farmers argue that Cranberries are native, it is a traditional farming method, and it is "no till." For most farmers, their Cranberry bogs are nestled amid thousands of acres of forested wetlands and upland Pine Barrens. Because the Cranberries require the purest of water, they believe they are the appropriate stewards for the eighty-four species of birds, fourteen species of mammals, fourteen species of reptiles and

70. Workers guide the Cranberries to conveyers to load into trucks. (Photo by Mark Robson)

amphibians, twelve species of fish, and numerous invertebrates that live there. After the signing of recent international treaties, the farmers are worried about competition from growers as far away as British Columbia and Chile, where environmental regulations are less severe and labor is less costly.

Some conservation organizations within New Jersey support modest expansion of the Cranberry bogs, arguing that it is a traditional crop and that it has far less of an impact than other farming practices or than residential subdivisions. Others, however, say the impact of creating more commercial Cranberry bogs in the Pine Barrens would have a significant detrimental effect. Everyone agrees that the issue is not chemical contamination, but manipulation of the natural environment. While Cranberries are native to these bogs, they do not naturally occur in the same density as in commercial bogs, nor are they the only plant in natural bogs, where there is a high variety of natural plants supporting a much greater biodiversity of aquatic organisms. Cranberry bogs are maintained as a monoculture and do not provide the structural diversity so important for native animals. We found evidence for this when we compared the diversity of birds and butterflies in and around managed bogs with those in abandoned bogs, where the monoculture is not maintained (fig. 71).

71. Cranberry bogs are quiet for most of the year. (Photo by J. Burger)

Further, the creating of additional Cranberry bogs may adversely impact Atlantic White Cedar, a native Pine Barrens tree that was exploited heavily from
the 1700s until the early 1900s for building materials. The wood of White
Cedar is rot resistant and was particularly useful for making shingles, fencing,
siding, and boats. It takes nearly one hundred years for White Cedar to reach
usable size. In a natural bog, the White Cedars shade the understory, creating
a mixed wetlands of small pines, gnarled Sheep Laurel, and wild Blueberry, as
well as Cranberries. The White Cedars normally grow in pure stands, but with
any human disturbance or fire, the White Cedars are quickly replaced by Red
Maples, also called Swamp Maples. For these bogs, expansion of commercial
Cranberries would eliminate a functioning ecosystem. Perhaps part of the so-
lution lies in rejuvenating old abandoned commercial Cranberry bogs, which
would increase the acreage under cultivation but not destroy pristine wetland
forests.

Double Trouble State Park also has a stretch of Cedar Creek where you can
canoe, with canoe/kayak access sites. Canoes can be rented just outside of the
park. Whites Bog Village, in Lebanon State Forest, also has a number of Cran-

berry bogs in different successional stages; in addition to the bogs, it contains a historical Cranberry and Blueberry farming village.

FOR MORE INFORMATION: Contact the Rutgers University Cranberry and Blueberry Center (current number is 609-726-1590; http://aesop.rutgers.edu:80/~bluecran/index.html), or call Double Trouble State Park (732-341-6662) or Whites Bog Preservation Trust (609-893-4646).

72. A short trail leads through deciduous woodlands to a bat-viewing platform. (Photo by J. Burger)

20

Bats at Hibernia Mine

In the gathering twilight, thousands upon thousands of dark, fleeting shapes emerge from the shadowy mine entrance and swirl into the sky. The bats course back and forth, forming courting and mating clusters of dark shapes, some close to the viewing platform, others at the limit of vision.

KEY LOCATIONS: The abandoned Hibernia Mine in the Wildcat Ridge Wildlife Management Area at Hibernia (Morris County).

DIRECTIONS: Take exit 37 off I-80 (6 miles west of I-287); turn north on Route 513 toward Hibernia (just over 4 miles), and then turn right onto Lower Hibernia Road. There is a parking area with a Wildcat Ridge sign and a well-marked trail to a viewing platform about 200 yards through the woods.

BEST TIME TO VISIT: Late summer and fall when the bats engage in evening mating flights before entering the mine for their winter hibernation. The large swarming groups can be observed from late August through mid-October from the viewing platform about 75 yards from the mine entrance.

PRIME HABITAT: Bats prefer to spend the winter hibernating in deep caves or old mine shafts; in summer they disperse throughout rural and suburban areas.

In the early morning, streams of dark shapes silhouetted against the dark sky make their way to the entrance of the Hibernia Mine, one of the few remaining places bats in northern New Jersey can roost without disturbance. Passing through the steel grate, they disappear into the dark interior without slowing down, swoop to a roosting crevice, and settle down to sleep away the daytime, hanging upside down in total darkness. There is some rustling and jostling for spaces, but mostly it is still.

In the shadowy light of late evening, the bats emerge quickly from the cave in an ethereal flight, for they pass close by without making a sound. Yet bats have a supersonic vocabulary and are constantly emitting ultrahigh-pitched sounds, far above the limits of human hearing, by which they detect their tiny insect prey and avoid striking objects such as wires and branches. These inoffensive creatures are associated with witchcraft and sorcery, with superstitions and fears. A bat trapped in a house, flying wildly to and fro, may seem out of control and fearsome, but it is merely frustrated and trying to escape. Outdoors, bats are beautiful and beneficial creatures who consume large quantities of unpleasant insects. In the tropics there are blood-eating Vampire Bats, but humans are not their favorite blood source. In New Jersey, a very small percentage of bats carry the rabies virus, and bats are therefore best left alone. The Chinese have the right idea; bats are a symbol of health, wealth, love, and a venerable old age.

Most of our bats are quite small, with mouse-sized bodies and Cardinal-sized wings, but there are tropical fruit-eating bats, called Flying Foxes, which are nearly eagle-sized. These huge creatures maintain a fruit diet, rendering their flesh tasty; in places like Indonesia, they are netted for food.

Perhaps we find bats enchanting because they are the only mammals that can truly fly, conquering a space we cannot traverse. They have greatly elongated forelimbs and "fingers" that support a thin membrane which forms their wings. Their angular shape, small head and big ears, and claw at the bend of their wings lends them an unfamiliar shape as they wing through the air.

Their tiny beadlike eyes peer into the darkness as they take flight out of their cave or mine at dusk, but they primarily navigate by an echolocation sonar system. The bats are very maneuverable as they fly in search of insects, and some stretch their tail membrane into a basket to catch unsuspecting prey.

Bats are an old and successful group of animals that evolved perhaps one hundred million years ago, probably from a tree-dwelling, insect-eating ancestor. They fly silently, and most people are unaware of their nightly forays in search of food. One quarter of all mammals are bats, and there are about one thousand species worldwide. Over forty species of bats live in the United States, and nine of them are regular residents in New Jersey. These include the year-round residents: Little Brown Bat, Big Brown Bat, Small-footed Myotis, Northern Long-eared Bat, and Eastern Pipistrelle Bat, as well as the federally endangered Indiana Bat. Three species, the Silver-haired, Hoary, and Red Bats, breed in New Jersey, but migrate south in the fall. Most of our bats are quite small. Our commonest species, the Little Brown Bat, weighs barely more than a nickel. Some of our bats live in trees during the summer (Red Bat, Hoary Bat, Pipistrelle, Silver-haired Bat), while the others live in caves, abandoned mines, or buildings.

Bats once had it easier because they could live in old caves and cavities in trees that were largely ignored by American Indians. With the arrival of the Europeans, bats started to use old buildings and mine tunnels. Even before the American Revolution, Morris County attracted a landed gentry class that operated iron mines in the mountains. More than four hundred iron mines were opened in northern New Jersey, but the mine shafts were heavily disturbed during mining operations. When Washington moved north into Morris County during the Revolution, there were between eighty and one hundred iron works. Iron from the Hibernia Mine was used for munitions, as well as shovels, axes, and other supplies. The Hibernia Mine was so valuable that mine employees were exempted from military service. Washington spent his first winter in Morristown at Jacob Arnold's Tavern and continued to acquire munitions from the Hibernia Mine.

Morris County had so many mines that by 1880 it was third in the nation in tons of iron produced. Two years later, however, the nation discovered that iron could be picked from the surface near Lake Superior, and mining moved west. The iron mines in Morris County tried to compete by digging deeper and deeper, but their fate was sealed. After going to a depth of 2,600 feet in search of iron, the Hibernia Mine closed in 1913, just seven years after a flood in one of the shafts drowned thirteen miners. Over the years, as supporting timbers decayed, the open shafts collapsed and vegetation gradually obscured the entrance.

The bats continued to use natural caves until the early 1900s, when they began to occupy the abandoned iron mines in northern New Jersey. These abandoned mines proved suitable for bats, and they quickly moved in and found the Hibernia and other mines particularly alluring. Mines are attractive for bats because they are unattractive to most people. They are dark, deserted, damp, and cold—perfect conditions for bats to hibernate. The air temperature in mines remains relatively constant all year in New Jersey, around 35 to 45 degrees Fahrenheit, and the different species seek different temperatures within the old mines. This is true everywhere, for over half of the bats found in the United States now hibernate in old mines.

As human disturbance in natural caves increased because of an interest in spelunking, bats were vulnerable to disturbance. They came to depend on abandoned mines as critical habitat for hibernating during the winter. However, concern for human safety has intervened. Mines can be lethal for people because of deadly gases, rotting timbers, falling structures, and gaping holes that may drop hundreds of feet. With increasing concern for wandering hikers and playing children, mine after mine was sealed up. Since the bats hibernate quietly over the winter, many mines were boarded up with thousands of bats still inside, their fate sealed by thoughtless and unknowing people. With no exit, they perished the next spring.

In the late 1980s, the owners of the Hibernia Mine started to secure the entrance of their mine with concrete to prevent people from entering. However, Joann Frier-Murza, Mike Valent, and others from the New Jersey Endangered and Nongame Species Program learned of the closure in time to save the bats that were sealed in the mine. Now people are prevented from entering the mine by an impenetrable steel grate, but small openings still remain so the bats can use the mine. A bat-friendly gate, designed by Roy Powers and constructed by

Powers, the U.S. Fish and Wildlife Service, and the Endangered and Nongame Species Program, now covers the opening and protects bats from human disturbance. In the past these disturbances were not intentional; people just wanted to explore the cave.

Now the Hibernia Mine is entered in late winter for periodic censuses, when all the bats are counted. Our participation in the censusing was one of our most thrilling adventures, although the cave is damp, cool, cramped, and incredibly dark. Under the light of headlamps, we painstakingly counted every bat (fig. 73).

The hibernating group of Little Brown Bats in the Hibernia Mine, which can total 25,000 or more, is one of the largest in the northeastern United States, and their nightly emergence is a spectacle well worth visiting in both the spring and fall, although the spring is far less predictable and there are fewer bats at any one time. There are a few tiny Eastern Pipistrelle Bats, as well as some Big Brown Bats and Northern Long-eared Bats among the Little Brown Bats. Indiana Bats are the truly exciting ones, however, for they are federally endangered, and between twenty and thirty-five have been counted in the Hibernia Mine, hibernating close together, more than two hundred yards from the entrance.

The mine itself once had more than fifteen levels that went deeper and deeper into the earth, but most have collapsed, and now only the top level is passable. The main chamber, not open to the public, is about six to eight feet

73. Mike Gochfeld counting a group of Little Brown Bats in the Hibernia Mine. (Photo by J. Burger)

high, and about eight feet wide. It extends more than two thousand feet into the granite rock. Mostly the bats crowd into small jagged hollows and side chambers drilled into the mine-shaft wall, probably to support beams. They also hang upside down in little drill holes left by the dynamite used to blast open the mine. These holes are about two to three inches in diameter and extend for a couple of feet. Here the bats throng together, each touching another. They pack into these small crevices in the dozens or even the hundreds. A square foot can have over one hundred bats, each clinging to the surface, crowded together for their long sleep. Others hang singly or in small groups, their hind claws clutching tiny irregularities in the rock wall. On some bats, a fine, whitish condensation of moisture covers their fur (fig. 74). This does not harm them.

In the fall, the bats concentrate near their hibernation caves in the thousands, engaged in an ancient mating ritual. After mating, the female stores the sperm but delays fertilization until spring. When the swirling mass of mating bats goes into the cave for the last time in the fall, they settle down to hibernate. They do not eat during this time, and they are mostly immobile. A stretch of a wing, an occasional yawn, or a squabble among close neighbors is the only motion. When spring arrives, delayed fertilization occurs, and the young develop rather rapidly, with a gestation period of thirty to sixty days. Finally, the hibernating bats wake up for the spring, and eventually most leave the caves and mines for the summer to spread out over the surrounding countryside, where they roost in smaller groups in trees or buildings during the day.

Females usually congregate in maternity colonies, where the disturbance is low and where they are protected from inclement weather. They form these small colonies in protected trees or buildings, where it is warm. The single young (rarely twins) are born in May or June, weighing nearly a quarter of the female's weight at birth. They grow relatively rapidly; within six weeks of birth the young can fly and begin to venture out on their own. By early summer, bats are more in evidence because the young are learning to fly, and they tumble into odd and unexpected places. The young sometimes flop to the ground, then have difficulty taking off. This is when humans are likely to encounter them. Often they are first encountered by house cats that proudly present the dead or injured bat to their owners. Bats should be left alone to fly away or to climb a tree where it is easier for them to take wing, or they should be moved by a wildlife nuisance expert or someone who has been immunized against rabies.

During the day the bats roost, hanging upside down, in social groups of up to three hundred bats in trees, under bridges, in attics, behind shutters, or in abandoned buildings. Formerly they roosted in belfries of old churches, sharing them with Barn Owls, but nowadays most of these have been boarded up. Some conservationists and state officials have designed bridges to provide sheltered maternity colonies for bats.

74. Little Brown Bats cling to slight irregularities in the rocks, in groups of tens to hundreds (*top*). Moisture clings to the stomachs of some bats, making their pale undersurfaces gleam in the flashlight (*bottom*). (Photos by J. Burger)

All of our bats forage on small, flying insects, including mosquitoes, midges, beetles, and bugs. For a small creature, they have a voracious appetite. Each night they can consume 50 to 100 percent of their body weight—a feat we would be hard pressed to accomplish. A Little Brown Bat regularly eats up to six hundred mosquitoes an hour, and can eat up to three thousand small insects in this time period. They serve an important role in controlling insects, including agricultural pests. They use sonar to echolocate their prey, and can zero in quickly on flying insects that reflect the sonar signal back to the bat. While bats eat a variety of insects, an assortment of predators eat them, capturing them either at their daytime roosts or in their evening flights. These include cats, Opossums, Skunks, Barn Owls, Great Horned Owls, Kestrels, Merlins, and Long-eared Owls. When Black Rat Snakes and Black Racers come across them in trees or buildings they avidly eat them.

Bats are sometimes found on the ground or in houses, unable to fly. These should never be handled, as they may be rabid. Rabies is a rare but fatal disease in humans. On average there are only two cases of human rabies in the United States each year. Only a small percentage (less than 2 percent in New Jersey) of bats carry rabies, but recently a death from bat-associated rabies occurred in New Jersey (the first since 1971). Therefore, even though the likelihood of encountering a rabid bat is small, the current recommendation from the Centers for Disease Control is to board up openings under eaves and in attics to discourage bats from entering houses. If one is prudent and avoids grounded or flightless bats, and stays out of the caves where they roost, there is no risk of getting infected. If bats need to be moved from a home, this should be done preferably by a professional nuisance-wildlife control person who has been immunized against rabies. However, bats have declined seriously in New Jersey, and it is particularly important to protect these inoffensive and useful animals by providing suitable habitat; in return, the bats will control unpleasant insects.

The spectacle of swirling bats engaged in a mating ritual in the magnificent scenery of Morris County is breathtaking. The bats are longtime residents of the caves and mines of New Jersey, and the soft swishing of wings as thousands upon thousands of them enter the Hibernia Mine for the winter is an awesome sight—one well worth experiencing.

Bat watching is becoming increasingly popular, although it has a long ways to go to approach either butterfly or bird watching. Nonetheless, it can be fascinating, particularly where large concentrations gather in the hour before or after sunset at their summer roosts. Before dawn they rush rapidly back to their roosts in caves or mines, and in the evening they spiral out again into the darkening sky.

The walk to the bat viewing platform at Hibernia takes about ten minutes over a flat trail that goes through a small woods and open field (fig. 75). The platform provides an excellent view of the swirling bats. Several other trails in

75. View from the Hibernia Mine entrance, showing the viewing platform. (Photo by J. Burger)

the Wildcat Ridge Wildlife Management Area lead to ridges with spectacular views of the forests and valleys of the highlands, particularly in the fall. Although the bats are only prominent in the spring and fall, the entire region is lovely at all times of the year, particularly from the Overlook Trail. Several of the overlooks along this trail provide good places to watch for migrating hawks in the spring and fall. On a clear day the New York City skyline is visible, and the spectacular views of the highland forests are encouraging because they suggest wilderness. These forests are providing some of the only remaining large, undisturbed tracts so necessary for nesting Neotropical migrants that require the tranquility of interior regions of forests to nest (see chapter 18).

Other trails lead past ponds created by Beavers, which build dams that create marshes and lakes for a wide variety of animals. While Beavers were trapped extensively throughout the Northeast, including New Jersey, in the last two centuries, their comeback in the past twenty-five years has provided habitat for a wide range of species. They have been credited with providing nesting and foraging habitat for Great Blue Herons, whose populations were very low following their exploitation for the millinery industry in the 1800s. It was the fashion to use plumes from herons and egrets to adorn fashionable ladies' hats, and often the birds were killed for only a few plumes.

The days of such carnage are over for migratory birds, but not so for bats. Although they are protected in most states, and some, such as the Indiana Bat, are federally endangered, they still are harassed and killed by unthinking and thoughtless people. With habitat decreasing, and more and more mines and caves being rendered inaccessible, they are having difficulties finding suitable hibernating sites for the winter. That makes the Hibernia Mine particularly important. With care, the wonderful and spectacular mass of thousands upon thousands of Little Brown Bats circling and fluttering in a swirling mass of courtship on a warm fall evening will continue far into the future.

FOR MORE INFORMATION: Call 908-735-8975 for information on guided tours to observe the bats. For information on rabies, call the New Jersey Department of Health (609-588-3121), or call your township or county health department.

Winter

76. From a high vantage point, it is possible to gaze over the Pine Plains, seeing the dense and low growth form. (Photo by J. Burger)

21

Dwarf Pine Plains

The tall Pitch Pines seem endless, broken only by sand roads and an occasional small stream that slowly meanders through the pines. Abruptly the tall trees give way to short, twisted pines that are barely ten feet tall, many are only head high. Here the dwarf pines are so thick you cannot walk through, although you can peer over them and see for a mile or more.

KEY LOCATIONS: There is only one Dwarf Pine Plains (also called Pygmy Pine Plains) in New Jersey, and there is another on eastern Long Island near Riverhead.

DIRECTIONS: From the north take Garden State Parkway to exit 67. Go west on Route 554 for 5 miles to the junction with Route 72. Continue west on Route 72 across Route 539. The Pine Plains begin about a mile west of 539. From the south, take exit 63 to Route 72 west and continue as above. Another section of the Pine Plains is accessible around milepost 8 on Route 539, 2 miles south of Warren Grove.

BEST TIME TO VISIT: Any time of year, but winter is lovely because it is so stark.

PRIME HABITAT: Dwarf Pine Plains is the only place in New Jersey to see these trees.

On a cold December day, with the snow falling gently, the Pine Barrens seem particularly desolate. There is little motion among the scrubby pines and oaks, no animals scurry over the pine needles, and no birds sing from the boughs lightly dusted with white. The bird diversity in the Barrens is low even during the breeding season, and the few animals that are present are seldom visible. The openings in the pines seem particularly empty, because there are no tracks in the fresh snow.

There is no hint of the Pine Snakes that are hibernating six feet below the sand surface in the complicated underground burrow systems they have constructed, nor of the Black Racers hibernating with them. There is no hint of the Red Squirrels that have followed the snakes into some of the hibernacula, dragging in shredded pine cones and seeds for the long winter. The snakes are far below the squirrels, at depths of five and six feet. The squirrels also use old abandoned skunk or fox dens, waiting out the cold and windy days. When the weather turns warm and sunny, they venture forth for a few hours, but then return to the warmth of the underground burrow.

Abruptly the tall pines give way to dwarf pines, most less than ten feet tall. The whole aspect changes; there are far fewer Scrub Oaks, and the pines are much denser and nearly impassable, although White-tailed Deer and other animals make trails through them. The Deer are safe here, for few hunters venture far within. The going is too difficult, the Deer are too few, and those they see are much smaller than Deer in north Jersey.

Sand roads lead off the paved road, rising slowly, allowing an even greater view of the surrounding dwarf forest that lies along the Burlington–Ocean County line near Warren Grove. Here it is possible to stand on the higher ridges and look for a mile over the short scraggly pines growing so close together that they are nearly impenetrable, their branches intertwined.

The transition of Pitch Pine uplands to Dwarf Pine Plains is abrupt, although the two dominant tree species are still Pitch Pine and Blackjack Oak. Our New Jersey Dwarf Pine Plains is quite unique, as there are only three truly Dwarf Pine Plains in the United States, where the trees are less than ten feet tall. These occur in the Long Island Barrens, in the New Jersey Pine Barrens, and in the Shawangunk Mountains in Pennsylvania. In all three cases, the dwarf pines grow only on the driest, sandiest, most nutrient-poor soil. In the heart of the Dwarf Plains, the Pitch Pines are not more than six feet tall, and some are half that (fig. 77). Even the oaks are short, and bent, and quite twisted. There are some shrubs, such as Black Huckleberry, Low-bush Blueberry, Broom Crowberry, Bearberry, Teaberry, and Hudsonia, but they are hardly visible in the dense tangle of the low canopy. This is the only place in New Jersey that Crowberry grows—it is an Ice Age relict of a plant more characteristic of Canadian forests.

Centuries of exposure to the truly barren, nutrient-poor, harsh conditions has resulted in a strain of Pitch Pine that is uniquely adapted to these environmental conditions. In other pine barrens farther south, there are forests that are relatively short, but not this short. The pines in the Scrub Pine habitat of Florida are usually twenty to thirty feet tall. Nothing really compares to the three dwarf pine forests in the Northeast. The three were connected during their development following the retreat of the last glaciers, but the intervening forests disappeared.

Ecologists love to argue over why the pines are so short and scraggly in the Dwarf Forest. The trees are as stunted as those in the harshest subarctic environments, such as just below the timberline of high mountains. If you look closely, the trunks of many of the pines are quite twisted, and even the branches come off at odd angles, a familiar growth form seen also just below the tree line. One explanation many people favor is that the short trees are

77. J. Burger standing at the edge of the Dwarf Pine Plains along Route 72.
(Photo by Paula Williams)

caused by arid conditions, infertile soils, exposure to strong winds, and repeated fires which occur more often here than in other Pine Barrens habitats,
including those that are relatively nearby. On average, the Dwarf Forest burns
every five to twenty years.

Recently, people have suggested that the trees here are genetically a dwarf
form, well adapted to the environmental conditions they face, and they do not
grow tall when transplanted to another habitat. Even when protected from
fire, and grown on soil with more nutrients, the dwarf pine form of the Pitch
Pine does not grow tall: it simply grows outward and becomes even more
scraggly. The presence of a genetic strain of Pitch Pine on the Pine Plains of
the New Jersey Pine Barrens, and in the Pine Barrens of Long Island, suggests
a long evolutionary history of adaptation to harsh environmental conditions.

The Pitch Pines in the Dwarf Forest are genetically adapted to the soil conditions. They are not short because they are young; some of the three-foot-
tall Pines in the Dwarf Pine Plains are thirty years old, while thirty-year-old
Pitch Pines in the upland barrens are much taller. The Pitch Pines here are able
to produce seeds at a very young age and have a high degree of cone serotony
(sealed by pitch, and opening only with fire), making them fire adapted. Their
ability to resprout from underground roots, trunks, and branches also makes
them adapted to a fire regime. It would be interesting to determine if those in
the two dwarf forests (New Jersey and Long Island) are part of the same genetic
continuum, but this mystery awaits further study.

78. Fire is a natural part of Pine Barren ecology. Sometimes the smoke is so dense that the sun is nearly blocked out. (Photo by J. Burger)

Fire is the common theme that runs through the ecology of the New Jersey Pine Barrens, as well as barrens everywhere (fig. 78). The vegetation has been shaped by fire. This is true of the entire Pine Barrens, including the Dwarf Forest. Before human settlement, lightning strikes caused widespread fires. When American Indians occupied the region, they set the pines afire to open up the pines, increasing the White-tailed Deer populations and providing open meadows where they could wait to ambush the Deer. Later, the early European settlers set fire to some of the pines while making charcoal. Still later, when the charcoal and glass industries were only a faint memory, fires were set by locomotives; sparks flew from the trains, burning large areas beside the tracks.

Dry pine needles are highly flammable and they burn readily, providing tinder for widely spreading fires. The fires burn off the needles (called "duff") on the forest floor, and burn up the trees, which are rich in flammable resins. After a fire, the pinelands look desolate and the Pitch Pine trunks are blackened. All the needles, many of the branches, and all the underbrush is gone. In particularly hot fires, the soil is bare, the trunks severely burned.

Because the pines and oaks are fire adapted, regeneration is rapid. When fires rip through the Dwarf Forest, the trees quickly rejuvenate: new trees grow from underground roots, and new branches sprout from the blackened trunks (fig. 79). A few months after a fire, small green tufts of needles grow from the base of Pitch Pine branches, and within a couple of years it is difficult to imagine the devastation that the fires had caused. Herbs and shrubs also grow from underground roots and runners. When fires occur frequently, there is little chance for the needle layer to accumulate, and the fires are not overly hot. The underground stems and roots are not damaged by these fires, and plant life can regenerate quickly.

However, when fire has been suppressed for many years, there is time for a thick layer of dried needles and leaves to accumulate. The next fire has plenty of fuel and burns so hot that it destroys much of the underground system that gives rise to fresh growth. These hot fires can whip through the pines, destroying the trees and root systems, leaving total devastation, with little chance of rapid recovery. As hard as it is for us to face, fire is a natural part of the ecosystem. The Dwarf Pines have evolved with fires, and suppressing them leads ultimately to more total devastation when a fire finally does occur, ignited by a careless person or a lightning storm.

The Dwarf Pines require more frequent fires to maintain them, on the order of a fire every five to twenty years, while the other barrens habitats do well with less frequent fires. The trees here are the same species that occur throughout the Pine Barrens, but they are more resistant to fire, as if they have evolved just for these conditions. The frequent fires, along with very old root systems, result in scraggly trees that in some places are only three or four feet high. When the fires have passed and the ground is cool, these species sprout from the root crown just below the soil, and the forest is soon green again.

Some pines require fires for their seeds to germinate because the cones do not open completely without intense heat. More importantly, a thick and dense layer of needles and oak leaves prevent the pine seeds from reaching moist soil where they can germinate. By contrast, the heavier acorns of the oak trees can easily penetrate the thick layer of leaves and needles, and they have no trouble germinating and growing under a dense canopy.

79. Following a fire, new branches sprout from the blackened trunks, shown here in pines along the Garden State Parkway. (Photo by J. Burger)

Fires are essential to the ecology of the Pine Barrens for another reason: they provide open places for other species, both plants and animals. Woodpeckers move in, taking advantage of some of the dead trees. Blueberries sprout, along with other short shrubs, providing browse for White-tailed Deer. Pine Snakes in New Jersey are at the northern limit of their range; they require open areas to dig their nests, for without complete sun penetration to the ground, their eggs will not hatch.

With the snow on the ground, it is hard to imagine that this bleak habitat with stunted pines hosts some birds. As the days warm in April and May, the dull green pine needles take on a more vibrant look, the brown leaves of the oaks will soon be pushed out by new green leaves, and the birds begin to arrive. The common species are Prairie Warblers, Field Sparrows, Brown Thrashers, and Towhees. Northern Harriers, also called Marsh Hawks, nest on the ground among the dwarf pines. This habitat has few amphibians and reptiles, although some Pine Snakes hunt below the pine thickets, searching for small mammals. Red Squirrels emerge, running from tree to tree, fighting over territories and searching for good dens. Red Fox, Skunks, and Opossums abandon their winter dens and wander the forests, searching for small mammals, bird eggs, and the fruits and berries that are their mainstay.

The Dwarf Pine Forest is worth visiting at any time of year. Indeed, we often select our route to include passage through these intriguing barrens on our way to other sites in southern New Jersey. It is not far from the Garden State Parkway, and is well worth the detour.

FOR MORE INFORMATION: There is no particular person or agency to call about the Dwarf Pine Plains. It is always there, and always open.

80. A flock of over a thousand Snow Geese taking flight at Brigantine (Edwin B. Forsythe National Wildlife Refuge). (Photo by Chris Williams)

22

Migrant Snow Geese at Brigantine

The crisp autumn winds whip across the marsh, bending the Cord Grass and rattling the Phragmites. Wisps of white foam blow across the waves. The salt marsh still bears shades of green as if it is not ready to face the cold winter ahead. Large flocks with hundreds upon hundreds of Snow Geese move slowly across the marsh, forming a lacy pattern against the gray sky. Their endless honking notes reach us faintly at first, then build to a crescendo as the flocks wheel out of the sky, touching down on the marsh in front of us. The large white birds, many still in family groups of three, land, anxious to eat after their long journey southward.

KEY LOCATIONS: The Brigantine Division of the Edwin B. Forsythe National Wildlife Refuge (Atlantic County). Also the Maurice River in Cumberland County. Large flocks of Snow Geese also winter in agricultural fields of southern New Jersey, but their location is not predictable.

DIRECTIONS: For Brigantine, take the Garden State Parkway to exit 48 to Route 9 south; go 6 miles and turn east onto Great Creek Road, and follow signs to the refuge entrance (0.6 mile).

BEST TIME TO VISIT: While Brigantine is always a pleasure to visit, the Snow Geese are on the marshes from November until the bays and impoundments freeze over. If it is a mild winter, the geese remain until April.

PRIME HABITAT: The geese alternate between the marshes where they forage and the open water of the impoundments where they rest.

A thousand snowy white shapes, slightly smaller than barnyard geese, walk slowly across the marsh. Their heads are bent downward as they pause to pluck the tender roots of the marsh grasses, a dark green tinged with pale browns and yellows. They pull and probe, nibbling on the roots, until they have cleared bare spots, and then they move on. They walk slowly, as if in a ballet choreographed by an unknown leader. Without looking up, they avoid one another, grazing quietly or communicating by loud cackling to announce their presence. Their "hounks" and "whhounks" echo across the marsh.

The arrival of the Snow Geese at Brigantine is one of the most exciting events of our year. First dozens and then hundreds of magnificent white geese dot the marsh, remaining in flocks. Within a few days the flock numbers in the thousands. As long as the water at Brigantine stays open, they will remain. When cold weather moves in and the bays and estuaries freeze, they migrate en masse, only as far south as required to keep ahead of the freeze-up. Maybe they find open water in Delaware, maybe in Virginia, maybe in North Carolina.

Like fall migrant shorebirds, the Snow Geese have traveled from their Arctic breeding grounds in extended long-distance flights without stopping. The geese fly high, often in large flocks, their calls barely audible. Unlike the shorebirds, however, when they reach New Jersey they are on their wintering grounds, or very near them. Only the ice and snow force them farther south. When they first arrive, however, New Jersey is hospitable for there are endless marshes for foraging, and acre upon acre of Cord Grass roots. Sometimes they even feed in farm fields in Cumberland County.

There are so many snowy shapes it is difficult to watch any one, and our eyes travel over and over the large flock, listening to the cackling and soft coos (fig. 81). As with an Escher puzzle, the massive flock gradually dissolves into family groups of three or more, now so very obvious. Each group contains a male and female, both the same size, and one or more young, their plumage shaded with gray. The young are as large as their parents and remain close to them so they can learn where to forage and derive some protection. Like most

81. A flock of Snow Geese at Brigantine, with Atlantic City in the background. (Photo by J. Burger)

geese, and unlike most other ducks, Snow Geese retain their mate for several years, and the family migrates together. The young follow the routes of their parents many years after the parents are dead. They are faithful to these traditional routes, and even after some ponds and marshes are gone, flocks stop at the old familiar places before seeking habitat elsewhere.

Looking closely, it is possible to see the geese as individuals. They are a handsome white goose, with black primaries or wing feathers. Standing, there is only a spot of black at the tip of their wings that mars their otherwise snowy plumage. Their bill and feet are a delicate pink, although most are muddied after the geese have been rummaging through the marsh mud. Their necks are longer than those of ducks, but far shorter than those of swans.

There are two subspecies of Snow Geese, the greater and the lesser, which are only slightly different in size. In New Jersey we have mostly the greater, which can weigh up to ten pounds. But here and there among the flock there is a decidedly smaller goose, a full snowy white adult, belonging to the lesser subspecies. We have to be careful, however, because in some winters a Ross's Goose has accompanied the Snow Geese from their Arctic breeding grounds. The Ross's Goose is very similar to the Snow Goose, but its beak is shorter, more slender, and pure pink, while the Snow Geese have a black line across the beak.

Far across the marsh, in the middle of the flock, a dark goose with a white head feeds with its family. It has slight tinges of white on a very few feathers, but overall it has a bluish-gray tinge, leading to its common name of Blue Goose. For many years, Blue Geese and Snow Geese were considered separate species, but the work of Canadian geneticist Fred Cooke demonstrated that they interbreed freely at their nesting colonies in northern Canada, and that there are actually two color forms of the same species. They are now called the white and blue morphs of Snow Geese. In New Jersey, the white form is much more common than the blue, but on wintering grounds in Louisiana the blue form is quite common.

The frenetic feeding of the first arrivals gives way to more leisurely foraging within a few days, as the Snow Geese settle into a daily routine that includes foraging on the exposed marshes at low tides and moving out to higher marshes and impoundments during high tides (fig. 82). Geese are more terrestrial than ducks and normally feed on marshes, where heavy grazing can create massive patches of bare mud. After the geese have eaten all the roots, no new Cord Grass may grow for years, leaving a bare patch of marsh mud.

As the geese move over the marsh, they eat the roots and rhizomes to a depth of ten inches. Even in areas where they do not completely eat out the roots, they decrease the productivity of the marsh grass root systems. In the spring, following grazing, the marsh is not quite as lush, not quite as luxuriant as the ungrazed areas. The balance between Snow Geese feeding and marsh productivity is delicate, and overgrazing can destroy a marsh as easily as cows can

82. A lone Snow Goose foraging intently. (Photo by J. Burger)

overgraze a pasture. However, the geese are here for only a few months, and they have vast marshlands they can visit. The relatively low harm they cause, however, is dependent upon having large expanses of marshes, allowing them to move about, thus reducing the damage to any one marsh in a given year.

While the geese can be detrimental to the marsh grasses, the marsh grasses can also harm the geese, for mercury and other contaminants, such as DDT, concentrate in the roots of Cord Grass. Mercury from industrial sources or sludge are carried in the air from power plants hundreds of miles away, and become deposits on marshes. Bacteria convert the mercury into methylmercury, which is readily taken up by the salt marsh grasses, and accumulates over time. Since the geese primarily eat the roots, they obtain mercury and bioaccumulate it in their tissues.

Mercury, and other contaminants, of course, affect a wide range of organisms, particularly those that are high on the food chain. One notable example of the dire consequences of contaminants is the Peregrine Falcon, which nearly disappeared from the United States in the 1960s due to DDT obtained from its prey. Populations plummeted because DDT affected eggshell thickness, and when the birds incubated, they broke their eggs; no young were raised for many years. By the 1960s all Peregrine Falcons east of the Rockies and south of the Arctic were wiped out—an area known to have supported at least four hundred pairs. Worldwide populations were severely threatened.

The decline of the Peregrine, and fish-eating birds such as Brown Pelicans and Bald Eagles, led to the ban on the use of DDT in Canada and the United

States in the early 1970s. The recovery of the Peregrine Falcon is a conservation triumph, led by Tom Cade of Cornell University, who founded the Peregrine Fund. By 1974 the Peregrine Fund was releasing the first captive-bred Peregrines on wooden towers on New Jersey salt marshes, a habitat deemed suitable though never used historically by the falcons.

The Peregrines took to the salt marshes. There were wide open spaces for hunting and an abundant supply of small birds for prey. The young Peregrines were placed in boxes on tall wooden towers and were provided with food in such a way that they could not see their providers. Instead, their boxes looked out across the wide expanses of marshes, and they learned that this was "their" habitat. After the young birds were able to fly, they were still provided food at the towers to supplement their diet during the period when they were still awkward at hunting. When the birds matured and perfected their hunting skills, the food supplementation was stopped, but the birds still considered the towers home. This is a procedure known as *hacking*. The success of this New Jersey program led to the use of hacking towers elsewhere in the East, and in 1979, the first introduced Peregrine Falcon returned to try to nest in one of New Jersey's salt marsh hacking towers. Although the initial breeding attempt failed, the birds bred successfully in subsequent years.

The Peregrine release program was a massive effort, and by 1981, 353 young falcons had been released at thirty-six locations in eleven eastern states. The program exceeded the most optimistic expectations. By 1985 forty pairs of Peregrines were observed, and they produced forty-seven young. By 1994, there were one thousand breeding pairs in thirty-five states, the result of the 4,700 releases; 104 pairs were nesting in the east. Today, about fifteen pairs are nesting in New Jersey, some in urban areas, some under bridges, and some in the salt marshes, including two pairs on towers at Brigantine itself. Their productivity in New Jersey is high: they raise well over one chick per nest. But there is still cause for concern. DDT and organochlorines are present in eggs that fail to hatch, and eggshell thinning hovers at around 16 percent, close to the point where breakage can be fatal.

While the Snow Geese feed placidly on the marsh at Brigantine, a male Peregrine sits on the nest platform, surveying his surroundings. It is thrilling to see a bird that was so close to extinction, peering around at the geese below, looking for smaller avian prey lurking in the bushes or foraging along the salt marsh creeks. Even the chilling wind that blows across the marsh is insufficient to dampen the incredible feeling inherent in the survival of this magnificent bird of prey.

Almost without warning, the Peregrine takes wing, flies swiftly across the marsh and makes a low pass, scaring up a small flock of feeding Dowitchers that has lingered past their normal migration time. The Dowitchers take wing in a dense flock, uttering "keek" alarm calls and flying low over the marsh, but not low enough to dissuade the Peregrine, which, turning over, singles out a

83. Snow Geese form endless lines when resting on the water at Brigantine. (Photo by Chris Williams)

straggler and swiftly grabs it in its talons. Returning to its perch, it begins to tear apart the Dowitcher, and the rest of the flock circles away to land on a distant mudflat where they resume feeding by probing in the mud. They are intent on fattening up for their southward journey.

The Snow Geese hardly stopped to peer into the sky at the passing falcon, a dark bullet that flew above their heads, and they quickly return to feeding. They are far too large to feel threatened by a Peregrine Falcon in their midst. Others, swimming leisurely in the water, barely pause to look up (fig. 83).

As winter approaches, the Snow Geese continue their daily rhythm. Influenced by the tides, they move from marsh to impoundment and back again. As the winds get colder and the breezes stiffen, they hunker down closer to the marsh, but still they feed. Ice begins to form on the edges of creeks and impoundments. Finally, snow comes and begins to cover the marsh in a blanket that is still thin enough for them to probe the muds for roots and rhizomes. With the shortening of daylight, they spend more and more of the day foraging, until they may be spending 90 percent of the daylight feeding. Geese are not very efficient at digesting plant material, and they digest only about 40 percent of the vegetative matter they consume. The rest passes out as feces, which fertilize the marsh. Since efficiency is low, they must forage for more and more time. It is a race against the clock, and it is important to have a wide range of available marshes so they can continue feeding for most of the day.

Finally the day comes when the marsh is covered with a blanket of snow that is too deep for them to penetrate, the water is covered with ice, and it is time to move south. Large flights of hundreds of Snow Geese take wing, careen into the air and disappear against the gray sky, their gabbling voices barely audible. But they will return in the spring on their northward journey, when the young are no longer with their parents but are searching for their own mates. In the spring, both immatures and parents will be interested in building up fat reserves for their long flight to the Arctic, where they face yet more snow and ice. The Arctic summers can be delayed, and if they are too late, the Snow Geese will not even begin to breed but will wander over the Arctic tundra in search of food and shelter. Usually, however, the snow melts, food is available, and they begin to breed in massive colonies. The cycle will begin anew.

FOR MORE INFORMATION: Call the U.S. Fish and Wildlife Service at the Brigantine Division of Edwin B. Forsythe National Wildlife Refuge (609-652-1665); http://bluegoose.arw.r9.fws.gov/.

84. Wintering gulls resting on a mud bar at Port Liberté, with New York City and the World Trade Center in the background. (Photo by J. Burger)

23

Wintering Gulls in Coastal New Jersey

A thousand gulls rise suddenly into the air, disturbed by a Red Fox trotting through the Phragmites beside the cove. The fox stops to watch as the loudly calling gulls circle again to land out on the thin ice breaking up just off the shoreline. They remain alert, heads upright, wings slightly out, ready to take flight. Disappointed, the fox turns and trots away into the vegetation.

KEY LOCATIONS: There are so many places to find large concentrations of gulls in New Jersey in winter that we take them for granted. Liberty State Park (Hudson County) is a good place. But there are also concentrations of gulls on the Raritan River sandbars in downtown New Brunswick (Middlesex County), near the mouth of the Shark and Manasquan Rivers along the Jersey shore (Monmouth County), and at the Florence landfill (South Trenton in Burlington County) on the Delaware River, visible from the boat ramp south of Bordentown in south Jersey. Gulls also concentrate on the inland lakes from Long Branch to Bayhead; since these lakes are only a block or two from the ocean, they seldom freeze.

DIRECTIONS: For Liberty State Park, take the New Jersey Turnpike Extension at exit 14, going east for 5 miles to exit 14B. Bear left after the toll booth, follow signs to Bayview Avenue; it is on Morris Pesin Drive in Jersey City. There are several parking lots from which you can view the bay.

For the Raritan River site in New Brunswick, take the turnpike to exit 9; follow Route 18 north. The highway runs along the river, and at low tide over two thousand gulls are likely to concentrate on the sandbar on the east or west of Route 27. Follow Route 18 over the John Lynch Bridge and take the first right turn into Johnson Park. Go about a mile and park near the pond (often many gulls and ducks are here), and walk around the pond to view the river.

For the inland lakes (North Shore route) take the Garden State Parkway to exit 117 and go east on Route 36 (this also provides access to Keyport and Keansburg on Raritan Bay) to Sandy Hook. Follow Route 36 south to Long Branch. It crosses the Navesink and Shrewsbury Rivers, both of which can have gull flocks. South of Long Branch begin to look for lakes on the inland side of Ocean Drive (a county street map would be valuable at this point). The first is Lake Takanassie. From there to Manasquan Inlet, you can encounter several lakes by staying close to the ocean. Periodically, take the streets to the east and check the ocean beaches and rock jetties for gull flocks and other wintering birds. After checking the north side of Manasquan Inlet, you must go inland to Route 35 to reach Point Pleasant and the south side of the inlet.

For the landfill at Florence, take Route 295 south from Trenton to the exit for Florence/Columbus, go west (right) a couple of miles (road becomes Delaware Avenue) to parks where the gulls are visible.

BEST TIME TO VISIT: September to March; the largest concentrations are in December to February.

PRIME HABITAT: Any place where open water is remaining in coastal lakes or bays, where the gulls can roost and forage. Open mouths of inlets, sandbars, and jetties are ideal, as are active landfills.

On a crisp, cold wintry day in late January, two thousand gulls stand silently on the thin ice near the inlet, facing into the wind to reduce the cold penetrating their feathers. Whitecaps rise on the open water, and two Great Black-backed Gulls pick sporadically at a dead fish floating on the surface. One much smaller Ring-billed Gull approaches tentatively and pecks at the fish head. The larger gulls chase it away, and one returns to pull flesh from the back, pick up a piece, and then flies off, pursued by another. The gulls career back and forth, screaming loudly, until the first gull drops the food, which is quickly picked up by the pursuer.

At first the gulls huddled together on the ice seem merely a mass of white bodies, but then the distinct shapes of different sizes and shades appear. Most have silvery gray backs and white heads, indicating they are adults. The larger and most numerous are the Herring Gulls; the smaller are Ring-billed Gulls, distinguishable by the black mark near the tip of their beaks. A few gulls stand out because of their black backs. These Great Black-backed Gulls are even larger than the Herring Gulls.

We look carefully until we find a Lesser Black-backed Gull, a European species that is still rare in North America. It is nearly as dark as a Great Black-backed but only the size of a Herring Gull. Meticulous scanning reveals another large gull, only this one seems pure white. It is not an albino, but is a Glaucous Gull, a species from the high Arctic which is also a rare winter visitor to our shores. Although gulls seem so similar to one another and so familiar, each has an interesting and different story.

We are used to hearing derogatory remarks about gulls, and one article we wrote about gulls was rejected because the editor thought they were more like rats than like birds. Indeed, gulls get a bad rap in general, but they are fascinating and highly social creatures that have adapted well to human society. In the mid-twentieth century, it became apparent that several species of gulls were increasing very rapidly in both Europe and North America, just at a time when many other species such as hawks (see chapters 16 and 17) and waterfowl (see next chapter) were declining drastically.

Gulls have learned to take advantage of garbage dumps (or refuse tips, as they are called in Europe), and clouds of gulls hovering over landfills are a very familiar sight. The rich and limitless source of food is especially beneficial to young gulls during the vulnerable months when they have not yet perfected their foraging techniques. Formerly the period between fledging and the end of the first winter was a time of high mortality for gulls, but thanks to human generosity, gulls survived this period and their populations soared. Now, in areas where landfills are being covered and even closed, the food availability for gulls has declined, and gull populations are declining significantly as well, returning to what are probably more normal levels. In our survey of the gulls of the world, we were surprised to find that there are quite a few species of gulls that are in trouble, and several are actually endangered.

Although both Herring and Great Black-backed Gulls now nest in New Jersey, this is a remarkably recent phenomenon. Formerly they bred only in eastern Canada and northern New England, but in the 1930s they began extending their range southward, and they arrived here as breeders only in the early 1950s. Farther north they nest on rocky or sandy islands, on cliffs, or on muskegs, but in New Jersey they quickly adapted to salt marsh islands, selecting the highest places away from tidal floods.

Ring-billed Gulls have also increased greatly since the 1970s, but they nest no closer than the Great Lakes, where many large colonies of densely nesting, loudly squawking Ring-bills can be found on rocky and wooded islands. They have increased so much that they are now considered a pest species and their populations are controlled in some places. In New Jersey, this has become the predominant inland species that one sees around grocery stores and parks in the winter.

Off to the side, on thin ice, not deigning to be part of the larger flock, is a small group of delicate gulls with cloudy gray remnants of the black head-feathering they sport in summer. These are Bonaparte's Gulls, which breed at the northern limit of the treeline where the spruce forests meet the Arctic tundra. These Bonaparte's Gulls are a bit smaller than our native Laughing Gull, a species familiar to everyone who visits the Jersey shore in summer. Now, almost all the Laughing Gulls are gone. They disappear in October, migrating south to Florida and even the West Indies, not to return until the end of April.

New Jersey is a wonderful place to watch gulls in the winter, for not only do we get large numbers of four common species—Herring, Ring-billed, Great Black-backed, and Bonaparte's—but rarities such as Glaucous and Lesser Black-backed also occur with some regularity.

The Bonaparte's Gulls take off and circle over the water near the jetty. They land and immediately begin dipping their bills into the water, seizing some small crustaceans that have come to the surface. Their calls are muted. They dip for a few seconds, then fly up to land nearby and begin dipping again. We search in vain for a slightly larger gull, with dark under the wings, for Black-headed Gulls have been seen here recently as well. We do spot a Little Gull, which has bold black marks across its wings and a black cap. This is mainly a European species that is even smaller than the Bonaparte.

When we used to hunt for such rarities as Little Gull, Black-headed Gull, and Lesser Black-backed Gull, we all assumed they were birds from Europe that had somehow gotten lost and strayed to North America. But each of these species has now been found to breed in North America, and the recent influx of Lesser Black-backed Gulls suggests that there are probably quite a few that breed here now.

While the hard-core bird-watchers look over every single gull among the thousands in a flock, trying to find one of the rare species, it is exhilarating simply to watch the gulls, both as individuals and as a flock, and to enjoy the majesty and splendor of the massive flock sitting on the ice floe. Such flocks can provide one ample amusement by watching their aggressive interactions, for it often seems to matter exactly where on the seemingly uniform ice each bird stands, which old piling it can claim, or which piece of the broken pier it can command as its roosting place.

The gulls that roost on ice floes, sandbars, isolated piers, or pilings are relatively safe from predators, for open water prevents dogs, foxes, and other mammals from reaching them. Such perches also provide an open view in all directions, all the better to watch for aerial predators and approaching people. Among birds of prey, only the Bald Eagle can kill an adult gull, although we have seen Great Black-backs preying on the recently fledged young of smaller species. It is the gulls that sit along the shoreline that must watch out for Red Foxes that move slowly through the Phragmites, Cattails, or other vegetation fringing the shoreline. Such stealthy predators move slowly and silently using the vegetation as a blind, and rarely they may be successful in snatching an unwary gull at the edge of the flock, particularly at night. For the most part, however, gulls seem to enjoy a carefree life. In the coldest winters when inland lakes, rivers, and even the bays freeze over, they can feed along the ocean or migrate southward to Delaware Bay or even the Chesapeake, keeping one step ahead of the ice.

Surprisingly, as New Jersey has become more and more crowded, and more and more people move to the shore to live, the number of predators has increased. People bring dogs and cats with them which can be formidable predators on birds, particularly young birds. Fifty years ago, the majority of the human population along the Jersey shore consisted of summer visitors, but today there are many permanent communities. Inadvertently, these enclaves provide food that maintains winter populations of Skunks and foxes. Red Foxes were never native to the barrier islands, so birds using these habitats did

85. A flock of mostly Ring-billed Gulls resting at the edge of a freshwater lake on the North Coast. Three Canada Geese and some Herring Gulls (the larger gulls) are also in the flock. (Photo by J. Burger)

not evolve with them. Foxes have now become a leading predator on gulls and other birds that nest along the Jersey shore, and a fox could easily kill several gulls a day if they roosted in an accessible area.

When the gusts of wind lessen, the gulls begin to take wing, to move out in search of food, usually nearby at the tide line, in the surf, and in the calm waters of coastal freshwater lakes. The flock of Bonaparte's Gulls has been feeding on the surface and now takes off in unison, flies to the nearby surf, and forms a swirling mass of gulls. They are hovering just above the surface, picking up small food items. Now and then they land again and alternate the different forms of feeding.

The Ring-billed Gulls associate with the flock of Bonaparte's Gulls but spend more time sitting on the water, dipping for food items. When they have finished eating, they return to nearby freshwater lakes to rest (fig. 85). The Herring and Great Black-backed Gulls feed mainly in the surf, searching for carrion or other food washed ashore. They are larger and more awkward than the smaller gulls, and much of their food is obtained from scavenging, although they sometimes capture starfish, crabs, and shellfish.

Although the different species of gulls share similar foraging methods, they have different skills and preferences. The smaller gulls are more agile and can readily obtain prey by hovering over the water and delicately picking up a small item from the surface. Both the smaller and intermediate-sized gulls spend a fair amount of time swimming on the surface of the water, picking up inverte-brates and other prey items. The larger gulls can forage in these ways, but they prefer feeding along the surf, picking up clams, crabs, or searching for dead fish or other carrion.

From our vantage point we can look up the river, where a lone female Gad-wall is swimming near the shore. Without warning, a pair of Great Black-backed Gulls swoop down on the Gadwall, surprising it before it can take flight. With angry slashes they force the duck under the water, again and again. The duck tries in vain to escape, but this species does not dive for long, and cannot escape under water. It tires quickly, and even before it is dead, one of the gulls seizes it by a wing and pulls it toward the rock jetty. Soon the gulls begin to tear it apart. Great Black-backed Gulls can be formidable predators when they are hungry, and this behavior indicates that food may be particu-larly scarce at the moment. Such predation is not limited to the cold winter months, for we have seen gulls feeding on tired songbird migrants struggling over the ocean to make their way toward land. The gulls force these warblers and sparrows onto the ocean, and swallow them whole.

When food really becomes scarce, the gulls head for alternative food sources, where the food is predictable. As mentioned above, many scientists at-tribute the increase in gull populations to the availability of food at garbage dumps during the winter, a time when mortality is usually high, especially for young. At a dump a young gull can find enough food in only an hour or two to last the day, and adults require even less time. Gulls have learned to turn over inedible items and tear open plastic bags. When laws required landfills to cover the garbage with dirt to keep down rat populations, the gulls learned to use the bulldozers as beaters. Massive flocks of gulls can usually be found near any landfill with active dumping, particularly of household refuse; we throw away enormous amounts of food every day.

Each year there are fewer and fewer garbage dumps. With the closing of many dumps in New Jersey, the gull populations have started to decline. With-out this readily available food source in all regions of the coast, some young are unable to find enough food and starve. We have found that the closing of landfills is hardest on the young birds because not only are they less able to compete with adults for natural foods along the shore, but they are less effi-cient at locating places to forage, finding prey items, capturing prey, and actu-ally eating the item once they find it. Taking a long time to eat or swallow a food item has a cost, since gulls are active pirates and willingly take food from another gull. Although young birds attempt piracy from other gulls, they are also less efficient at pirating food from others, even other immatures. This has forced some young birds to visit the local supermarket or fast-food restau-rants, searching for handouts or food people have left about carelessly. If that fails, they begin to pilfer dumpsters and tear apart garbage bags.

86. Herring Gulls forage in the shallow surf along a jetty. (Photo by J. Burger)

The flock of Herring Gulls feeding along the shore seems oblivious to the people walking on the nearby pier, but when the people descend to the sand and begin walking toward them, the gulls fly off in one flock, to land about a half mile down the beach. While gulls are fairly habituated to people, their close approach is not tolerated. In the winter, however, there are many cold blustery days with very few people around. On a warm winter day with lots of human activity, the gulls may be frequently disturbed, and people displace the birds over half of the time. People with dogs, joggers, and anyone in fast motion are the most upsetting and are most likely to stimulate immediate flight. Such disturbances are easy to prevent, for the birds show signs of nervousness long before they fly; they stop feeding, they look around more frequently, and they start moving their wings in readiness for flight. Retreating at this point or giving the flock a wide berth usually allows them to resume feeding. Many people may not see any point to worrying about gull welfare, not realizing that the short day-length of winter limits the time available for feeding, and each disturbance requires the gulls to expend energy to fly away (figs. 86–87).

Many gulls remain along the coast, feeding in the surf or out in the open water. They forage at all times of day and even feed at night. We found that most species of gulls are active on moonlit nights, and if food is particularly scarce, they forage even on dark nights. On such nights we have used "night-vision" telescopes with image intensifiers that make everything appear in shades of green. Depending on the species, we found that gulls forage on 48 to 88 percent of the nights.

Through the scope we can watch the green shapes fly along the shore, land at the green surf, and peck at green items too small for the night telescope to reveal. Sometimes they fly in flocks, their greenish wings nearly touching one another. For the most part they are silent, sailing through the dark night in search of crabs or carrion.

FOR MORE INFORMATION: Call New Jersey Audubon (908-766-5787) or the New Jersey hotline for rare winter gulls (908-766-2661, or 609-861-0466 for Cape May). You can also call Liberty State Park (201-915-3401). For New Jersey Audubon: www.nj.com /audubon /.

87. Gulls hover while foraging. (Photo by J. Burger)

88. Brant drinking at a freshwater stream along the edge of a coastal bay. (Photo by J. Burger)

24

Brant and Other Waterfowl on the North Shore

As the tide falls, a cacophony of cackling echoes across the leads of open water, over the thin ice, to the shoreline where small drifts of snow nestle against the Phragmites. Five thousand noisy Brant begin to agitate, preparing to leave the safety of the open water to fly in long strings of endless dark shapes, bound for shallow water to feed on Eelgrass.

KEY LOCATIONS: There are many places one can find wintering waterfowl, such as the ocean front at Sandy Hook and the coves, as well as the North Shore. Along the lakes and shoreline of New Jersey's North Shore, from Long Branch to Bayhead, several inlets and over a dozen freshwater lakes are located only a block or two from the Atlantic Ocean.

Barnegat Inlet, Brigantine National Wildlife Refuge, and the mouth of the Maurice River in Cumberland County are also excellent places for viewing waterfowl.

DIRECTIONS: You might start the North Shore tour at Sandy Hook: take Garden State Parkway to exit 117 and go east on Route 36 (this also provides access to Keyport and Keansburg on Raritan Bay). Follow signs for Sandy Hook. Check both the southern end (Spermaceti Cove) and the upper end (Horseshoe Cove) of Sandy Hook. Depending on the winds, the ducks may be close to the shore or can be seen as mere bobbing shapes at a distance.

Return to Route 36 (Ocean Avenue) and follow it south to Long Branch. It crosses the Navesink and Shrewsbury Rivers, both of which have waterfowl flocks. Once you are south of Long Branch, begin to look for lakes on the inland side of Ocean Boulevard (a county street map would be valuable at this point). The first is Lake Takanassie; from here to Manasquan Inlet, all the lakes can be encountered by staying close to the ocean. After checking the north side of Manasquan Inlet, one must go inland to Route 35 to reach Point Pleasant and the south side of the inlet.

To start the North Shore tour at Point Pleasant, take exit 98 off the Garden State Parkway and follow Route 34 south.

For Barnegat Light, take exit 63 from the parkway. Go east on Route 72 to Long Beach Island, then go north about 5 miles to Barnegat Light. Park in the State Park parking lot and walk to the jetty.

Brigantine National Wildlife Refuge is also good for waterfowl. From the Garden State Parkway, take exit 49 to Route 9 south, turn east onto Great Creek Road, and follow signs to the refuge entrance (0.6 mile).

For the Maurice River, take Route 47 to Belmont, turn west on Glade Road, which becomes Heislerville Road. Turn right onto Dorchester Road, followed soon by a left onto May's Landing Road.

BEST TIME TO VISIT: December to March.

PRIME HABITAT: Inland lakes along the coast, which usually remain at least partly open throughout the winter, as well as the mouths of rivers and bays.

Masses of black bodies crowd together, some in tens and twenties, others in the hundreds, still others in numbers too high to count. Their soft gabbling and cackling calls waft across the waters, rising and falling. The large rafts of Brant are away from shore, but many linger near the edge. A few float atop the water, peering about, but many individuals are upended, their dark wings and white tails bobbing about as they pull at the Eelgrass and other vegetation in the shallows. The Brant, our smallest goose, have arrived on the Jersey shore from their northern breeding grounds and are prepared to spend the winter. The moderating effect of the ocean prevents the Jersey bays and estuaries from freezing in all but the coldest winters, and when the Brant first arrive they feed on the beds of Sea Lettuce along the banks, or on the green algae blown up on shore. Brant prefer the tidal bays, whereas most other geese seek freshwater lakes and brackish water impoundments. The Brant thrive on the Eelgrass beds that grow wherever there is a sandy bottom. At low tide, the Brant spread out along the shore, in bays, inlets, and river mouths, and return to large rafts in the middle of open water when high tides make foraging more difficult. There they rest until the tidal waters retreat once again.

Only when prolonged cold sets in does the ice begin to form, slowly creeping across the shallows, restricting access to food. Even then there are some leads open where the tidal reach is particularly strong or where running water flows into the bay. Falling tides still provide foraging opportunities, but the Brant are often concentrated over a few beds, and if the freeze continues, the geese can destroy the beds, eating all the Eelgrass roots. In particularly bad years, some Brant slowly starve, and die-offs occur. When taken by surprise, Brant get caught with dwindling food supplies and little energy to migrate. Usually, however, the Brant have warning of impending cold weather and migrate farther south. In some cold winters, conservation groups and public officials prevent wholesale starvation in Barnegat Bay by providing supplemental forage, dropped off on the thick ice. In recent years, open water has persisted all winter, allowing the Brant to remain in area bays.

89. Ducks, including domestic ducks, gulls, and even pigeons, readily approach people for food. (Photo by J. Burger)

The Brant concentrate in a few predictable places, particularly in years when there is a lot of open water. The large expanse of water where the Shark River flows through Belmar is a consistently fruitful place.

Although several species of ducks (Mallards, Gadwall, Black Ducks, and Blue-winged Teal) breed in New Jersey, there is a far greater diversity of ducks in winter, when migrants from the northern tier of states and Canada swell our waterfowl populations. The many lakes and ponds offer easy viewing, and when the ice forms in the middle, the ducks are confined to the unfrozen leads close to the shoreline, where running water enters (see appendix C).

While the Brant concentrate in estuarine waters, many of the ducks move to the freshwater lakes that are only a block or two from the ocean and remain open for much of the winter, except during periods of extreme cold. There are about a dozen such lakes from Long Branch to Bayhead with exciting populations of ducks, swans (see next chapter), and other waterbirds. On many ponds, ducks have become panhandlers and readily approach anyone who seems interested in providing them with food (fig. 89). Although signs are posted to discourage feeding of waterfowl, feeding continues to be popular, for the ducks universally ignore the signs. Feeding encourages abnormally high concentrations, which can lead to fouling of the lakes and increases the possibility of diseases causing major die-offs. Nonetheless, at some favored feeding sites, the ducks rapidly approach anyone who steps out of the car. This affords a good opportunity for viewing and photographing, although the ducks quickly assess the situation and move away if food is not forthcoming.

One of the problems waterfowl face is lead poisoning because of the extensive use of lead shot by waterfowl hunters. Since a shotgun shell has dozens of pellets, only a few are needed to kill a duck. The remaining shot falls into the water and sinks to the bottom of lakes and ponds, to remain for many years. Many species of ducks forage by pulling up vegetation from the bottom of shallow ponds or lake edges, or scoop up grit from the bottom, and they inadvertently ingest the lead shot. Because of their lifestyle, many different species of waterfowl are affected by lead shot, and die-offs involve hundreds of birds at one time. In the late 1950s, estimates were that 3 percent of the annual mortality in waterfowl was due to lead poisoning.

This tremendous loss led to the banning of lead shot for waterfowl hunting. Most areas are now "steel shot only" zones. Nonetheless, the problem remains because of the persistence of lead shot in aquatic environments, and because lead shot is not banned for other types of shooting. In addition, one or two lead pellets may not be enough to kill a bird immediately, but the lead gradually dissolves from the pellet, is absorbed into the bloodstream, and spreads throughout the body, affecting vigor, appetite, flying ability, and eventually causing death. Even low levels of lead in the body can cause birds to lose weight, exhibit cognitive dysfunctions, leading to lower reproductive success, and if they survive, they are more vulnerable to hunting in future seasons. Lead causes decreases in egg size, increased mortality of embryos and nestlings, decreased growth rates, and contributes to lowered fledging rates. Some of these effects are even apparent in the second generation, in young whose mothers were not directly exposed to lead. The banning of lead shot for waterfowl in the United States was absolutely essential, but the problem will remain with us for many years.

Fortunately for the ducks that spend the winter in the freshwater lakes in the densely populated north Jersey shore communities, there is no hunting and thus little possibility of exposure to lead shot. Every year we find it exciting to visit these coastal lakes, stopping as well at the bays, river mouths, and ocean front to look for Brant, loons, bay ducks, and rare gulls. The scenes become more familiar and endearing with each passing year, and although we note the houses that line the lakes and crowd the shore, we look beyond to the wild ducks and geese that can survive amid our chaos. The sight of a hundred ducks waddling rapidly toward us, the feeling of a hundred slate gray Coots scuttling across the grass, and the cackling sound of five thousand Brant erupting into endless lines flying off to foraging grounds is exciting and intoxicating (fig. 90).

A tour of the North Shore can begin or end at Sandy Hook (be aware that the park police rigorously enforce posted speed limits), where there are several parking lots. Some ducks, such as Buffleheads, are widespread but not numerous and can be found anywhere along the route. Others, such as Goldeneye,

90. Coot frequent the inland lakes along the North Shore, sometimes forming dense flocks. (Photo by J. Burger)

are found only in a few places, particularly at Sandy Hook and Belmar. Along the ocean there may be flocks of White-winged and Surf Scoters with even a few Black Scoters. On the inland side of Sandy Hook, in Horseshoe Cove, there is almost always a huge flock of Greater Scaup, sometimes several thousand. Among them there may be a Tufted Duck, a rare visitor from Europe that can be distinguished easily by its all-black back. The cove is a good place to see large numbers of Black Ducks. This used to be the most abundant freshwater duck in New Jersey, but its numbers have declined alarmingly in the last fifty years, possibly due to competition from the Mallard which, conversely, used to be very rare. There are often hundreds of Brant in the cove as well. Common Goldeneye are often seen at Sandy Hook, and there may be several hundred in the cove near the tip of the Hook. In recent winters, a single male Barrow's Goldeneye has been spotted here with some regularity.

One can easily spend several hours at Sandy Hook, but in winter the days are short so one most move quickly if the entire route is to be covered. The next stop is the Navesink River, just at the base of the Hook. Here is the place to find a large flock of Scaup if they were absent in Horseshoe Cove.

Along the coast of Monmouth County, from Long Branch to Manasquan Inlet, there are many places to find ducks in the several natural and man-made lakes. Most of these are completely encircled by roads, which offer easy and complete viewing. The first is Lake Takanassie, followed by Deal and Sylvan Lakes. South of Sylvan Lake is Shark River Inlet. The mouth of the inlet often

91. Line of Brant in the open water. (Photo by J. Burger)

has Red-breasted Mergansers and Bufflehead, as well as Common and Red-throated Loons and Horned Grebes. Occasionally, Harlequin Ducks are found near the jetty. But the big waterfowl concentration is about a mile to the west where Shark River widens into a large, odd-shaped lake that extends from Neptune south to Belmar. The marina offers good viewing of waterfowl, often at very close range. Great Cormorants, a dwindling species, are still found here in winter. There are often large flocks of American Widgeon in the western part of the lake, visible from Marconi Road. Bufflehead and Ruddy Duck are often seen at close range in the marina. A careful look may reveal a Horned Grebe, a species that was much more numerous twenty years ago.

Returning back to the coast, one can visit Silver Lake and Lake Como. The extremely elegant Hooded Merganser is often in evidence here. As one approaches Sea Girt, swing inland to check Spring Lake and then back to Wreck Pond and Stockton Lake. Finally, in Manasquan one should check both the north and south sides of the inlet. Farther up the river between the Route 35 and Route 70 bridge there may be waterfowl, including Canvasbacks, Gadwalls, and Redheads.

South of the inlet is Old Sams Pond and Twilight Lake. An additional highlight, worth the long drive, is the jetty at Barnegat Light, where Harlequin Ducks and Purple Sandpipers are usually present and where one may see Eiders as well.

Wherever we start, we are always thrilled to see so many different species of waterfowl in a wide array of habitats. The dunes of Sandy Hook, fringing a sometimes violent and often icy ocean, can be as picturesque as any coastal scene. The river mouths, often with long rafts of cackling Brant, are exciting (fig. 91). The inland lakes, surrounded by houses yet packed with a wide variety of ducks, are interesting to visit because the birds are so calm and allow careful observation. The breakwater at Barnegat Inlet is always exciting, for the surf laps against the rocks, splashing Purple Sandpipers that feed on the salt-washed algae. We never tire of searching for the diversity of waterfowl that can be found in a single day.

FOR MORE INFORMATION: Call Division of Fish, Game and Wildlife (609-292-9400), or call New Jersey Audubon (908-766-5787) or New Jersey hotline for rare ducks (908-766-2661, or 609-861-0466 for Cape May).

92. Tundra Swans on Whites Bog, where several hundred overwinter. (Photo by J. Burger)

Swans at Whites Bog
and Coastal Lakes

Only the slow, graceful movement of a hundred pure white Tundra Swans breaks the calm waters, each leaving a delicate wake. With their necks held elegantly upright, the statuesque swans sail effortlessly across the water, a flotilla of pure white against the steel-gray water.

KEY LOCATIONS: Whites Bog in Burlington County (Whistling or Tundra Swans); Mannington Marsh in Cumberland County; and Wreck Pond and other lakes along the North Shore in Monmouth County (Mute Swans).

DIRECTIONS: For Whites Bog (written as Whitesbog on some road maps), from Route 70 take Route 530 west toward Brown Mills. After 1.2 miles turn right at the entrance to Whites Bog Village.

For Mannington Marshes, use the Salem-Woodstown Highway (Route 45). Several other roads (Route 540 and Route 620) also cross the marsh. Take the turnpike south to exit 1; go south on 540 across the marsh and north on Route 45 toward Woodstown.

For the coastal lakes, take Garden State Parkway to exit 98 and go southeast on Route 34, exit left onto Route 524 into Sea Girt (see chapter 24). The largest concentration of Mute Swans is often on Wreck Pond on the north edge of Sea Girt. Mute Swans also occur on many of the other coastal lakes between Manasquan Inlet and Long Branch. Drive north on Ocean Avenue and check Spring Lake, Sylvan Lake, Lake Como, and Lake Takanassie. Drive around Shark River from Belmar and find Swans (all seasons) and wintering ducks and Brant.

BEST TIME TO VISIT: Tundra Swans are present from late fall until the bogs freeze, usually in late January or February. If the bogs remain open all winter, the swans linger until they depart, usually in March, for their breeding grounds.

Mute Swans are present all year on coastal lakes but are concentrated in large numbers in the winter.

PRIME HABITAT: Lakes with open water and abundant vegetation to provide roots and tender shoots for food.

Snow lies in shallow drifts along the grassy margin of the bog, golden brown in the winter sunlight, and piles against the trunks of long-barren trees. The dark water is roughened by the wind. Fringed by pale tan vegetation, and then by tall pines, the bog impoundments are extensive, and occasional brown stems emerge, evidence that the bog was once lush and green. The rectangular shapes of some of the ponds, separated by narrow sandy dikes, reflect their use as Cranberry bogs. The straight edges of the nearer bogs give way to more distant ones, unkept, uneven, and largely hidden by trees.

The serene scene is completed by the presence of 250 Tundra Swans, also known as Whistling Swans, drifting in a flotilla across the water, faint trails forming V's behind them. Most are pure white, and with their gracefully straight necks they contrast starkly with the browns and grays of the wintry marsh. About a third of the birds have grayish plumage, indicating they are young birds accompanying their parents on their first migration (fig. 93). Graced by these ethereal shapes, the splendor of the Whites Bog scene is stunning.

The flock stops, and lazily the birds begin to dip their bills into the water and extend their necks downward, searching for tender shoots and rhizomes. With only their curved back showing, they look like dollops of whipped cream, motionless, floating gently. First one, and then the next, lift their heads, holding their necks upright, peering around, their jet-black bills adding color that only emphasizes their whiteness. With flapping wings, one reaches upward,

93. Close view of Tundra Swans, showing the slight gray tinge on some young of the year. (Photo by J. Burger)

stretches, and returns to feeding. Stretching is contagious, and soon several are extending their head skyward, raising their bodies with their waving wings. Some birds nearly touch one another, but most are a foot or two apart, remaining in the safety of the flock. Slowly the gathering glides across the open water, feeding intently.

The relative quiet is broken by their occasional gabbling and soft cackling notes that waft across the water. The noise increases and on some unknown cue, many birds leap upward, stretching their wings and necks, and flapping vigorously. Their wings beat a rhythmic "wuff-wuff-wuff" in the winter air. Slowly, the birds lift from the water, their heads pointed straight ahead, their necks fully extended. The white seems even more snowy, more billowy, and more brilliant against the dark green pine trees, and the pale blue sky. In flight the Swans raise their voices "woo-hoo" "woo-hooo." The old name "Whistling" Swans was derived from their high-pitched cooing, often heard high overhead before the migrating flocks of swans are visible to the naked eye. Most people do not think of it as whistling, any more than the calls of the Trumpeter Swan sound like trumpets. The airborne swans circle over the water, gaining altitude, and fly off to another part of Whites Bog, forming a ribbonlike flock of pure white splendor.

The remaining Swans swim effortlessly toward a far bank. Some dip their heads beneath the surface, continuing to feed on the succulent roots. They also eat stems, seeds, and the fleshy tubers of aquatic plants. Their habit of dredging up aquatic roots often results in their consuming some animal matter, but they prefer the roots. With their long neck, they can feed in water up to three feet deep, allowing them to graze where other waterfowl cannot. On their migration, flocks of swans descend into agricultural fields and may consume crops, including waste grain left on the fields, or winter cereals.

Like many species, their winter and summer food preferences are similar. On their Arctic breeding grounds, Tundra Swans also submerge their heads and necks, upending to browse along the margins of lakes. Sometimes they even graze in tundra meadows, although they prefer aquatic vegetation. They forage most of the day, when they are not engaged in breeding, and sometimes they feed by the light of a bright moon.

Tundra Swans are the most numerous and widespread of all swans in North America. They breed in the high Arctic, along the land-water margins, nesting from James Bay all the way around the coast of Alaska. The Tundra Swans in Whites Bog travel several thousand miles to the muskegs of northern Canada to breed. They are a large bird; males weigh up to twenty-two pounds, but the females are smaller. Their black legs, feet, and bill contrast sharply with their all-white plumage.

Swans are family oriented. They are highly monogamous, maintaining the same mate from year to year. Recent research has shown that in many kinds of birds, males try to breed with females other than their mates, and females accept copulations from neighbors. However, in swans there is no evidence of extra-pair copulation; their attention is riveted only on their mate. They feed in family groups on the tundra, migrate in family groups, overwinter in family groups, and return to their tundra breeding sites in the same family groups. Only then do the immatures leave their families to find a mate, unless they happened to find one while wintering with another family group. Once on the breeding ground, they take up territories, usually including at least part of a lake, for foraging. Their actual arrival on a breeding territory is somewhat related to the season; they must wait for the snow and ice to disappear before setting up housekeeping. Both parents establish and defend the territory, incubate, and care for the young. Their usual territory size of up to a square mile is maintained throughout the breeding season until the young are fully able to fly.

The male, called a *cob*, selects the nest site within the territory, usually a hummock that is slightly higher than the surrounding tundra. The height protects the nest and eggs from flooding, as well as providing a better vantage point for predator detection. It is the female, called the *pen*, that constructs most of the nest, although the male adds a few pieces of vegetation. They build a substantial nest, usually by pulling bits of vegetation from within ten feet of the nest, and continue to add material throughout incubation, shifting their body from side to side to make a nice nest cup.

The parents take turns incubating, but there is almost always one parent at the nest to protect the eggs from harm. The three to six eggs in a clutch are a blue-green when they are first laid, but they bleach to a pure white in the Arctic sun. They hatch in about thirty days, under the watchful eye of the female, who during this vulnerable time refuses to relinquish the nest to the male.

The hatchling swans are quite able to take care of themselves, and after drying off, they walk about the nest area, waiting impatiently for their siblings to hatch. Within a day or two of hatching, the young swans, called *cygnets*, leave the nest with their parents. The awkward, ungainly, pale gray balls of fluff are not nearly so elegant as their pure white parents, as immortalized in Hans Christian Andersen's "Ugly Duckling" story.

When cold winds whip across the tundra marshes, the parents brood their chicks, and do so until they are a week or two old. The chicks follow one or both parents to the water, where the parents often dig up rootlets and paddle furiously to bring them to the surface, which allows the young to forage on their own. The young mostly dabble at the surface, following their parents about, waiting for them to make food available. The siblings compete for the vegetation uprooted by their parents, and sometimes the smallest one starves to death. The chicks continue to stay with their parents, although sometimes one parent goes in one direction and the other in another, each with one or two trailing chicks. Young swans make a tasty meal for Arctic predators such as foxes and Snowy Owls, and although the parents defend them vigorously, they usually cannot safeguard the entire brood. Most of the family groups we see on the wintering grounds have only one or two young birds.

With the cold temperatures of late September, ice begins to form on their high Arctic ponds, snow covers the tundra, and it is time to migrate. The young fly south with their parents, and long strings of swans fly higher than any other migrant, well over 10,000 feet above the flatlands. They fly non-stop to their wintering areas, where they rest for the first day or two without eating, and then slowly begin to dip their heads below the water, searching for food.

It is not unusual to see two hundred or three hundred Tundra Swans at Whites Bog, and even nowadays, the numbers can reach five hundred. One of the most severe threats these birds face is hunting. In many states, including New Jersey, hunting by swan permit is allowed, although usually each hunter is limited to only one. Hunting has been justified by increasing swan populations, concerns about damage to agricultural crops, and for trophy hunting.

Swans, of course, are also exposed to contamination, largely through spent lead shot. Since many waterfowl, including swans, are shot over water, shot that does not hit a bird falls into the water. It sinks to the bottom and is eaten by waterfowl that forage on the bottom muds. This makes swans particularly vulnerable because most of their foraging occurs in this zone. For example, in one refuge in North Carolina in the 1970s, an estimated one thousand Tundra Swans died annually from lead-shot ingestion. This problem is less severe today because lead shot is banned for waterfowl hunting in the United States. However, shot expended over the preceding decades still remains in the sediment of many ponds and marshes and is available to the swans. Swans also ingest lead from soil, particularly near mining and smelting complexes, and can accumulate enough to show signs of lead poisoning, including mortality.

For the most part, however, Tundra Swan populations seem to be increasing. Biologists estimate the eastern North American population to be about 90,000, which has doubled over the last thirty-five years. While the recent doubling may be true, it is difficult to obtain estimates of their populations before the heavy gunning that began in the late 1880s. The recent doubling may simply be due to recovery from previous lows. The U.S. Fish and Wildlife Service keeps tabs on swan numbers, and any decrease would be quickly noted.

Another swan spectacle occurs in the coastal lakes along the North Shore of New Jersey—the Mute Swans (fig. 94). They are much larger than Tundra Swans and can weigh up to thirty-five pounds, although they usually weigh about twenty-five. While Tundra Swans are native to North America, the Mute Swans on the coastal lakes and Mannington Marshes are feral, a European species that was imported to North America long ago. These swans happily grace many park ponds, and they breed well in New Jersey. As lovely as they are, they are considered pests in some coastal communities because they terrorize other

94. Adult Mute Swan in a freshwater lake along the North Shore of New Jersey. (Photo by J. Burger)

waterfowl, destroy the vegetation, foul swimming areas, and annoy beach-goers. For the most part, however, people appreciate them for their beauty and majesty.

Mute Swans are distinguishable from Tundra Swans by their larger size and orange rather than black bills. They typically swim with their neck in a sensual S-curve, compared to the straight neck of the Tundra Swan. They are, however, no less elegant as they gracefully glide across the coastal lakes. Often they raise their wings partially arched over their backs, from which posture the term "swan boat" is derived. Their habitat is interesting because of its stark contrast with Whites Bog. Whites Bog is a tranquil, working Cranberry bog, but the coastal lakes are surrounded by houses, circled by highways, and bordered by mowed lawns. While you may not encounter a soul on a wintry weekday at Whites Bog, a jaunt along the Jersey shore lakes is clearly suburban, and you are always surrounded by houses and cars. The view of a coastal lake, however, is magnificent when forty or fifty Mute Swans are serenely sailing across the lake, their feathers unruffled, their necks arched as gracefully as those of the Tundra Swans.

Mute Swans are native to Eurasia and were introduced to North America from the mid-1800s to the mid-1900s because they were considered a lovely addition to city parks and private estates. Today, thousands of swans populate coastal lakes from Maine to South Carolina, with smaller flocks in the Pacific Northwest and the Great Lakes. They are increasing at what some people consider alarming rates, and their ranks have swelled to well over one thousand in coastal New Jersey.

Mute Swans prefer lakes with shallow shorelines that provide abundant submerged vegetation for food. They stay in pairs for much of the year, but courtship begins in late January through March, making this time of year particularly interesting. Although the male usually joins the female on her natal territory, or nearby if that is occupied, he actually selects the nest site. They usually prefer to place their nests near open water but out of the way of flooding; a small island in a lake is ideal because there are no mammalian predators. Since their nests are on the ground, they are vulnerable to mammals, even though swans are able to defend their nests vigorously by arching their necks, hissing, and charging at intruders. As with Tundra Swans, the female builds most of the nest, adding dried grasses to the nest from within bill distance. The nest can be as much as two feet high. Egg laying in New Jersey is usually from mid-March to mid-April.

After an incubation period of about thirty-six days, the eggs hatch into chicks that can be either dusty gray or white. Like Tundra Swans, they follow their parents into the water and soon learn to pick up pieces of floating vegetation that the parents have dislodged from the lake bottoms. The parents also pull vegetation from the sides of lakes and ponds and even break off pieces overhanging the water. Small young often ride on their parent's back, nestled between the wings, which Tundra Swans never do. Mute Swans are very territorial, and the young of different broods do not intermingle; parents will even kill other young that wander into their territory.

Young Mute Swans become independent at about four to five months, but sometimes they remain with their parents throughout the winter. Since they do not migrate long distances unless a particularly cold snap freezes all the open water, the young can passively remain with them. Usually, however, they disperse from the area. Although they might try to return to their natal territory the following spring, males especially are driven off by their parents. A lake must be quite large to allow more than a single pair of swans to nest, and the young are forcibly expelled to find their own territory, often on a nearby lake.

Mute Swans are monogamous like Tundra Swans, maintaining the same mate for life unless death results in the need to find a new one. The oldest-known Mute Swan in North America was nearly twenty-seven years old. Unlike Tundra Swans, they are not hunted in North America, and most states, including New Jersey, actively protect them. However, some states, such as New Hampshire, Delaware, Minnesota, North Carolina, and Virginia, have declared them a nuisance, allowing some control. In England, we are told, Mute Swans technically belong to the queen and are protected.

The coastal lakes are interesting to see because the Mute Swans, like other waterfowl, have grown accustomed to humans and often allow close approach, especially if they think you have food. They continue to feed by dipping their

95. Mute Swans engaged in feeding. (Photos by J. Burger)

heads in the water, even though people are nearby (fig. 95). Their habitat is certainly suburban. By contrast, Whites Bog is truly a magical environment. A visit to the bogs in early fall (September) allows you to watch the Cranberry bogs during harvest, as well as visit the farming village. But it is late fall or winter that is truly enchanting. On a cold wintry day, with the lake partially frozen and delicate snowflakes drifting slowly downward, the Tundra Swans are a magnificent sight. A hundred Tundra Swans floating lazily on the water, dipping down to pull roots and tender shoots from below the water, is a spectacular sight, especially as their gabbling drifts across the water. The whole ambiance is the spectacle, a mood that sets off the swans, transporting you to some frozen Arctic tundra thousands of miles away.

FOR MORE INFORMATION: Call New Jersey Audubon (908-766-5787).

96. A lake covered with Water Lilies in the New Jersey Pine Barrens. (Photo by J. Burger)

Other Spectacles

The spectacles described so far are wonderful, fairly predictable, and merit a visit every year. There are many other spectacles in the state that bear mentioning, for you may well encounter them, and it is worth pausing to enjoy their excitement, beauty, or majesty. We will briefly mention only a few that were candidates for our "top 25" list. Some of these are widespread and can be found in many parts of the state. Canada Geese, for example, are so widespread and numerous that people pass them by without a second glance. Yet a generation ago, the migratory flocks of geese honking their way northward were truly a spectacle. There are many other nature spectacles that are not predictable in time or place; one just happens upon them by chance.

White Water Lilies

On a warm July day in southern New Jersey, almost any roadside ditch, small pond, or lazy lake is covered with a carpet of White Water Lilies (fig. 96). In some places they are so thick they seem to grow over one another, but in other places, each plant is distinguishable, a lovely pattern of oval, glossy leaves spiraling from a center where two or three pure white flowers lie on the water's surface, facing the sun. The forest-green leaves can be up to ten inches across and have a v-notch at one side. They usually lie flat on the water, unless they are forced to stand upright because there is so little space.

White Water Lilies are native to New Jersey and can grow so dense they compete with one another for both nutrients and light. When they are crowded, the leaves and flowers are smaller. In the narrow ditches along some sandy roads in the Pine Barrens they grow so thick that the water is barely visible. They are wonderful because they grow in so many different aquatic habitats, cedar bogs, Cranberry bogs, ponds, slow streams, and lakes, and they flower from July through September. The pure white flowers do not like the afternoon sun, however, and they usually close by three in the afternoon.

Interspersed among the lilies is Yellow Spatterdock, casting a yellow buttery glow to the marsh. The leaves are narrower and a darker green than the water lilies and are only up to eight inches across. They are far less showy and a bit understated. Their brilliant yellow flower, about the size of a golf ball, never quite opens. Still, it serves to make the White Water Lilies that much more elegant.

If you fail to find White Water Lilies anywhere else, a good place to look is the pond on your way into Brigantine Refuge (see chapter 22 for directions). Here the lakes are fringed by Cattails, a few Bayberries, and even some Persimmon Trees.

Herring Runs

In the spring, as the water temperatures begin to rise, herrings (both Alewife and Blueback Herring), travel upriver, mainly at night, to spawn in freshwater. The Blueback Herring seek fast currents over hard substrates, while the Alewife spawn in sluggish waters in the shallows at the bends of small rivers.

The herring eggs float just above the bottom, or adhere to roots, branches, rocks, sand, and gravel in shallow water along the shoreline. Eggs hatch in only two to four days, although if temperatures are low, they can take up to fifteen days. Eventually the tiny fish move upriver, where they remain in schools until late summer or early fall. They stay near the top of the water and can tolerate some salinity, but generally they remain in freshwater. They feed on zooplankton, crustacean eggs, small insects, and small fish, and are themselves food for a variety of large predatory fish. In the fall, juvenile herring migrate back to marine waters.

In the estuaries the small herring grow slowly, remaining in the bays or swimming out onto the continental shelf. The young fish linger in the upper levels of the water column, although as they age they seek the bottom. Males reach sexual maturity at three to four years, while females usually require four to five. Once they reach adulthood, they move back to the streams, rivers, and ponds where they were hatched. Adults usually move upstream in "runs" from April to early July. At this time of year, the herring are about ten inches long. Although herring occur from Greenland to North Carolina, the massive runs occur only from Massachusetts to New Jersey.

Like American Shad (see chapter 2), herring have been impacted by dams that stopped their spring migration upriver to spawn. Recently this problem has been addressed by building lifts and fish ladders, such as the one at Sunset Lake on the Cohansey River at Bridgeton (Cumberland County), and at Cooper River Lake at Camden (Camden County; fig. 97). These were constructed by Public Service Electric & Gas (PSE&G), which has also built other fish ladders in Delaware. These efforts are contributing to conservation and management of herring in the Delaware Bay estuary. Every year more and more fish make their way up these ladders to spawn in their traditional breeding grounds. With time, the massive runs are being restored.

Characteristics used by PSE&G to select suitable spawning habitats where dams have prevented herring access include water depth, velocity of water movement, substrate, temperature during the spawning period, salinity, pH, and dissolved oxygen levels. Herring require a firm, muddy bottom that contains detritus and vegetation for spawning. They spawn when the water temperatures are between 54 and 68 degrees Fahrenheit. Once suitable spawning habitat is identified, fish ladders can be constructed downriver to allow fish to bypass dams and other obstructions.

The fish ladder at Sunset Lake allows the fish to swim up over nine feet from the Cohansey River to the lake, while the one at Cooper River brings them up about five feet. Restoration of herring includes natural movement of the herring up the fish ladders, lifting additional herring from below the ladder to the lake, and transplanting gravid adults, ready to spawn, from elsewhere. For example, in 1998 gravid adult herrings from Union Lake (see chapter 2) were restocked by PSE&G into Cooper Lake (about seven hundred) and into Sunset Lake (about one thousand) with the assistance of the New Jersey Aquarium personnel. The construction of fish ladders, with associated viewing platforms and information boards, is very important not only from a conservation viewpoint, but also from a cultural one. It is critical to restore herring because they are an integral part of the heritage of New Jersey.

Union Lake in Millville also has a fish ladder to move the herring up to the lake, although the local fishermen note that the run is not as good as it was before the dam was rebuilt. They believe the flow is not as strong, making it more difficult for the fish to swim up the ladder. The fish swim up the Maurice River through salt marshes and eventually through deciduous woodland. At Union Lake, the fish ladder is constructed of concrete and zigzags back and forth, moving the fish up about twenty feet to the lake. Several species of fish use the Union Lake fish ladder, including Striped Bass, Alewife, and Blueback Herring.

As with any restoration program, progress is slow, but each year more adults spawn in these lakes and more juveniles are observed. Fish ladders also provide passageways for the juveniles to migrate downstream from the spawning lakes, leading to the successful restoration of herring "runs" in these rivers. Since juveniles hatched in Union, Sunset, and Cooper River lakes take several years to mature, populations continue to swell as these adults return to their natal habitat (fig. 98).

The two fish ladders built by PSE&G in New Jersey can be visited at Sunset Lake and Cooper River Lake. At Sunset Lake, a nature trail at the Cohanzick Zoo in the Bridgeton City Park leads to the fish ladder. The fish ladder at Silver Lake in Dover, Delaware, is also worth a visit. Because you can walk across the top of the dam at Silver Lake, it is possible to see the top and the bottom of the ladder. A wire grate covers the ladder to protect the herring swimming slowly up. When the herring are running, you can watch them as they reach the top. Their swirling silver bodies gleam as they twist and turn. There are information signs about the fish ladder, and people fish nearby during the herring run. Dover is about an hour south of the end of the New Jersey Turnpike.

The fish ladder at Union Lake Dam, constructed by the New Jersey Department of Environmental Protection, is at the end of Sharp Street in Millville, at the head of the Maurice River in Cumberland County. For the Union Lake fish ladder, take Route 55 south through Vineland; take exit 24 to Route 49 west toward Millville. After crossing Route 47, go one mile and take a right on Sharp Street. Park in the Green Acres parking lot across from the spillway. A trail leads down to the fishing dock, and across the street is the fish ladder (do not climb onto the ladder). Also see chapter 2 for directions to the Easton fish ladder, which has underwater viewing windows.

97. Fish ladder at Sunset Lake, constructed by PSE&G for river herring (*facing page*), and at Union Lake, constructed by NJ DEP. Union Lake photo shows the dam with a side view of a fish ladder (*top photo*), and top view of the ladder (*bottom photo*). (Photos by J. Burger)

98. Striped Bass, one of the other species observed around fish ladders. River Herring are sometimes caught to be used as bait for Striped Bass. (Photo by J. Burger)

Diamondback Terrapin Seeking Nest Sites

In the waning days of spring, Diamondback Terrapins turn their attention to love. The Terrapins spend nearly all of their time solitarily in salt marsh creeks and estuaries until it is time for them to mate. From mid-June to mid-July they gather off suitable nesting beaches. The females are nearly twice the size of males, an adaptation that allows the female to lay fairly large eggs. The males patrol the shallow water, searching for females. After mating, most females wait for several days for the fertilized eggs to mature. Then the females leave the safety of the estuarine waters to search for a nest site on the dunes.

The gravid females wait for the tide to rise higher and higher on the beaches, and an hour or so before high tide they come ashore. Turtles that are separated from their nesting beaches by roads must cross the pavement to reach the sandy areas. At this time, many are killed by cars. Some thoughtless people kill them on purpose, as if being able to hit a small, defenseless turtle is an indication of prowess. Roads that have a curb are particularly lethal, for the turtles cannot climb over obstacles greater than a few inches.

The females move slowly over the sand dunes, searching for just the right nest spot (fig. 99). Coming in at high tide ensures that the female lays her eggs well above high tide, above any threat of tidal inundation, and it also reduces the distance she has to crawl to find a nest site. This in turn reduces the time she is on land exposed to people, predators, and the drying heat of the sun. She sniffs the ground periodically, turns around, and tests a bit of sand with her back feet, webbed into flippers. Turning, she sniffs again, and dissatisfied, moves on to another place, and then another.

Finally her quest is satisfied, she begins the hour-long process of digging with her hind legs, scooping out dirt first with one back foot, and then the other, until she has a nest that is about six inches deep. She deposits about ten oval, leathery, white eggs and begins to cover the nest, pulling in the sand with her hind legs. Satisfied, she smooths out the surface of the sand, obliterating any visual signs of the nest. Her chore completed, she trundles as quickly as possible back to the surf. Silently she disappears, not to return until next year.

The eggs take about sixty to eighty days to hatch, depending on whether the nest is in full sun and how deep it is. On some beaches, predators find the nests and destroy up to 90 percent of them. This is particularly a problem since the number of Red Foxes, Raccoons, and Skunks on the New Jersey coast has increased greatly. Most Diamondbacks nest on barrier island beaches, a habitat that was once far more open and which had far fewer predators before people built bridges that provided the predatory animals easy access.

Early in the twentieth century, Diamondbacks were harvested so extensively for food that they nearly disappeared. They brought well over a hundred dollars a dozen in the early 1900s. In the middle of the century, this pressure was

99. Female Diamondback Terrapin searching the dunes for a suitable nest site. (Photo by J. Burger)

100. Turtle-crossing sign on a road near Tuckerton, warning drivers to avoid the female turtles crossing the road. (Photo by J. Burger)

greatly reduced and the Terrapin began to recover. However, populations have declined again recently due to loss of beach nesting habitat, increases in nest predators, accidents with boats in our bays, and the increase in crab traps, which also trap and drown the turtles.

Still, when the weather turns warm in late June, and the tides are high, the remaining Diamondback Terrapins leave the safety of the water to engage in the ancient ritual of digging their nests above the tideline. Then Terrapins can often be seen crossing the coastal roads, with peak numbers from about June 20 to about July 10, usually around high tide. Good places to view them include Seven Bridges Road leading to Tuckerton through the Great Bay Boulevard Wildlife Management (see chapter 10 for directions), Brigantine Refuge dikes, and the roads near the Stone Harbor marshes (fig. 100).

Spring Songbird Migration

Before the first orange-red rays rise above the treeline, the dawn chorus begins. Chirps, chips, and squeaks waft through the forest as the birds literally drop out of the sky into the treetops. Dozens of different species join the chorus until it is almost impossible to decide where to look.

Spring migration is one of the highlights of the naturalist's year. Depending on weather conditions, large concentrations of migrating birds may descend in almost any wooded part of the state. Certain areas have proven repeatedly favorable for seeing a large variety of these birds, only a few of which will remain in New Jersey to nest. Excellent places include Stokes Forest, Scherman-Hoffman Sanctuary, Princeton Woods, and, of course, Cape May.

In early April, when the cool breezes are still blowing off the Atlantic, the first spring Neotropical songbirds begin to arrive. It is true that the Red-winged Blackbirds, which winter nearby, arrived in late February and began searching the wet ground where the snows just melted; the Bluebirds and Song Sparrows also came back in late March, returning north from more southern regions of the United States. But it is the warbler migration that holds the mystery. These small, five- to six-inch colorful, vociferous birds fill the skies, cover the trees, and even land on the ground when they are too exhausted to care.

When the fresh leaves have just emerged from the trees in mid-April, and an army of tiny caterpillars of various species hatch from eggs that overwintered, the migrants return just in time to consume them. Most of the insect-eating birds spent the winter in Mexico, Central America, the Caribbean Islands, and South America. Some have traveled over two thousand miles to reach New Jersey, and when they arrive, they have little time for anything but searching for prey.

Hundreds upon hundreds of warblers filter into extensive forests, making a landfall where they can find abundant food and a place to rest for a few days. Coming from the tropics, most are bound for the evergreen forests of the north, primarily Canada, where they spread out to breed and raise their young. Some thirty-five different species of warblers move through New Jersey each spring. First, Yellow-rumped (Myrtle) and the Palm Warblers arrive in mid-April, flitting through the trees, providing quick glimpses of their bright yellow. The yellow-and-black breeding plumage is in marked contrast to the dull, streaky plumage of the few Yellow-rumps that spend the winter in New Jersey. The next arrival is the ground-dwelling Louisiana Waterthrush, a warbler that looks more like a thrush. With its brown back and spotted breast, it blends into the leaves and twigs of the forest. It hops merrily on rocks in streams, giving its musical song that begins with three loud, clear whistling notes that echo from the shallow sides of streams or through the forest.

By late April, the Myrtle and Palm Warblers have been joined by Prairie, Black-throated Green, Yellow, and Black-and-White Warblers. The pace of the migration quickens, the trees are more laden with warblers every day, and the early morning chorus is louder and more diverse, as more and more of the resident birds begin to breed. The larger and more colorful songbirds begin to arrive in early May: Baltimore Orioles, Scarlet Tanagers, and Rose-breasted Grosbeaks, each with its loud, pure, musical songs. Their bright reds and oranges are spectacular. Some secretive and shy birds arrive also, Veerys and Wood Thrushes that will skulk through the underbrush, challenging you to find them. These thrushes breed in New Jersey and their voices join the morning chorus, adding an eerie, flutelike, ethereal quality. Their close relatives, such as the Swainson's Thrush, are usually silent, for they have a long distance yet to fly to their northern breeding ground.

These colorful migrants are joined by Kingbirds, Least Flycatchers, and several other flycatchers—drabber birds that often fail to catch our eye or engage our imagination. They are magnificent, however, when they sally forth from a perch to snatch an insect out of the air, dutifully returning to the same perch where they can be watched for hours. The delicate Ruby-throated Hummingbird makes its appearance in early May, looking like a tiny helicopter with too far to go in too short a time.

By mid-May, other species too numerous to mention arrive. Some remain to breed, others are with us for only a few days. Warblers, thrushes, vireos, orioles, sparrows, woodpeckers, wrens, and flycatchers abound in the forests and in the nearby fields. It is at this time that bird-watchers try for a "Big Day," finding more than one hundred species in a twenty-four-hour period, and New Jersey Audubon sponsors its "World Series of Birding," when international groups of competitors try to see two hundred species in a single day.

By the end of May, the migration has slowed to a trickle, but morning song is at its fullest. It is a challenge to sort out the voices of Robins, Orioles, Tanagers, and Wrens. The list goes on and on, and with experience, one can identify twenty to thirty species of birds singing from a single spot.

Unlike the shorebirds that fly several thousand miles non-stop to reach the beaches of Delaware Bay en route to their Arctic breeding grounds, most migrant land birds make a series of short night flights, starting shortly after dusk, landing wherever they can in the predawn hours. With the first light they may reevaluate their position, looking for higher-quality habitat nearby. This mass movement of migrants trying to find suitable, high-quality feeding habitat is called the "morning flight." In searching for high-quality habitat, birds need to balance nutritional and immediate energy needs with the risk from predators. Many stopover sites feature a high concentration of prey and predators, and both require large amounts of food to put on enough fat to fuel their northward migration.

Food availability is clearly key, although some songbirds eat a greater range of foods on migration than they do during the breeding season. Birds that normally eat only insects often eat a bit of fruit on migration. Those birds that have a more flexible diet during migration show faster rates of weight gain, allowing them to be on their way quicker. Even so, most land birds show strong habitat preferences.

Cape May County is ideal because it provides a wide variety of habitats in a small area, but some of these habitats are threatened. Larry Niles, Mandy Dey, and others in the Endangered and Nongame Species Program developed a Landscape Project to investigate both habitat use by nesting Neotropical migrants and habitat loss, with an aim to protecting a mixture of appropriate habitats before it is too late to save them.

Mid-May is the peak of the spring migration, and for the discerning wildlife watcher, it is a real thrill. However, the birds are not as easy to see as they are during autumn migration when they literally fall from the sky and have time to tarry. In the spring, the birds are bound for northern breeding grounds and spend much of their time high up in the trees, searching for insects. If it has been a warm spring and the trees are in full leaf, they are difficult to find, and by mid-May it can be intensely frustrating to catch a glimpse of some songster hidden high in the canopy. Still, it can be very thrilling to listen to the spring chorus and watch for the birds flitting through the vegetation.

Any forest with associated open fields and streams nearby is suitable, preferably along the coast, along the migratory pathway. Outstanding places to view spring migration include Stokes Forest (see directions to Sunset Mountain in chapter 16), Scherman-Hoffman Sanctuary (see directions in chapter 11), Princeton Woods, and of course, Cape May. Some birders consider Princeton Woods to be the best place for spring migrants. For Princeton Woods (the Charles Rogers Wildlife Refuge and Institute Woods), take U.S. 1 south through Princeton and turn right onto Alexander Road; go about 0.7 mile to West Drive and turn left, go about a quarter mile, following the left fork into the Rogers Refuge. For Cape May, visit the same spots that are mentioned in chapter 18 for fall migration.

Nesting Osprey on Delaware Bay and Barnegat Bay

Flying gracefully above the waters of Barnegat Bay, the young Osprey suddenly veers and swoops downward, splashes the surface with outstretched legs, and seizes an eight-inch fish in its talons. Much less gracefully, it flaps vigorously, struggling to rise from the water and to gain altitude, and then flies to perch on the red buoy marking the channel. Peering around to look for competition that might steal it away, it finally turns its attention to the fish. Holding the fish down with one foot, it begins to tear it apart with its beak, swallowing each strip of flesh and skin, bones and all. On another nearby buoy, another young Osprey, nearly in adult plumage, with its brown back, white underparts, and white head with bold dark markings from forehead across its eye, without moving a muscle, watches the boats moving past. Only if a boat approaches too closely or lingers too long does the Osprey take wing (fig. 101).

For most people who live along the shore, this scene has become commonplace in Barnegat Bay, along the Delaware Bayshore, and in other lakes, creeks, and estuaries along our coast. But it was not always so. Although Ospreys were abundant in the early twentieth century, they suffered severe reproductive failure after the 1950s from pesticides that accumulated in their tissues and resulted in females laying thin-shelled eggs that collapsed during incubation. The population in New Jersey plummeted to only about fifty pairs, most failing to reproduce. Once a familiar sight, the Ospreys disappeared from the inland

101. Osprey gliding gracefully above the water. (Photo by Sherry Meyer)

lakes completely, and only a few birds remained along the shore. The buildup of DDT and other chlorinated pesticides is still a problem for long-lived species such as Osprey, because once the females became contaminated, they continue to lay contaminated eggs with thin eggshells year after year. The pesticide residues are eliminated from their bodies very slowly.

The Osprey populations in New Jersey were so low that the Endangered and Nongame Species Program developed a recovery plan that included building nest platforms in predator-free places and bringing in eggs from other states where the levels of DDT and other contaminants were not as high. Aided by this intensive management effort and by the general decline in DDT levels in the environment after the pesticide was banned in the early 1970s, Ospreys resumed successful breeding. Gradually, the population built back up, as the remaining New Jersey birds successfully raised the introduced eggs and their own pesticide levels declined. Finally, in 1985 they were removed from the state's endangered species list. Ospreys are a true success story for New Jersey conservation.

In bygone years, Ospreys built their nests in the tops of large cedar trees, for they require a sturdy object with a large surface to build their bulky stick nests, which they continue to use for many years. But the cedar trees are all gone from the shore. Today, many of their nests are on channel markers (fig. 102) or on artificial structures, platforms supported on telephone poles placed at strategic positions along the coast. Some of these were dropped from helicopters so they would sink into the mud of bays, standing upright, surrounded by water. Other Ospreys build their nests on buoys in inland waterways. Some of the nests in Barnegat Bay are so close to the water that it is possible to see the incubating parents clearly, and later their growing chicks.

In the spring, the male begins to court his female by bringing her back a big fish, and then another, and another. This courtship feeding continues for many days, allowing the female to assess the ability of the male to provide food for her young. The more food the male brings back, the earlier egg laying takes place. Finally, after repeated copulations, the eggs are laid, and the pair settles down to incubation and chick rearing.

102. Ospreys often nest on channel markers in Barnegat Bay and other coastal waterways. (Photo by J. Burger)

Once the young hatch, the male brings back a fish, passes it to the female, and then flies off to find more. She tears the fish into smaller pieces to feed the young. Even when only a few days old, a brood of four can eat eight to ten pounds of fish a day, and with each succeeding day, their demands are greater. The young birds grow quickly and soon learn to tear apart fish on their own. Eventually the full-grown and fully feathered young can be seen standing on their nests and flapping their broad wings, accompanied by jumps. Finally the day arrives when they try flying, and although they are awkward, they somehow careen back to the nest. In the ensuing days they increase their wing strength, perfect their maneuverability, and soon make tentative tries to catch fish on their own. They continue to use the nest for many weeks, for the parents feed them while they are mastering the skills of fishing.

It is relatively easy to see breeding Ospreys along the coast of New Jersey, for the number of nesting pairs now exceeds 240 and reproduction is quite high, averaging more than one young per nest, which is enough to maintain healthy populations for years to come. Reproduction continues to increase on the Delaware Bayshore, the area where contaminants have posed the greatest problem for Osprey.

With powerful beats of their long, broad wings, the eagle-sized Ospreys can climb high in the sky, sweep rapidly to the water to pick up a fish, or glide gracefully to a nest. With a wing spread of five to six feet, they are truly marvelous, and a spectacle to behold.

Wintering Bald Eagles

In the tall trees, twelve Bald Eagles sit proudly in the winter sun. Most are adults with starkly white heads, but several are all-brown birds which may be anywhere from one to four years of age. It is thrilling to see so many eagles in one place along the Delaware River. One eagle picks at a dead fish washed up on the shore. Suddenly another takes wing, flies over the open water in a nearby cove, and swoops down, slamming an unwary Black Duck against the water and seizing it with its feet. The eagle struggles briefly with powerful thrusts of its wings to rise from the water, and then wheels around to carry its helpless prey back to its perch. The eagle lands, and holding down the hapless duck with its claws, it bends to pluck off breast feathers and begins ripping the flesh.

In our childhood in the Hudson Valley, it was not unusual to see a half-dozen eagles sitting on ice floes on a January day. But by the mid-1960s that phenomenon was a thing of the past, and any eagle sighting was unusual. This change occurred in New Jersey as well. In the 1950s it was not unusual to see Bald Eagles here, for quite a few pairs nested in the state, but by the 1970s the number of nesting Bald Eagles dwindled until there was but a single pair nesting in southern New Jersey.

Like the Ospreys, Peregrine Falcons, and other top avian predators, the Bald Eagles were victims of pesticides, particularly DDT. These birds eat mainly large fish and other birds, and as top predators were exposed to the highest concentration of pesticides that bioamplified through the food chain. This was the phenomenon described graphically by Rachel Carson in her landmark book, *Silent Spring,* published in 1962. Although the link to pesticides was not universally accepted at that time, Carson provided compelling evidence adduced from a variety of sources that pesticides such as DDT were the underlying cause of reproductive failure in eagles and many other species—particularly those high on aquatic and terrestrial food chains.

It seems ironic that the Bald Eagle, our national symbol, was one of the major victims of the post-World War II romance with chlorinated pesticides. The eagles had such high levels of DDT that it interfered with their estrogen cycle and with egg formation. Fertility declined. Some eggs were fertile, but the eggshells were deficient in calcium, resulting in eggs so thin that they broke under the weight of the incubating parents. Some embryos developed normally but died during the hatching process. This was one of the most dramatic examples of what we now call "endocrine disruption."

Throughout most of the Bald Eagle's range, the sad story was repeated. Adults returned to their nests, repaired them, and mated, but no young were produced. Year after year, the counts of wintering eagles showed a decreasing proportion of young birds, until it became obvious that our national emblem was in crisis. Aided by the banning of persistent pesticides, management programs succeeded in turning the tide of nesting failures. Reproduction resumed in the 1980s, abetted by aggressive wildlife management programs that reintroduced eagles into various places they had formerly inhabited.

In 1992 New Jersey began its eagle management program under Larry Niles of the Department of Environmental Protection. Niles, Kathleen Clark, and others developed a program that has raised New Jersey's breeding eagle numbers from a single nest in the early 1980s to nearly twenty nests today. Eagle populations with relatively low pesticide levels were identified in various places around the country. Fertilized eggs were taken from the nests of these birds and placed in the nests of eagles in more contaminated areas. The original birds mated again and laid new eggs, while the recipients also succeeded in raising their adopted offspring. In addition, young eagles that hatched elsewhere or in captivity were "hacked" in New Jersey. This involves raising the young on a tower and then releasing them while continuing to provide food on the tower. The provision of food assures their survival, and the hope is that the tower will be viewed as home. Indeed, several hacked eagles survived to adulthood.

Over the years, as the contaminants were gradually eliminated from the eagles' bodies, more and more pairs were capable of reproducing on their own. Security around eagle nests was also upgraded to prevent them from being disturbed or shot. The result was greatly increased nesting success. In New Jersey, the population has recovered from the single pair in south Jersey twenty years ago, to eighteen pairs nesting both in the north and the south today. Although not each pair succeeds in raising young, overall fledging success is high. Each year more eagles are raised in New Jersey. Some of these birds have returned to breed when they reached adulthood, a good sign for our future populations. The outlook is much more favorable than it was twenty years ago.

While the number of Bald Eagles nesting in New Jersey has increased dramatically in the past fifteen years, eggs that fail to hatch still show elevated levels of DDD and DDE, two of the metabolites of DDT, as well as PCBs (polychlorinated biphenyls). The PCB levels in eggs are up to three times higher than the level known to reduce eagle productivity. If these levels continue to rise, the encouraging reproductive success of the New Jersey eagles may take a turn for the worse. Increasing pesticide levels probably also account for the poor reproductive success of some of New Jersey's Peregrine Falcons; concentrations of PCBs and dioxin equivalents are at levels that cause behavioral abnormalities such as poor incubation performance in adults.

Bald Eagles are fledging from New Jersey in ever-increasing numbers; now over twenty young are fledged each year. They are learning to fish and are eventually returning to breed in the state. Our wintering population is also increasing, and between 150 and 200 Bald Eagles rest on ice floes, perch in trees, and fish in the open water, particularly in southern New Jersey, which hosts most of our wintering population, but also on the large reservoirs in the north. Large expanses of open water and relatively warmer temperatures provide ideal conditions along Delaware Bay, which normally hosts over half of the wintering population.

For winter viewing of eagles in central New Jersey, visit Poxono Island, Wallpack Bend, and the Route 206 bridge near Milford (Pennsylvania) on the upper Delaware. For other winter viewing of eagles in southern New Jersey, visit the upper Delaware Bay in Salem County and the Cohansey and Mullica Rivers. The Brigantine National Wildlife Refuge often has one or two eagles that can be seen from the auto tour route. Eagles should not be approached too closely. Even at a distance these majestic birds are a spectacular sight.

Canada Geese

Some of our commonest birds gather in large flocks whose numbers are truly staggering. Robins gather by the hundreds during fall migration. Red-winged Blackbirds and Grackles form flocks of thousands, while winter roosts of Crows and Starlings contain tens of thousands. The arrival and departure from the roost can be breathtaking. Sometimes a half million Starlings explode from their roost over a period of a few minutes.

103. Canada Geese gather on lawns to forage and then rest on inland lakes and rivers. (Photo by J. Burger)

Among other spectacles, the Canada Goose deserves special mention. Once they nested farther north in Canada, but New Jerseyans felt they were magnificent and clipped the wings of some geese, forcing them to spend the winter. In the next spring, these geese paired and raised healthy broods. Since young geese learn their migration routes from their parents, the young learned that they need only move from one large lawn to another. Now there have been generations of geese that believe they should not migrate, and so they remain, by the thousands, on our lawns and lakes, where they are often considered pests (fig. 103). They are, however, still magnificent.

Living in the Northeast, we have seasonal identifiers. The honking skeins of migrating Canada Geese, flying so high we can barely detect them, mark both the coming of spring and the approach of winter. A flight of Canada Geese is a thrilling, tingling spectacle. Although we see our local geese every day of the year, we still marvel when a loud honking flock floats by on heavily beating wings, forming long V's, black chevrons against a darkening sky.

FOR FURTHER INFORMATION: Call the Endangered and Nongame Species Program (609-292-9400), New Jersey Audubon (908-766-5787; www.nj.com/audubon), Cape May Bird Observatory (609-861-0700), American Littoral Society (732-291-0055 in north Jersey; 609-294-3111 in south Jersey; www.alsnyc.org), or PSE&G (888-627-7437), depending on the subject.

Epilogue:
People at the Mall

New Jersey is a remarkable state. It is the most heavily industrialized state and has the highest population density in the nation, yet it has a wide range of habitats, from the Jersey shore to the mountains. It has the Pine Barrens, a unique treasure of global importance, and more forest now than it had a century ago. As is clear from the diverse range of nature spectacles discussed in this book, New Jersey is ecologically blessed. It is also obvious, however, that many of the nature spectacles involve plants, amphibians, birds, and even invertebrates, but none involve mammals. This is because we have few large mammals, at least few that are spectacular *and* are predictable.

White-tailed Deer used to be scarce, but with the protection afforded by suburbanization, deer numbers have skyrocketed in recent decades. Hunters kill over 50,000 deer in New Jersey each year, roughly a third of the population at the start of the hunting season, but that is not sufficient to manage the population. In many communities, including those where hunting is prohibited, deer are widely considered pests. More serious are the increasing numbers of deer-auto interactions, almost always fatal to the deer, and potentially fatal to the auto's inhabitants. Deer are partly responsible for our high Lyme disease rates and for an enormous range of damage to agricultural and wildlands, not to mention our backyards. They do not seem thrilling enough to warrant their own chapter, although the curious naturalist can find spectacular numbers at the Duke Estate, where they were never controlled but were provided with food in many winters.

Black Bears are an exciting mammal, as well as a conservation success story. Both deliberate introductions and natural immigration across the Delaware River resulted in an increase in the number of bears in northwestern New Jersey. Bears are usually nocturnal and hard to see, and they are mainly solitary. That does not make the damage they do any less irksome. The excitement of seeing a bear in one's backyard is giving way to concern for bird feeders, pets, and people. The Department of Environmental Protection issues educational notices to respect bears and to avoid feeding them so they will not habituate so quickly to human presence.

Both deer and bear are attractive and entertaining in their proper setting, when viewed from a safe distance. Although Northeasterners have not dealt adequately with the downside of their population increases, we surely must.

Also, they do not occur predictably in numbers sufficient to label them a spectacle. New Jersey's most spectacular mammal happening is us! We occur everywhere in the state, in all seasons, and dominate the landscape. Like deer and bears, we can be attractive and entertaining in our appropriate habitat, and like those species, we can be incredibly damaging, wreaking complete havoc on New Jersey's landscapes.

What is the appropriate habitat for observing the human spectacle? Our daily migration corridors are certainly spectacular enough, particularly if there is a toll booth or a tipped tractor trailer in the way. But we are most impressed with the habitat known as the Mall. Below we examine "People at the Mall" as one of New Jersey's spectacles, one we can all enjoy, both as observers and as participants.

People at the Mall

In the bright lights so typical of their habitats, a bustle of bodies moves swiftly by, like ants on a march, seemingly engaged in some serious goal-oriented activity. Some stop briefly to peer through panes of glass, others to loiter with friends. Many are silent, while others vocalize continuously. A few are solitary, hurrying to some unknown destination, others move more languorously in small groups. Here are people engaged in one of the most popular activities in New Jersey, visiting the mall.

KEY LOCATIONS: There is a mall in every region of the state, but a few truly large ones include Paramus in north Jersey, Bridgewater Commons in Somerset County, Menlo Park Mall in Edison, and Cherry Hill in south Jersey. One can compare behavior at different times of the year, in large versus small malls, and at indoor versus outdoor malls.

DIRECTIONS: No one needs directions to the nearest mall, which is one of the amazing aspects of this spectacle.

BEST TIME TO VISIT: Halloween afternoon, the day after Thanksgiving ("Black Friday"), or the three weeks just before December 25 of any year. Malls are also good in the summer when individuals concentrate in the early morning to walk rapidly without a destination. Highest concentrations are found in the evening from 7 to 9 P.M.

PRIME HABITAT: The largest mall in a region, located next to a major thoroughfare. Observations are easiest where viewing platforms, in the form of benches, allow people to habituate to your presence.

104. Typical New Jersey mall at Bridgewater Commons in Somerset. (Photo by J. Burger)

Under bright lights, cool air from large fans rustle through the shiny bulbs tied to bright green artificial pine boughs, and thin silvery metallic strands tinkle, brushing lightly together. A faint scent of fresh pine wafts by. A solitary pine cone falls with a faint echo, unnoticed by the throng hurrying toward their own destinations, caught in one of the oldest of rituals, in a newly created habitat. People are rushing in every direction. Like Chickadees, they gather at feeding stations known as Food Courts to enjoy seeds and suet and other tasty delicacies offered to them by the caring people who spend long hours catering to customer whims and fancies. Parents call loudly to their offspring: "No, No" or "Come here now" are popular vocalizations.

It is the day after Thanksgiving at a New Jersey mall, and people are beginning their quest for gifts for loved ones, family, friends, and the postman. They are particularly foraging for elusive bargains. While the behavior of presenting gifts is very old indeed, the manner of obtaining those gifts has surely changed over the years, both for those who inhabited New Jersey ten thousand years ago, and for those who migrated when aggression forced them to leave the shores of other continents, or when low food supplies in Ireland and elsewhere made migration a necessity.

Those who remained in the old habitat faced starvation, lowered their reproductive success, and had lower survival. Many starved, fewer young reached reproductive age, and those that did, raised fewer young themselves. Migration to the New World did not exactly meet the expectations of an easy life. Those who migrated to the new habitat in New Jersey faced competition from previous residents, as well as from the next wave of immigrants that was sure to follow. But there was more space, there were more trees and other natural resources, and it was easier to establish a territory.

People who reached the new habitat established colonies, initially thirteen, and selected territories. Selection was resource-based, and optimum sites were near water bodies that assured fresh water for drinking as well as access to transportation routes. Many severed ties with their old countries. Through a wide range of social interactions, leaders emerged, and the colonies prospered and grew. The colonists used a wide range of tools to manipulate the habitat, increasing food supplies and creating newer and more diverse industries.

Finding gifts for family and friends once meant going out into the woods and shooting game, tanning leather, or building objects. But as the natural habitat became more and more restricted, commerce became more diversified, and people began searching elsewhere for gifts. At first these could be obtained from neighbors, and later they were obtained from small neighborhood general stores. Finally, gifts were obtained in large stores, where variety was highly prized. The largest stores attracted the most people, and these gradually out-competed the smaller stores, starving them out of existence. Soon the small stores disappeared from neighborhoods, and then from the towns.

A new habitat emerged: some people put several large stores together, called a *strip mall*, a form of shopping that was founded in New Jersey. For a while they prospered, but then people built even larger malls, and the smaller malls fell on hard times, with many facilities remaining vacant.

New Jersey is in transition. The old habitat of small stores has dwindled, even the small malls are disappearing, being replaced by larger and larger malls, and by new habitat, the enclosed, all-weather-comfort mall. Village stores are being converted to more specialized uses. Without government regulation and intervention, only the large malls will remain.

In some towns, people banded together and passed zoning laws that forbid the building of large malls in their midst, and some small boutiques and stores survived. But the same people also retained the privilege of visiting the malls in nearby towns. As the number of stores increased, so did the number of people. Human density increased, and increased, and increased.

Today, large concentrations of people can be found at malls at most times of the day, although the numbers generally increase in the late afternoon and peak in the early evening. While most people visiting the malls are interested in shopping, and they bustle about, going from store to store, some individuals make coming to the mall a pastime in itself. Some malls open early to allow senior citizens to walk; the terrain is level, the distances long, and the climate controlled. For others, visiting the mall is a social occasion, where males can meet females, and both can find friends from previous mall visits. Here one can observe much of the human life cycle: courtship, parental care, and exercising among the elderly.

105. Children at a mall (from left to right: Elizabeth, Erik, and Emily Burger). (Photo by J. Burger)

There are age and gender differences in the way people behave at malls. The very young remain with adults, trailing along behind. Some young are carried or pushed, while others are dragged, kicking and screaming. Presentation of small stuffed animals known as "BeanieBabies" sometimes quiets down the noisy young, but often persistent howling attests to gifts denied. Slightly older children, young adults really, still gaze at the BeanieBabies, not yet beyond the age of collecting specimens of the latest craze in cards or figurines (fig. 105).

Still older young, apparently near fledging, are left alone by their parents. They gather in groups, sometimes all males, sometimes all females, and sometimes mixed. These groups assemble in the late afternoon and often remain in the same spot until darkness descends. The noise level is higher in these groups of fledglings. Sometimes the groups roam slowly through the passageways, foraging on the available food.

There are also gender differences in behavior among the groups of young fledglings. Our research has indicated that approach distance varies depending upon the sex of both the approacher and the approachee. Approach distance is the distance that remains between two individuals after one has stopped approaching the other. The greatest distance is maintained when a male approaches a female, and the shortest distance is maintained when a female approaches a male. This means that when a male approaches a stationary female, he remains farther away from her than if she were doing the approaching. This is peculiar, since the usual assumption with human behavior is that males are dominant over females and would therefore approach them as close as they like.

This difference in approach distance is not due to age, since similar results were found with older adults, distinguished by their partially gray hair. The differences may be due to the need of males to reduce the threat caused by their greater size, since in a direct conflict involving physical contact, the larger individual would win. By remaining farther away, the male indicates a willingness not to engage in aggression or exert dominance.

There are differences in behavior as a function of group size. In most animals, such as Baboons, Zebras, and White-tailed Deer, vigilance decreases with group size: with more eyes to look for predators, each animal can spend less time looking. However, in these human groups, vigilance increases with numbers, but mostly with respect to other groups of similar ages. Apparently, when human groups reach a certain critical size, the possibility for competition and interactions between groups increases, and each group must be wary of approaching danger. Aggression between groups has become a special (though unwelcome) attribute at some malls.

While most activity at a mall is hurried and noisy, some is more subdued. Early in the morning, senior citizens come to the mall for their daily walk, and although some hurry, most walk leisurely back and forth. Peculiar lines also form early in the morning outside of booths that sell tickets for plays or concerts, and some people arrive the minute the doors to the mall open. Other lines form outside of stores that sell currently popular toys. While the people waiting at the booths seem to be strangers to one another, those waiting for the stuffed animals seem to know one another, and exchange information on where the latest releases are available. In the early evening long lines form for the movie theaters, but these lines move quickly. All these lines provide wonderful opportunities to watch group behavior.

Food Courts offer additional opportunities to observe behavior because people are generally more relaxed and engaged in pleasurable activities. Competition for food is usually limited because there are so many choices. Moreover, people remain for only a short period, making it possible to watch many different people quickly. We used to examine gender differences in smoking behavior in Food Courts, but fortunately, smoking is now prohibited in most malls. Instead, people gather outside the doorways, huddled in small groups, smoking before they can return to shopping. Adults smoke quickly, anxious to be on their way, while groups of teen-agers linger, spending most of their time holding their cigarettes conspicuously, as if signaling that they have reached adulthood.

While fledglings appear to be coming to the mall for social interactions, adults seem bent on purchasing goods. Some know exactly what they need, go from their car to the store, and from the store back to their car. Others "shop," checking out many stores but making relatively few purchases. They are largely uninterested in social interactions. Some adults move rapidly from store to store, picking up packages at nearly every place. They can be seen exiting the mall, carrying goods toward their cars. As the number of shopping days to December 25 becomes smaller, the pace of movement quickens, the number of packages picked up increases, and the competition for items increases.

Partially the competition increases because the resources are becoming more limited. The variety in items, and quality of each item, is larger right after Thanksgiving, and seems to decrease toward December 25. For example, while there might be numerous sweaters in every size and color early in December, by December 20 few remain of any size or color. Thus it is critical to quickly obtain the item once it has been spotted. This results in many adults grabbing for the same item, with loud vocalization and shoving. As with most studies in animal behavior, it is difficult to observe direct competition because the presence of so many people makes it trying to see the interactions between the individuals in the center. Piracy (the stealing of an object from one individual) occurs very rapidly, and it is difficult to predict exactly when the most hostile interactions will occur. Long hours of observation are necessary, but since the greatest number of individuals are present from about 4 to 9 P.M., in the three weeks before December 25, this is an optimal time to record aggression.

Like gulls and other animals whose piracy is an important form of acquisition, there are specialists who obtain nearly all of their gifts and other goods in this manner. Since the pirate is attempting to steal from another, the behavior is often surreptitious and therefore difficult to quantify. Nonetheless, careful observation from one or two sites can provide quantitative data, and because large numbers of people gather at malls, this is an excellent place for such observations. Malls provide some of the best places to watch human behavior. It is possible to find suitable observation sites, and people habituate to your presence when you remain in the same place.

People walk by rapidly without giving you a glance, ignoring the open notebook where you are recording their behavior. There are many things to observe: how close people come to one another, gender and age differences determining how close people walk to one another, the number of times different people make eye contact with their friends or perfect strangers, how fast different people walk, how often they stop to look at different store windows, the response of people to being brushed accidentally, who will stop to pick up an object dropped by someone—the possibilities are endless.

Sometimes a lone toddler ambles by, obviously separated from its parent. Innocently, she stops to look at the stuffed animals and games in a store window, walks over to the nearest display, and grabs at the bright green stuffed bear. Still no parent appears. A caring saleswoman in her early fifties bends to ask the child where her mother is. She looks up blankly, and returns to playing with the bear. After calling a security guard, the woman waits with the child, talking about the bear in soft, reassuring tones. An announcement comes over the mall system, "Lost little girl in front of BeanieBaby stall." Within minutes a harried mother with two other small children rushes up, and, after reuniting, the family hurries away, unaware that the little girl still clutches the BeanieBaby. With a smile the salesclerk takes out a five and walks to the register to pay for the early Christmas gift to a bewildered and once-lost child.

Somewhere between nine and ten at night, the light levels begin to decrease in most malls, the number of open stores decreases, and the number of people scurrying about declines, until only the twelve-screen theaters are occupied. Oddly, fledglings are the last to leave, and they often remain in close-knit groups until they are asked to leave by others wearing uniforms. Finally, however, even these groups depart, and the lights are dimmed. Only shadows remain—the shadows of the tiny balls dangling from the pine boughs that hang from the ceilings. All is quiet: the people have left the mall. But they will return at the same time the next morning, for visiting the mall is a highly synchronous event, and a highly predictable one.

FOR MORE INFORMATION: Information on suitable viewing hours can be obtained by calling your local mall, or by asking a teen-age relative or neighbor.

Appendix A
Scientific Names of Species
Mentioned in Text

Plants

Alder	*Alnus* spp.
Alfalfa	*Medicago sativa*
Arrowhead	*Sagittaria* spp. (*S. latifolia*)
Atlantic White Cedar	*Chamaecyparis thyoides*
Bayberry	*Myrica pennsylvanica*
Beach Grass	*Ammophila breviligulata*
Bearberry	*Arctostaphylus uva-ursi*
Beech	*Fagus grandifolia*
Birch	*Betula* spp.
Black Huckleberry	*Gaylussacia baccata*
Black Knapweed	*Centaurea nigra*
Blackjack Oak	*Quercus marilandica*
Bladderwort	*Utricularia* spp.
Blueberry	*Vaccinium* spp.
Bluestem Grass	*Andropogon, Schizachyrium*
Bog Asphodel	*Narthecium americanum*
Bog Clubmoss	*Lycopodium inundatum*
Bracken Fern	*Pteridium aquilinum*
Broom Crowberry	*Corema conradii*
Butterfly Bush	*Buddleia davidii*
Butterfly Weed	*Asclepias tuberosa*
Cattail	*Typha* spp.
Cherry	*Prunus* spp. (especially *Prunus serotina*)
Coneflower	*Echinacea* spp.
Cord Grass	*Spartina alterniflora*
Cosmos	*Cosmos* spp. (*C. bipinnatus*)
Cranberry (American)	*Vaccinium macrocarpon*
Curly-grass Fern	*Schizaea pusilla*
Daffodil	*Narcissus* spp.
Daisy	*Chrysanthemum* spp.
Dangleberry	*Gaylussacia frondosa*
Dill	*Anethum graveolens*
Eelgrass	*Zostera maritima*
Fennel	*Foeniculum vulgare*
Fir (Mexico)	*Abies oyamel*
Gerardia (Purple)	*Gerardia* spp. (*G. purpurea*)

Golden Club	*Orontium aquaticum*
Golden Crest	*Lophiola americana*
Grass Pink	*Calopogon pulchellus*
Hackberry	*Celtis occidentalis*
Hemlock	*Tsuga candensis*
Highbush Blueberry	*Vaccinium corymbosum*
Holly (American)	*Ilex opaca*
Honeysuckle	*Lonicera japonica* and *L. tartarica*
Horned Bladderwort	*Utricularia cornuta*
Hudsonia	*Hudsonia tomentosum*
Licorice (American)	*Glycyrrhiza lepidota*
Lotus (American)	*Nelumbo lutea*
Lowbush Blueberry (Early)	*Vaccinia vacillans*
Maple	Family Aceraceae
Marsh Elder	*Iva frutescens*
Milkweed (Common)	*Asclepias syriaca*
Mountain Laurel	*Kalmia latifolia*
Oak	*Quercus* spp.
Orange Milkweed	*Asclepias tuberosa*
Peach	*Prunus persica*
Persimmon	*Diospyros virginiana*
Phragmites (Common Reed)	*Phragmites communis* (= *P. australis*)
Pipevine (Dutchman's Pipe)	*Aristolochia durior*
Pitch Pine	*Pinus rigida*
Pitcher-plant	*Sarracenia purpurea*
Poison Ivy	*Rhus radicans*
Purple Coneflower	*Echinacea purpurea*
Red Cedar	*Juniperus virginiana*
Red Maple	*Acer rubrum*
Rose Mallow	*Hibiscus moscheutos*
Round-leaved Sundew	*Drosera rotundifolia*
Sacred Lotus	*Nelumbo nucifera* (India), *Nymphaea lotus* (Egypt)
St. Peter's Wort	*Ascyrum stans*
Salt Hay	*Spartina patens*
Sassafras	*Sassafras albidum*
Scrub Oak	*Quercus ilicifolia*
Scrub Pine	*Pinus virginiana*
Sea Lettuce	*Ulva latuca*
Seaside Goldenrod	*Solidago sempervirens*
Sedum	*Sedum* spp.
Shadbush (Juneberry)	*Amelanchier canadensis*
Sheep Laurel	*Kalmia angustifolia*
Spatterdock	*Nuphar variegatum*
Spatulate-leaved Sundew	*Drosera intermedia*
Sphagnum Moss	*Sphagnum* spp.
Sundews	Family Droseraceae
Swamp Maple	*Acer rubrum*
Swamp Milkweed	*Asclepias incarnata*

Sweet Pepperbush	*Clethra alnifolia*
Sycamore	*Platanus occidentalis*
Tamarisk	*Tamarix gallica*
Teaberry	*Gaultheria procumbens*
Thread-leaved Sundew	*Drosera filiformis*
Tulip Poplar	*Liquidambar styraciflua*
Turkey Beard	*Xerophyllum asphodeloides*
Turtlehead	*Chelone glabra*
White Fringed Orchid	*Habenaria blephariglottis*
White Water Lily	*Nymphaea odorata*
Yellow Spatterdock	*Nuphar variegatum*
Zinnia	*Zinnia elegans*

Butterflies and Moths

Admirals	*Limenitis* spp., *Vanessa* spp.
American Lady	*Vanessa virginiensis*
Anglewings	*Polygonia* spp.
Aphrodite Fritillary	*Speyeria aphrodite*
Baltimore Checkerspot	*Euphydryas phaeton*
Black Swallowtail	*Papilio polyxenes*
Buckeye (Common)	*Junonia coenia*
Cabbage White Butterfly	*Pieris rapae*
Cloudless Sulphur	*Phoebis sennae*
Comma (Eastern)	*Polygonia comma*
Common Wood Nymph	*Megisto cymela*
Copper (American)	*Lycaena phlaeas*
Coral Hairstreak	*Satyrium titus*
Emperors	*Asterocampa* spp.
Eyed Brown	*Satyrodes eurydice*
Fritillaries	*Speyeria* spp.
Giant Swallowtail	*Papilio cresphontes*
Great Spangled Fritillary	*Speyeria cybele*
Gypsy Moth	*Lymantria dispar*
Hackberry Emperor	*Asterocampa celtis*
Hairstreaks	*Satyrium* spp.
Harvester	*Feniseca tarquinus*
Little Wood Satyr	*Megisto cymela*
Little Yellow	*Eurema lisa*
Long-tailed Skipper	*Urbanus proteus*
Monarch	*Danaus plexippus*
Mourning Cloak	*Nymphalis antiopa*
Northern Broken-dash	*Wallengrenia egeremet*
Northern Pearly Eye	*Enodia anthedon*
Orange Sulphur	*Colias eurytheme*
Painted Lady	*Vanessa cardui*
Pearl Crescent	*Phyciodes tharos*
Pipevine Swallowtail	*Battus philenor*
Plain Ringlet	*Coenonympha tullia*

Red Admiral	*Vanessa atalanta*
Silver-spotted Skipper	*Epargyreus clarus*
Skippers	*Hesperiidae*
Snout	*Libytheana carinenta bachmani*
Spicebush Swallowtail	*Papilio troilus*
Spring Azure	*Celastrina ladon*
Tawny Emperor	*Asterocampa clyton*
Tiger Swallowtail	*Papilio glaucus*
Viceroy	*Limenitis archippus*

Other Invertebrates

Ant	Family Formicidae
Bee	Family Apidae
Barnacles	Subclass Cirripedia (mainly *Balanus* spp.)
Blue Crab	*Callinectes sapidus*
Blue Mussel	*Mytilus edulis*
Brackish-water Fiddler Crab	*Uca minax*
Conch	*Strombus* spp.
Fiddler Crab	*Uca* spp.
Flies	Order Diptera
Globe Trotter	*Pantala flavescens*
Grasshopper	Orthoptera Family
Green Darner	*Anax junius*
Green-head Fly	*Tabanus americanus*
Horseshoe Crab	*Limulus polyphemus*
Hummingbird Clearwing Moth	*Hemaris thysbe*
Mites	Family Acaridae
Mosquitoes	Family Culicidae
Mud Fiddler Crab	*Uca pugnax*
Ribbed Mussel	*Modiolus demissus*
Saddlebags	*Tramea* spp.
Salt Marsh Mosquito	*Aedes solicitans*
Sand Fiddler Crab	*Uca pugilator*
Shadow Darner	*Aeshna umbrosa*
Slipper Shell	*Crepidula fornicata*
Snowberry Clearwing Moth	*Hemaris diffinis*
Soft-shelled Clam	*Mya arenarum*
Sponges	Phylum Porifera
Ticks	*Dermacentor* spp.
Wooly Aphids	Family Eriosomatidae: *Schizoneura, Pemphigus*

Fish

Alewife	*Alosa pseudoharengus*
Anchovy	*Anchoa mitchilli*
Atlantic Sturgeon	*Acipensar oxyrinchus*
Blueback Herring	*Alosa aestivalis*
Bluefish	*Pomatomus saltatrix*

Bullheads	*Coltidae*
Eel (Common)	*Anguilla rostrata*
Eel (European)	*Anguilla anguilla*
Gizzard Shad	*Dorosoma cepedianum*
Glass Eel (American Eel)	*Anguilla rostrata*
Herring (Blueback)	*Alosa aestivalis*
Killifish	*Fundulus* spp.
Pompano	*Trachinotis carolina*
Rainbow Smelt	*Osmerus mordax*
Sea Lamprey	*Petromyzon marinus*
Shad (American)	*Alosa sapidissima*
Short-nosed Sturgeon	*Acipensar brevirostrum*
Silversides	*Menidia* spp.
Striped Bass	*Morone saxatilis*
Summer Flounder	*Paralicthys dentatus*
Tuna (Bluefin)	*Thunnus thynnus*
Weakfish	*Cynoscion regalis*

Amphibians

Bullfrog	*Rana catesbeiana*
Carpenter Frog	*Rana virgatipes*
Chorus Frog	*Pseudacris triseriata*
Cricket Frog	*Acris crepitans*
Four-toed Salamander	*Hemidactylium scutatum*
Fowler's Toad	*Bufo woodhousei*
Gray Treefrog	*Hyla versicolor*
Green Frog	*Rana clamitans*
Southern Leopard Frog	*Rana utricularia [sphenocephala]*
Pine Barrens Treefrog	*Hyla andersonia*
Southern Leopard	*Rana utricularia*
Spring Peeper	*Pseudacris [Hyla] crucifer*
Wood Frog	*Rana sylvatica*

Reptiles

Black Racer	*Coluber constrictor*
Black Rat Snake	*Elaphe obsoleta*
Diamondback Terrapin	*Malaclemys terrapin*
Garter Snake	*Thamnophis sirtalis*
Loggerhead Sea Turtle	*Caretta caretta*
Pine Snake	*Pituophis melanoleucus*

Birds

Alder Flycatcher	*Empidonax alnorum*
Bald Eagle	*Haliaeetus leucocephalus*
Baltimore Oriole	*Icterus galbula*
Barn Owl	*Tyto alba*

Barrow's Goldeneye — *Bucephala islandica*
Belted Kingfisher — *Ceryle alcyon*
Bittern (American) — *Botaurus lentiginosus*
Black-and-white Warbler — *Mniotilta varia*
Black-bellied Plover — *Pluvialis squatarola*
Black-crowned Night Heron — *Nycticorax nycticorax*
Black Duck — *Anas rubripes*
Black-headed Gull — *Larus ridibundus*
Black-legged Kittiwake — *Rissa tridactyla*
Black Scoter — *Melanitta nigra*
Black Skimmer — *Rynchops niger*
Black-throated Green Warbler — *Dendroica virens*
Black Vulture — *Coragyps ater*
Bluebird (Eastern) — *Sialis sialia*
Blue Jay — *Cyanocitta cristata*
Blue-winged Teal — *Anas discors*
Bonaparte's Gull — *Larus philadelphia*
Brant — *Branta bernicula*
Broad-winged Hawk — *Buteo platypterus*
Brown-headed Cowbird — *Molothrus ater*
Brown Pelican — *Pelecanus occidentalis*
Brown Thrasher — *Toxostoma rufum*
Bufflehead — *Bucephala albeola*
California Gull — *Larus californicus*
Canada Goose — *Branta canadensis*
Canvasback — *Aythya valisneria*
Cardinal — *Cardinalis cardinalis*
Caspian Tern — *Hydroprogne caspia*
Cattle Egret — *Bubulcus ibis*
Chickadee — *Parus atricapillus, P. carolinensis*
Chipping Sparrow — *Spizella passerina*
Clapper Rail — *Rallus longirostris*
Clay-colored Sparrow — *Spizella pallida*
Cooper's Hawk — *Accipiter cooperi*
Coot — *Fulica americana*
Crow (Common) — *Corvus brachyrhynchos*
Double-crested Cormorant — *Phalacrocorax auritus*
Dowitcher — *Limnodromus griseus*
Dunlin — *Calidris alpina*
Eider (Common) — *Somateria mollisima*
Eurasian Wigeon — *Anas penelope*
Evening Grosbeak — *Hesperiphona vespertina*
Field Sparrow — *Spizella pusilla*
Fish Crow — *Corvus ossifragus*
Flicker — *Colaptes auratus*
Flycatchers — Family Tyrannidae
Forster's Tern — *Sterna forsteri*
Franklin's Gull — *Larus pipixcan*

Fulvous Whistling Duck	*Dendrocygna bicolor*
Gadwall	*Anas strepera*
Glaucous Gull	*Larus hyperboreus*
Glossy Ibis	*Plegadis falcinellus*
Golden Eagle	*Aquila chrysaetos*
Goldeneye (Common)	*Bucephala clangula*
Goshawk (Northern)	*Accipiter gentilis*
Grackle (Common)	*Quiscalus quiscala*
Great Black-backed Gull	*Larus marinus*
Great Blue Heron	*Ardea herodias*
Great Cormorant	*Phalacrocorax carbo*
Great Egret	*Egretta americana*
Great Horned Owl	*Bubo virginianus*
Greater Scaup	*Aythya marila*
Green Heron	*Butorides virescens*
Green-winged Teal	*Anas crecca carolinensis*
Grosbeak (Mexican)	*Pheucticus* sp.
Gull-billed Tern	*Gelochelidon nilotica*
Harlequin Duck	*Histrionicus histrionicus*
Herring Gull	*Larus argentatus*
Hooded Merganser	*Lophodytes cucullatus*
Horned Grebe	*Podiceps auritus*
House Wren	*Troglodytes aedon*
Iceland Gull	*Larus glaucoides*
Ivory Gull	*Pagodroma eburnea*
Kestrel (American)	*Falco sparverius*
Killdeer	*Charadrius vociferus*
King Eider	*Somateria spectabilis*
King Penguin	*Aptenodytes patagonicus*
King Rail	*Rallus elegans*
Kingbird (Eastern)	*Tyrannus tyrannus*
Kirtland's Warbler	*Dendroica kirtlandii*
Laughing Gull	*Larus atricilla*
Least Flycatcher	*Empidonax minutus*
Least Tern	*Sterna antillarum*
Lesser Black-backed Gull	*Larus fuscus*
Lesser Scaup	*Aythya affinis*
Little Blue Heron	*Egretta caerulea*
Little Gull	*Larus minutus*
Long-eared Owl	*Asio otus*
Loon (Common)	*Gavia immer*
Louisiana Waterthrush	*Seiurus motacilla*
Mallard	*Anas platyrhynchos*
Marsh Hawk (Northern Harrier)	*Circus cyaneus*
Marsh Wren	*Cistothorus palustris*
Merganser (Common)	*Mergus merganser*
Merlin	*Falco columbarius*
Mew Gull	*Larus canus*

Mockingbird	*Mimus gilvus*
Mourning Warbler	*Oporornis philadelphia*
Mute Swan	*Cygnus olor*
Myrtle Warbler	*Dendroica coronata*
Northern Harrier (Marsh Hawk)	*Circus cyaneus*
Northern Pintail	*Anas acuta*
Oldsquaw	*Clangula hyemalis*
Oriole (Mexican)	*Icterus sp.*
Osprey	*Pandion haliaetus*
Ovenbird	*Seiurus aurocapillus*
Oystercatcher (American)	*Haematopus palliatus*
Palm Warbler	*Dendroica palmarum*
Peregrine Falcon	*Falco peregrinus*
Pheasant	*Phasianus colchicus*
Piping Plover	*Charadrius melodus*
Prairie Warbler	*Dendroica discolor*
Purple Sandpiper	*Calidris maritima*
Raven	*Corvus corax*
Red-breasted Merganser	*Mergus serrator*
Red Knot	*Calidris canutus*
Red-shouldered Hawk	*Buteo lineatus*
Red-tailed Hawk	*Buteo jamaicensis*
Red-throated Loon	*Gavia stellata*
Red-winged Blackbird	*Agelaius phoeniceus*
Redhead	*Aythya americana*
Ring-billed Gull	*Larus delawarensis*
Ring-necked Duck	*Aythya collaris*
Ring-necked Pheasant	*Phasianus colchicus*
Robin	*Turdus migratorius*
Rose-breasted Grosbeak	*Pheucticus ludovicianus*
Ross's Goose	*Chen rossii*
Ross's Gull	*Rhodostethia rosea*
Rough-legged Hawk	*Buteo lagopus*
Royal Tern	*Thalasseus maximus*
Ruby-throated Hummingbird	*Archilochus colubris*
Ruddy Duck	*Oxyura jamaicensis*
Ruddy Turnstone	*Arenaria interpres*
Ruffed Grouse	*Bonasa umbellus*
Sabine's Gull	*Xema sabini*
Sanderling	*Calidris alba*
Sandhill Crane	*Grus canadensis*
Scarlet Tanager	*Piranga olivacea*
Semipalmated Plover	*Charadrius semipalmatus*
Semipalmated Sandpiper	*Calidris pusilla*
Sharp-shinned Hawk	*Accipiter striatus*
Short-billed Dowitcher	*Limnodromus griseus*
Shoveler (Northern)	*Anas clypeata*
Snow Goose	*Chen caerulescens*

Snowy Egret	*Egretta garzetta*
Song Sparrow	*Melospiza melodia*
Sora Rail	*Porzana carolina*
Spotted Sandpiper	*Actitis macularia*
Starling	*Sturnus vulgaris*
Surf Scoter	*Melanitta perspicillata*
Swainson's Hawk	*Buteo swainsonii*
Swainson's Thrush	*Catharus swainsonii*
Tanagers	Family Thraupidae
Tern (Common)	*Sterna hirundo*
Thrushes	Family Turdidae
Towhee	*Pipilo erythrophthalmus*
Tree Swallow	*Iridiprocne bicolor*
Tri-colored Heron	*Egretta tricolor*
Trumpeter Swan	*Cygnus buccinator*
Tufted Duck	*Aythya fuligula*
Tundra Swan	*See* Whistling Swan
Turkey Vulture	*Cathartes aura*
Veery	*Catharus fuscescens*
Vireos	*Vireo* spp.
Virginia Rail	*Rallus limicola*
Warblers	Family Parulidae
Whistling Swan	*Olor columbianus*
White-breasted Nuthatch	*Sitta carolinensis*
White-fronted Goose	*Anser albifrons*
White-winged Scoter	*Melanitta deglandi*
Widgeon (American, Baldpate)	*Anas americana*
Widgeon (Eurasian)	*Anas penelope*
Wood Duck	*Aix sponsa*
Woodpeckers	Family Picidae
Wood Thrush	*Hylocichla mustelina*
Wren	*Troglydytes aedon*
Yellow-breasted Chat	*Icteria virens*
Yellow-crowned Night Heron	*Nycticorax violacea*
Yellow-rumped Warbler	*Dendroica coronata*
Yellow Warbler	*Dendroica petechia*
Yellowthroat	*Geothlypis trichas*

Mammals

Baboon	*Papio* spp.
Beaver	*Castor americanus*
Big Brown Bat	*Eptesicus fuscus*
Black Bear	*Ursus americana*
Buffalo	*Bison bison*
Cat	*Felis domesticus*
Coyote	*Canis latrans*
Flying Fox	*Pteropus* spp.

Hoary Bat	*Lasiurus cinereus*
Indiana Bat	*Myotis sodalis*
Lion	*Panthera leo*
Little Brown Bat	*Myotis lucifugus*
Northern Long-eared Bat	*Myotis evolis*
Opossum	*Didelphis virginiana*
Pipistrelle Bat (Eastern)	*Pipistrellus subflavus*
Raccoon	*Procyon lotor*
Rats	*Rattus* sp.
Red Bat	*Lasiurus borealis*
Red Fox	*Vulpes vulpes*
Red Squirrel	*Tamasciurus hudsonicus*
Rhinoceros	*Diceros bicornis*
Silver-haired Bat	*Lasius borealis*
Skunk (Striped)	*Mephitus mephitus*
Small-footed Myotis	*Myotis subulatus*
Squirrel (Gray)	*Sciurus carolinensis*
Vampire Bat	Subfamily Desmodontinae
White-tailed Deer	*Odocoileus virginianus*
Wolf	*Canis lupus*
Zebra	*Equus burchelli*

Appendix B
Gulls Found in New Jersey

Gulls with White Heads in Breeding Season

Glaucous Gull: large, white-winged, a few each winter
Iceland Gull: smaller than Herring Gull, a few each winter
Great Black-backed Gull: our largest gull, very common, breeds.
Lesser Black-backed Gull: size of Herring Gull, a few each winter, fewer in summer, becoming more common
Herring Gull: the typical seagull, and abundant breeder but declining
California Gull: size of a Ring-billed; accidental visitor
Ring-billed Gull: our commonest inland gull in winter, increasing
Mew Gull: accidental, similar to Ring-billed
Ivory Gull: accidental
Black-legged Kittiwake: rarely seen offshore, mainly November
Ross's Gull: accidental

Gulls with Blackish Heads in Breeding Season

Black-headed Gull: rare, mainly in winter; larger than Bonaparte's
Laughing Gull: familiar and abundant summer breeder
Franklin's Gull: accidental visitor in fall and winter
Bonaparte's Gull: common winter visitor
Little Gull: very rare, mainly in winter
Sabine's Gull: accidental

Appendix C
Waterfowl Found in New Jersey

Mute Swan: several North Shore ponds (see chapter 22)
Whistling [Tundra] Swan: Whitesbog, usually not on shore (see chapter 22)
Canada Goose: omnipresent, throughout most of New Jersey
Brant: several coastal estuaries, particularly Sandy Hook, Shark River, Manasquan
White-fronted Goose: accidental
Snow Goose: Brigantine
Ross's Goose: accidental at Brigantine
Fulvous Whistling Duck: accidental, no recent records
Mallard: omnipresent
American Black Duck: scattered, declining, mainly Sandy Hook
Gadwall: scattered, Manasquan area
Northern Pintail: scattered, North Shore lakes, uncommon
Green-winged Teal: scattered, North Shore lakes, uncommon
Blue-winged Teal: breeds in summer, absent in winter
Eurasian Wigeon: accidental, usually one or two along North Shore, e.g. Belmar; look
    for it in American Wigeon flocks
American Wigeon: common, widespread along North Shore
Northern Shoveler: scattered, North Shore lakes, sometimes common
Wood Duck: breeds in summer, rare in winter, not usually on North Shore
Redhead: scattered, North Shore lakes, rare
Ring-necked Duck: scattered, North Shore lakes, common
Canvasback: scattered, North Shore lakes, fairly common
Greater Scaup: Sandy Hook, Navesink, Shark River, sometimes huge flocks; declining
Lesser Scaup: scattered, North Shore lakes, rare
Tufted Duck: accidental, look in large flocks of Greater Scaup
Common Goldeneye: common at Sandy Hook and Shark River
Barrow's Goldeneye: very rare; look in flocks of Common Goldeneye
Bufflehead: widespread but not numerous, more in rivers than in lakes
Oldsquaw: anywhere on ocean, but mainly in Sandy Hook
Harlequin Duck: regular at Barnegat Light jetty; rare at other jetties
Common Eider: rare and few, but often at Barnegat Light
King Eider: rare and few, but often at Barnegat Light
White-winged Scoter: more often in migration than in winter, Sandy Hook
Surf Scoter: more often in migration than in winter, Sandy Hook
Black Scoter: rare, mainly at Sandy Hook
Ruddy Duck: scattered, North Shore lakes, uncommon
Hooded Merganser: scattered, North Shore lakes, fairly common
Common Merganser: rare along coast, common on inland rivers and lakes
Red-breasted Merganser: widespread and common along shore, more on ocean and
    estuaries than on lakes

Selected References

General and Introduction

Boyd, H. P. 1991. *A Field Guide to the Pine Barrens of New Jersey.* Medford, N.J.: Plexus Publishing Company.

Boyle, W. J., Jr. 1986. *A Guide to Bird Finding in New Jersey.* New Brunswick: Rutgers University Press.

Brown, M. P. 1997. *New Jersey Parks, Forests, and Natural Areas: A Guide.* New Brunswick: Rutgers University Press.

Burger, J. 1996. *A Naturalist along the Jersey Shore.* New Brunswick: Rutgers University Press.

Burger, J. 1999. *Animals in Towns and Cities.* Dubuque, Iowa: Kendall-Hunt Publishing Company.

Di Lionno, M. 1997. *New Jersey's Coastal Heritage.* New Brunswick: Rutgers University Press.

Gruzlovic, H., and A. Cradic. 1994. *Natural Wonders of New Jersey: A Guide to Parks, Preserves and Wild Places.* Castine, Maine: Country Roads Press.

Lippman, H., and P. Reardon. 1991. *Enjoying New Jersey Outdoors: A Year-round Guide to Outdoor Recreation in the Garden State and Nearby.* New Brunswick: Rutgers University Press.

Pettigrew, L. 1998. *New Jersey: Wildlife Viewing Guide.* Helena, Montana: Falcon Press.

Scherer, G. 1998. *Nature Walks in New Jersey.* Boston: Appalachian Mountain Club Books.

Serro, J. 1992. *Nature's Events: A Notebook of the Unfolding Seasons.* Harrisburg, Penn.: Stackpole Books.

Walter, E., and J. Wallen. 1996. *The Smithsonian Guides to Natural America—Mid-Atlantic States.* Washington, D.C.: Smithsonian Books.

Westergard, B. 1998. *New Jersey: A Guide to the State.* New Brunswick: Rutgers University Press.

1. Chorusing Frogs

Dunne, M. 1989. New Jersey toads. *New Jersey Outdoors* 16:40.

Pechmann, J.H.K., and D. B. Wake. 1997. Declines and disappearances of amphibian populations. In *Principles of Conservation Biology* (G. K. Meffe and C. R. Carroll, eds.). Sunderland, Mass.: Sinauer Associates.

Stolzenburg, W. 1997. The naked frog. *Nature Conservancy* 47:24–27.

Zappalorti, R. T. 1982. Spring voices in the night. *New Jersey Outdoors* 9:11–13.

Zappalorti, R. 1989. Frogs. In *New Jersey Wildlife Profiles,* 88. Trenton: New Jersey Department of Environmental Protection.

Zipko, S. J. 1977. Patterns of reproduction in New Jersey amphibians. Occasional Paper No. 128. *New Jersey Audubon* 3:144–50.

2. Shad Run on the Delaware River

Able, K. W., and M. P. Fahay. 1998. *The First Year in the Life of Estuarine Fishes in the Middle Atlantic Bight.* New Brunswick: Rutgers University Press.

Atlantic States Marine Fisheries Commission. 1985. *Fishery Management Plan for American Shad and River Herrings.* Washington, D.C.: Atlantic States Marine Fisheries Commission, Fisheries Management Report 6.

Boriek, M. 1998. Overview of the 1998 Delaware River American Shad run. *N.J. Fish and Wildlife Digest* 12:28.

Page, L. M., and B. M. Burr. 1991. *Freshwater Fishes.* Norwalk, Conn.: Easton Press.

Serro, J. 1992. *Nature's Events: A Notebook of the Unfolding Seasons.* Harrisburg, Penn.: Stackpole Books.

Division of Fish, Game and Wildlife. *Annual Reports.* Trenton: Division of Fish, Game and Wildlife, Department of Environmental Protection.

Waldman, J. R., K. Nolan, J. Hart, and I. J. Wirgin. 1996. Genetic differentiation of three key anadromous fish populations of the Hudson River. *Estuaries* 19:759–768.

3. Glass Eels at Cheesequake

Able, K. W., and M. P. Fahay. 1998. *The First Year in the Life of Estuarine Fishes in the Middle Atlantic Bight.* New Brunswick: Rutgers University Press.

Chanda, D. 1989. American Eel. In *New Jersey Wildlife,* 100. Profiles. Trenton: New Jersey Department of Environmental Protection.

Moonsammy, R. Z., D. S. Cohen, and L. E. Williams (eds.). 1987. *Pinelands Folklife.* New Brunswick: Rutgers University Press.

4. Spawning Horseshoe Crabs

Botton, M. L., and R. E. Loveland. 1989. Reproductive risk: High mortality associated with spawning by Horseshoe Crabs (*Limulus polyphemus*) in Delaware Bay, USA. *Marine Biology* 101:143–151.

Burger, J. 1996. *A Naturalist along the Jersey Shore.* New Brunswick: Rutgers University Press.

Burger, J. 1997. Heavy metals in eggs and muscle of Horseshoe Crabs (*Limulus polyphemus*) from Delaware Bay. *Environmental Monitoring and Assessment* 46:279–287.

Loveland, R. E., and M. L. Botton. 1992. Sexual dimorphism and the mating system in Horseshoe Crabs, *Limulus polyphemus* L. *Animal Behavior* 44:907–916.

McLain, P. 1994. The living fossils of Delaware Bay. *New Jersey Outdoors* 21:25–27.

Schrading, E., T. O'Connell, S. Michels, and P. Perra. 1998. *Interstate Fishery Management Plan for Horseshoe Crab.* Washington, D.C.: Atlantic States Marine Fisheries Commission.

Shuster, C. N., Jr., and M. L. Botton. 1985. A contribution to the population biology of Horseshoe Crabs, *Limulus polyphemus* L. in Delaware Bay. *Estuaries* 8:363–372.

Staff. 1999. April migrations. *Natural History* 108:16–18.

5. *Migrant Shorebirds at Delaware Bay*

Botton, M. L., R. E. Loveland, and T. R. Jacobsen. 1994. Site selection by migratory shorebirds on Delaware Bay, and its relationship to beach characteristics and abundance of Horseshoe Crab (*Linulus polyphemus*) eggs. *Auk* 111:605–616.

Burger, J. 1986. The effect of human activity on shorebirds in two coastal bays in northeastern United States. *Environmental Conservation* 13:123–130.

Burger, J. 1993. Shorebird squeeze. *Natural History* 93 (May):9–14.

Burger, J. 1996. *A Naturalist along the Jersey Shore.* New Brunswick: Rutgers University Press.

Burger, J. 1997. *Oil Spills.* New Brunswick: Rutgers University Press.

Burger, J., and M. Gochfeld. 1991. Vigilance and feeding behavior in large feeding flocks of Laughing Gulls, *Larus atricilla*, on Delaware Bay Estuaries. *Estuarine, Coastal and Shelf Science* 32:207–212.

Clark, K. E. 1991. Jersey: A way station for migratory birds. *New Jersey Outdoors* 18:28–31.

Clark, K. E., L. J. Niles, and J. Burger. 1993. Abundance and distribution of migrant shorebirds in Delaware Bay. *Condor* 95:694–705.

Cordell, H. K., N. G. Herbert, and F. Pandolfi. 1999. The growing popularity of birding in the United States. *Birding* 31:168–176.

Harrington, B. 1983. The migration of the Red Knot. *Oceanus* 26:44–48.

McLain, P. 1987. Sanderlings. *New Jersey Outdoors* 14, no. 12:23–25.

Myers, J. P. 1983. Conservation of migrating shorebirds: Staging areas, geographic bottlenecks, and regional movements. *American Birds* 37:23–25.

Myers, J. P. 1993. Sex and gluttony on Delaware Bay. *Natural History* 95:68–77.

Tsipoura, N., and J. Burger. 1999. Shorebird diet during spring migration through Delaware Bay. *Condor* 101:635–644.

Tsipoura, N., C. G. Scanes, and J. Burger. 1999. Corticosterone and growth hormone levels in shorebirds during spring and fall migration stop-over. *Journal of Experimental Zoology* 284:645–651.

6. *Mountain Laurel*

Grimm, W. C. 1957. *The Book of Shrubs.* New York: Bonanza Books.

Jaynes, R. A. 1997. *Kalmia: Mountain Laurel and Related Species.* 3rd ed. Portland, Oregon: Timber Press.

Serro, J. 1992. *Nature's Events: A Notebook of the Unfolding Seasons.* Harrisburg, Penn.: Stackpole Books.

7. *Nesting Herons at Avalon*

Burger, J. 1978. The pattern and mechanism of nesting in mixed-species heronries. In *Wading Birds*, 45–58. New York: National Audubon Society, Report 7.

Burger, J. 1979. Resource partitioning: Nest site selection in mixed-species colonies of herons, egrets and ibises. *American Midland Naturalist* 101:191–210.

Burger J., and M. Gochfeld. 1993. When is a heronry crowded: A case study of Huckleberry Island, New York. *Journal of Coastal Research* 9:221–228.

Burger, J., M. Gochfeld, and L. J. Niles. 1995. Ecotourism and birds in coastal New Jersey: Contrasting responses of birds, tourists, and managers. *Environmental Conservation* 22:56–65.

Hancock, J., and J. Kushlan. 1984. *The Herons Handbook*. New York: Harper and Row.

Stone, W. 1937. *Bird Studies of Old Cape May*. New York: Dover.

Wander, W., and S. A. Brady. 1979. A closer look at New Jersey's wading birds. *New Jersey Outdoors* 6:10–11.

8. Laughing Gulls at Stone Harbor

Belant, J. L., and R. A. Dolbeer. 1993. Population status of nesting Laughing Gulls in the United States, 1977–1991. *American Birds* 47:220–224.

Bongiorno, S. F. 1970. Nest-site-selection by adult Laughing Gulls (*Larus atricilla*). *Animal Behavior* 18:434–444.

Burger, J. 1996. Laughing Gull. In *Birds of North America* 225:1–28. Washington, D.C.: American Ornithologists' Union, and Philadelphia: Academy of Natural Sciences.

Burger, J. 1996. *A Naturalist along the Jersey Shore*. New Brunswick: Rutgers University Press.

Burger, J., and M. Gochfeld. 1991. Vigilance and feeding behavior in large feeding flocks of Laughing Gulls, *Larus atricilla*, on Delaware Bay. *Estuarine, Coastal and Shelf Science* 32:207–212.

Montevecchi, W. A. 1977. Predation in a salt marsh Laughing Gull colony. *Auk* 94: 584–586.

9. Nesting Terns and Skimmers

Burger, J. 1996. *A Naturalist along the Jersey Shore*. New Brunswick: Rutgers University Press.

Burger, J., and M. Gochfeld. 1990. *Black Skimmer: Social Dynamics of a Colonial Species*. New York: Columbia University Press.

Burger, J., and M. Gochfeld. 1992. Terns for the better. *Natural History*, June, 45–47.

Burger, J., C. D. Jenkins, Jr., and K. Staine. 1992. Beach nesting birds: Optimism for the future. *New Jersey Audubon*, Summer, 9–11.

Galli, J. 1979. The Least Tern. *New Jersey Outdoors* 16:24–25.

Gochfeld, M., and J. Burger. 1994. Black Skimmer. In *Birds of North America* 108:1–28. Washington, D.C.: American Ornithologists' Union, and Philadelphia: Academy of Natural Sciences.

Thompson, B. C., J. J. Jackson, J. Burger, L. A. Hill, E. M. Kirsch, and J. Atwood. 1997. Least Tern. In *Birds of North America* 290:1–32. Washington, D.C.: American Ornithologists' Union, and Philadelphia: Academy of Natural Sciences.

Weidner, D. S. 1991. Champagne Island, Hereford Inlet. *New Jersey Audubon* 17:20–21.

10. Fiddler Crabs at Low Tide

Bertness, M. D. 1985. Fiddler Crab regulation of *Spartina alterniflora* production on a New England salt marsh. *Ecology* 66:1042–1055.

Burger, J. 1992. Immediate effects of an oil spill on behavior of Fiddler Crabs (*Uca pugnax*). *Archives of Environmental Contamination and Toxicology* 20:404–409.

Burger, J. 1994. Immediate effects of oil spills on organisms in the Arthur Kill. In Burger, J., ed., *Before and After an Oil Spill: The Arthur Kill*, 115–129. New Brunswick: Rutgers University Press.

Burger, J., J. Brzorad, and M. Gochfeld. 1991. Effects of an oil spill on emergence and mortality in Fiddler Crabs *Uca pugnax*. *Environmental Monitoring and Assessment* 22:107–115.

Crane, J. 1975. *Fiddler Crabs of the World*. Princeton, N.J.: Princeton University Press.

Katz, L. C. 1980. Effects of burrowing by Fiddler Crabs, *Uca pugnax* (Smith). *Estuarine and Coastal Marine Science* 11:233–237.

Teal, J. M. 1958. Distribution of Fiddler Crabs in Georgia salt marshes. *Ecology* 39: 185–193.

11. Butterflies in Gardens

Glassberg, J. 1993. *Butterflies through Binoculars: Boston to Washington D.C. Region*. New York: Oxford University Press.

Glassberg, J. 1995. *Enjoying Butterflies More*. Marietta, Ohio: Bird Watchers' Digest Press.

Glassberg, J. 1999. *Butterflies through Binoculars: Eastern North America*. New York: Oxford University Press.

Gochfeld, M., and J. Burger. 1997. *Butterflies of New Jersey*. New Brunswick: Rutgers University Press.

Pyle, R. M. 1992. *Handbook for Butterfly Watchers*. Boston: Houghton Mifflin.

Stokes, D., L. Stokes, and E. Williams. 1991. *The Butterfly Book: An Easy Guide to Butterfly Gardening, Identification, and Behavior*. Boston: Little, Brown and Co.

Sutton, P. 1990. How to create a butterfly and hummingbird garden. *New Jersey Audubon* 16:1–4 (reprint available from Cape May Bird Observatory).

Tekulsky, M. 1985. *The Butterfly Garden*. Boston: Harvard Common Press.

Xerces Society/Smithsonian Institution. 1990. *Butterfly Gardening: Creating Summer Magic in Your Gardens*. San Francisco: Sierra Club.

12. Grass Pink at Webb's Mill

Boyd, H. P. 1991. *A Field Guide to the Pine Barrens of New Jersey*. Medford, N.J.: Plexus Publishing Company.

Collins, B. R., and K. H. Anderson. 1994. *Plant Communities of New Jersey*. New Brunswick: Rutgers University Press.

Fox, W. E. 1979. Little orchids of the Pine Barrens. *New Jersey Outdoors* 6:10–12.

Redington, C. B. 1994. *Plants in Wetlands*. Dubuque, Iowa: Kendall-Hunt Publishing Company.

13. American Lotus at Mannington Marsh

Collins, B. R., and K. H. Anderson. 1994. *Plant Communities of New Jersey*. New Brunswick: Rutgers University Press.

Pierson, G., and G. Zimmermann. Restoring Jersey's Atlantic White-cedar. *New Jersey Outdoors* 20:17–19.

Radis, R. 1998. New Jersey plants: Bog candles. *New Jersey Audubon* 24:22–23.

Stone, W. 1911. *The Plants of Southern New Jersey.* Trenton: Annual Report of the New Jersey State Museum.

Sturtevant, B., and N. Griscom. 1993. Unraveling the mysteries of Webb's Mill Bog. *New Jersey Outdoors* 20:16–19.

14. Coalescing Terns and Skimmers

Burger, J. 1976. Daily and seasonal activity patterns in breeding Laughing Gulls, *Larus atricilla. Auk* 93:308–323.

Burger, J., and M. Gochfeld. 1990. *Black Skimmer: Social Dynamics of a Colonial Species.* New York: Columbia University Press.

Burger, J., and M. Gochfeld. 1992. Terns for the better. *Natural History* 6/92:45–47.

Burger, J., and K. Staine. 1993. Nocturnal behavior of gulls in coastal New Jersey. *Estuaries* 16:809–814.

Erwin, R. M. 1977. Black skimmer breeding ecology and behavior. *Auk* 94:709–717.

Weidner, D. S. 1991. Champagne Island, Hereford Inlet. *New Jersey Audubon* 17:20–21.

15. Migrating Monarchs at Cape May

Burger, J. 1996. *A Naturalist along the Jersey Shore.* New Brunswick: Rutgers University Press.

Gochfeld, M., and J. Burger. 1997. *Butterflies of New Jersey.* New Brunswick: Rutgers University Press.

Hunter, H. 1998. A Monarch researcher tests her wings. *Peregrine Observer* (Cape May Bird Observatory) 20:23–25 (February 1998).

Malcolm, S. B., and M. P. Zalucki (eds.). 1993. *Biology and Conservation of the Monarch Butterfly.* Los Angeles Natural History Museum, No. 38.

Marriot, D. L. 1994. Tracking North American Monarchs. Part 2, The West. *American Butterflies* 2(2):16–19.

Scott, J. V. 1996. Orange snow on the mountains: Monarchs in Mexico. *American Butterflies* 4(1):4–8.

Swengel, A. 1998. Where the Monarchs are: 4th of July butterfly count column. *American Butterflies* 6(3):46.

Treviño, R. 1997. Children of Mexico welcome the Monarchs. *American Butterflies* 5(4):19–21.

Urquhart, F. A. 1987. *The Monarch Butterfly: International Traveler.* Chicago: Nelson Hall. Reprinted 1998 by Wm. Caxton Ltd., Ellison Bay, WI.

Walton, R. 1993. Tracking North American Monarchs. Part 1, The East. *American Butterflies* 1(3):11–16.

16 and 17. Migrant Hawks

Aquila, C. 1992. Chimney Rock: The little-known hawk watch. *New Jersey Audubon* 18:20–21.

Aquila, C., and S. Byland 1995. A five year analysis of autumn hawk migration at Chimney Rock, Martinsville, N.J. *Records of New Jersey Birds* 21:26–27.

Bildstein, K. 1995. Redtail 0877-17127. *Hawk Mountain News,* No. 83:8–11.

Boyle, W. J., Jr. 1986. *A Guide to Bird Finding in New Jersey.* New Brunswick: Rutgers University Press.

Broune, M. 1948. *Hawks Aloft: The Story of Hawk Mountain.* Kutztown, Penn.: Kutztown Publishing Co.

Burger, J., M. Gochfeld, and L. J. Niles. 1994. Ecotourism and birds in coastal New Jersey: Contrasting responses of birds, tourists, and managers. *Environmental Conservation* 22:56–64.

Clark, W. S., and B. K. Wheeler. 1987. *Hawks.* Peterson Field Guide Series. Boston: Houghton Mifflin.

Conn, R. 1996. Chimney Rock: Some records and recollections. *Records of New Jersey Birds* 22:2–4.

Dunne, P. 1989. *New Jersey at the Crossroads of Migration.* Bernardsville, N.J.: New Jersey Audubon Society.

Dunne, P. J., and W. S. Clark. 1977. Fall hawk movement at Cape May Point, N.J., 1976. *New Jersey Audubon* 3:114–124, Occasional Paper No. 120.

Dunne, P., and C. Sutton. 1986. Population trends in coastal raptor migrants over ten years of Cape May Point counts. *Records of New Jersey Birds* 12:39–43.

Dunne, P., D. Sibley, and C. Sutton. 1988. *Hawks in Flight.* New York: Houghton Mifflin.

Hawk Migration Association of North America: http://www.hmana.org/.

Kerlinger, P. 1986. Habitat requirements of migrating hawks. *New Jersey Audubon* 12:12–13.

Kerlinger, P. 1989. *Flight Strategies of Migrating Hawks.* Chicago: University of Chicago Press.

Niles, L. J., J. Burger, and K. E. Clark. 1996. The influence of weather, geography, and habitat on migrating raptors on Cape May peninsula. *Condor* 98:382–394.

Niles, L. J., K. Clark, and D. Ely. 1991. Breeding status of Bald Eagles in New Jersey. *Records of New Jersey Birds* 17:2–5.

Sibley, D. 1993. *The Birds of Cape May.* Cape May: New Jersey Audubon Society's Cape May Bird Observatory.

Snyder, N., and H. Snyder. 1991. *Birds of Prey: Natural History and Conservation of North American Raptors.* Stillwater, Minn.: Voyageur Press.

Sutton, C. 1988. Wintering raptors and waterfowl on the Maurice River. *Records of New Jersey Birds* 14:42–51.

Sutton, C., V. Elia, and J. Dowdell. 1998. Status and trends in wintering raptors and waterfowl on the Maurice River: A ten year study. *Records of New Jersey Birds* 24:26–35.

Sutton, P. 1998. Birding bucks piling up in Cape May, NJ. *Peregrine Observer* 20:12.

18. Migrant Songbirds at Cape May

Dunne, P. 1989. *New Jersey at the Crossroads of Migration.* Bernardsville, N.J.: New Jersey Audubon Society.

Gustafson, M. 1987. Passerine habitat use at Higbee Beach Wildlife Management Area, 1985. *Records of New Jersey Birds* 12:62–66.

Robbins, C. S., D. K. Dawson, and B. A. Dowell. 1989. Habitat area requirements of breeding forest birds in the Middle Atlantic states. *Wildlife Monographs* 103:1–34.

Sibley, D. 1993. *The Birds of Cape May.* Cape May: New Jersey Audubon Society's Cape May Bird Observatory.

19. Cranberries in the Pine Barrens

Boyd, H. P. 1991. *A Field Guide to the Pine Barrens of New Jersey.* Medford, N.J.: Plexus Publishing Company.

Eck, P. 1990. *The American Cranberry.* New Brunswick: Rutgers University Press.

Miller, P. S. 1994. *Double Trouble: A Pine Barrens Preserve.* Toms River, N.J.: Ocean County Cultural and Heritage Commission.

Moonsammy, R. Z., D. S. Cohen, and L. E. Williams (eds.). 1987. *Pinelands Folklife.* New Brunswick: Rutgers University Press.

NJDEP. 1996. *Double Trouble State Park.* Trenton: Division of Parks and Forestry.

Schmidt, R. M. 1991. *Cranberry Cookery.* 2nd ed. Barnegat Light, N.J.: Pine Barrens Press.

Wilson, H. F. 1953. *The Jersey Shore: A Social and Economic History of the Counties of Atlantic, Cape May, Monmouth and Ocean.* New York: Lewis Historical Publishing Company.

20. Bats at Hibernia Mine

Burger, J. 1999. *Animals in Towns and Cities.* Dubuque, Iowa: Kendall-Hunt Publishing Company.

Clayton, D. M. Bats. In *New Jersey Wildlife Profiles,* 46–47. Trenton: New Jersey Department of Environmental Protection, Division of Fish, Game and Wildlife.

Cunningham, J. T. 1994. *This Is New Jersey.* New Brunswick: Rutgers University Press.

Dutko, R. 1993. Going to bat for a misunderstood mammal. *New Jersey Outdoors* 20: 21–27.

Fenton, M. B. 1983. *Just Bats.* Toronto: University of Toronto Press.

Graham, G. I. 1994. *Bats of the World.* New York: Golden Press.

Harvey, M. J. 1992. *Bats of the Eastern United States.* Cookeville, Tenn.: Arkansas Game and Fish Commission / Tennessee Technological University.

Stolzenburg, W. 1996. Out of sight, out of mine. *Nature Conservancy,* September/ October 1996, 16–21.

Valent, M. 1996–97. Surveying New Jersey's abandoned mines for bats. *Conserve Wildlife* 7 (Winter 1996):4–5.

21. Dwarf Pine Plains

Boyd, H. P. 1991. *A Field Guide to the Pine Barrens of New Jersey.* Medford, N.J.: Plexus Publishing Company.

Collins, B. R., and E.W.B. Russell. 1988. *Protecting the New Jersey Pinelands.* New Brunswick: Rutgers University Press.

Collins, B. R., and K. H. Anderson. 1994. *Plant Communities of New Jersey: A Study in Landscape Diversity.* New Brunswick: Rutgers University Press.

Forman, R.T.T. 1998. *Pine Barrens: Ecosystem and Landscape.* New Brunswick: Rutgers University Press.

McPhee, J. 1968. *Pine Barrens.* New York: Noonday Press.

22. Migrant Snow Geese at Brigantine

Bartlett, D. 1975. *The Flight of the Snow Geese.* New York: Stein and Day.

Burns, M. 1996. *The Private Eye: Observing Snow Geese.* Vancouver: University of British Columbia Press.

Cade, T. J., J. H. Enderson, C. G. Thelander, and C. M. White. 1988. *Peregrine Falcon Populations: Their Management and Recovery.* Boise, Idaho: Peregrine Fund, Inc.

Cooke, F., R. F. Rockwell, and D. B. Lank. 1995. *The Snow Geese of La Perouse Bay: Natural Selection in the Wild.* Oxford: Oxford Ornithology, vol. 4.

Johnsgard, P. A. 1974. *Song of the North Wind: A Story of the Snow Goose.* Lincoln: University of Nebraska Press.

Palmer, R. S. 1976. *Handbook of North American Birds: Waterfowl.* New Haven, Conn.: Yale University Press.

Tordoff, H. B. 1995. Return of the Peregrine. *Hawk Mountain News* No. 83:7–11.

23. Wintering Gulls

Burger, J. 1988. Jamaica Bay studies, 8: An overview of abiotic factors affecting several avian groups. *Journal of Coastal Research* 4:193–393.

Grant, P. J. 1982. *Gulls: A Guide to Identification.* Vermillion, S.D.: Buteo Books.

Griffin, W. D. 1978. Winter birds at the Jersey shore. *New Jersey Outdoors* 5:10–11.

24. Brant and Other Waterfowl

Burger, J., R. Trout, W. Wander, and G. Ritter. 1983. Jamaica Bay Studies, 4: Abiotic factors affecting abundance of Brant and Canada Geese on an East Coast estuary. *Wilson Bulletin* 95:384–403.

Ditch, R. 1991–92. The North Shore. *New Jersey Audubon* 17:18–20.

Griffin, W. D. 1978. Winter birds at the Jersey shore. *New Jersey Outdoors* 5:10–11.

Kirby, R. E., and F. Ferrigno. 1980. Winter, waterfowl, and the saltmarsh. *New Jersey Outdoors* 7:10–13.

Sutton, C., V. Elia, and J. Dowdell. 1998. Status and trends in wintering raptors and waterfowl on the Maurice River: A ten year study. *Records of New Jersey Birds* 24:26–35.

25. Swans at Whites Bog

Himber, C. P. 1998. Whitesbog's winter visitors. *New Jersey Outdoors* 25:18–21.

Ciaranca, M. A., C. A. Allin, and G. S. Jones. 1997. Mute Swan. In *Birds of North America* 273:1–28. Washington, D.C.: American Ornithologists' Union, and Philadelphia: Academy of Natural Sciences.

Limpert, R. J., and S. L. Earnst. 1994. Tundra Swan. In *Birds of North America* 89:1–20. Washington, D.C.: American Ornithologists' Union, and Philadelphia: Academy of Natural Sciences.

26. Other Spectacles

Able, K. W., and M. P. Fahay. 1998. *The First Year in the Life of Estuarine Fishes in the Middle Atlantic Bight.* New Brunswick: Rutgers University Press.

Burger, J. 1976. Behavior of hatchling Diamondback Terrapin, *Malaclemys terrapin*. *Copeia* 1976:742–748.

Burger, J. 1977. Determinants of hatching success in Diamondback Terrapin, *Malaclemys terrapin*. *American Midland Naturalist* 97:444–464.

Burger, J., and W. A. Montevecchi. 1975. Nest site election in the terrapin, *Malaclemys terrapin*. *Copeia* 1975:113–119.

Clay, C. H. 1995. *Design of Fishways and Fish Facilities*. Boca Raton, Fla.: Lewis Publishers.

Cordell, H. K., N. G. Herbert, and F. Pandolfi. 1999. The growing popularity of birding in the United States. *Birding* 31:168–176.

Dunne, P. 1989. *New Jersey at the Crossroads of Migration*. Bernardsville, N.J.: New Jersey Audubon Society.

Garber, S. D. 1988. Diamondback Terrapin protection. *Plastron Papers* 19:35–40.

Gustafson, M. 1986–87. Passerine habitat use at Higbee Beach Wildlife Management Area, 1985. *Records of New Jersey Birds* 12:62–66.

Leck, C. 1975. *The Birds of New Jersey*. New Brunswick: Rutgers University Press.

Niles, L., K. Clark, and D. Ely. 1991. Breeding status of Bald Eagles in New Jersey. *Records of New Jersey Birds* 17:2–5 (spring).

Public Service Electric and Gas. 1999. *Fish Ladders* (Appendix G-5). Newark, N.J.: PSE&G.

Segars, H. 1986. The Osprey. *New Jersey Outdoors*, July/August, 28–30.

Staff. 1999. April migrations. *Natural History* 108:16–18.

Epilogue

Fox, K. 1993. *Pubwatching with Desmond Morris*. Dover, N.H.: Alan Sutton.

Gooddall, J. 1988. *In the Shadow of Man*. Revised edition. Boston: Houghton Mifflin.

Morris, D. 1967. *The Naked Ape*. New York: Dell Publishing.

Morris, D. 1987. *Man Watching: A Field Guide to Human Behavior*. New York: Equinox Books.

Morris, D. 1998. *Bodytalk: The Meaning of Human Gestures*. New York: Crown.

Morris, D. 1998. *The Human Sexes: A Natural History of Man and Woman*. New York: Thomas Dunne Books.

Tiger, L. 1984. *Men in Groups*. New York: Marion Boyars.

Tiger, L., and R. Fox. 1997. *The Imperial Animal*. Revised; originally 1971. New Brunswick: Transaction.

Wasser, S. K. 1983. *Social Behavior of Female Vertebrates*. New York: Academic Press.

Subject Index

Taxonomic Index